THE
BLIND MAN'S
ELEPHANT

THE
BLIND
MAN'S
ELEPHANT

ESSAYS
ON THE CRAFT
OF POETRY

KURT BROWN

CONUN
DRUM
PRESS

AN IMPRINT OF BOWER HOUSE

DENVER

Designed by Margaret McCullough

Library of Congress Control Number 2019938019
ISBN 978-1-942280-54-5

10 9 8 7 6 5 4 3 2 1

A Special Thanks to

Laure-Anne Bosselaar-Brown

David Roahen

Sara Roahen

David Rothman

Maelle de Schutter

Mathieu de Schutter

TABLE OF CONTENTS

TABLE OF CONTENTS

ADDENDUM

INTRODUCTION

Kurt Brown and the Love of the Actual

by David J. Rothman

> The poet is still the singular, passionate observer we
> need in order to translate the world into penetrating,
> accurate language that somehow makes reality
> available to our minds in a way in which experience
> alone cannot thoroughly provide.

> "Poetry and the Language of Adam"

1.

Criticism is by definition always in a crisis, both words descending from
the Proto-Indo-European root *krei-*, which means literally "to sieve," but
also, by ancient extension, "to discriminate or distinguish." Criticism is
the place where we must make choices, like Frost in his yellow wood. The
stakes for anyone who cares about the relationship between language and
reality are always high. And in the present crisis of our criticism, Kurt
Brown's posthumous collection of essays, *The Blind Man's Elephant,* is
a vital book, offering a powerful and coherent vision of what it can mean
to read poetry now. Although the books are different and the two poets
might have eyed each other warily across the room at a party, in its range
and scope, its passion, its erudition coupled with extraordinary rhetorical
clarity when discussing complicated subjects, and especially its precise
presentation of how to think about poetry and why it matters, I can think of
no book as powerful, and as likely to attract a wide audience, since Dana
Gioia's *Can Poetry Matter?,* which came out in 1992.

This collection represents a lifetime of work. While Kurt published
many essays not included here, he did make this selection before his un-
timely death in 2013. He published quite a few other strong essays (I

have copies of at least half a dozen and there are many others out there, both in print and in manuscript), but those will have to wait for a more comprehensive collection of his work. For now, at least we have the book Kurt wanted us to have.

2.

Kurt did not publish a great deal before he was in his mid-40s, but then did so at an impressive rate, producing many volumes of original work, editing innovative anthologies, and bringing out a wide range of essays that grew stronger and stronger over time. Kurt and his wife, the poet Laure-Anne Bosselaar, were also tremendously generous to younger poets and poetry institutions across the country.

I met Kurt in early 1980, when I was just twenty and spending a year off from college living in Aspen, ski racing, working odd jobs, scribbling madly, and thinking about how to become a writer. Kurt taught a community course at the Aspen Institute on contemporary poetry (Kinnell, Walcott, and Snyder, among others), and we became inseparable friends. Kurt was about fifteen years older than me, and one of the most passionate, knowledgeable, committed poets I have ever known. He lived and breathed poetry. Why he had decided to do so in Aspen, I'm not sure, as he was not a skier, but while there he not only edited *Aspen Anthology*, he also founded the Aspen Writers' Conference and later the organization that became Writers' Conferences & Centers (WC&C), now the national membership organization for such groups.

Kurt took me under his wing as an assistant editor at *Aspen Anthology* and taught me the ropes of editing, from opening the mail to proofing the pages; he edited my first poems to be published in national journals; he taught me how to write a book review and published my first one; he gave me my first job helping to run a literary festival. Mostly we sat around in the cluttered office of the magazine in the decaying Wheeler Opera House and talked and talked and talked about poetry during afternoons that seemed to last forever.

We stayed in touch as I bounced around the country figuring life out, and then ten years later, during the summer of 1990, I worked with Kurt again, taking a break from my graduate studies to spend several weeks in

Aspen, now helping him run the 15th Aspen Writers' Conference. It was, like everything Kurt produced, memorable. The work, however, as before and as it always is in running such events, was not exactly glamorous. I helped with every kind of administrative and event management detail imaginable, from finding chairs and setting them up then putting them away, to transportation, to meals, to directions, to buying the booze (and caring for the boozed), to trouble-shooting. You name it, I and my fellow assistants did it. And the writers were impressive. I don't remember everyone who was there, but they included my former teacher Derek Walcott, along with Charles Simic, Al Young, Carolyn Forché, Cyra McFadden, James Welch, and others, a gifted and vivacious faculty, along with scores of eager students from all over the country, everyone seemingly infected by Kurt's creativity, enthusiasm, and good will. There were seminars, lectures, readings, workshops, parties, hikes, dinners, conversations, arguments, the usual kinds of ultimately harmless bad behavior, and lots of words, what seemed like an ocean of words, new ones, old ones, the good, the bad, the dull and more, spilling out of people in every direction. It was intoxicating in the way that it was supposed to be.

On the final weekend, as people were packing up and leaving, I remember that Kurt approached me with a look in his eye that I recognized.

"I have a great idea," he began. Great, I thought. While I was interested, I knew that Kurt's ideas usually meant work...for me. And I was tired. I had hardly slept for weeks. My liver was ailing. I had thought we were done.

"Did you know," he went on, "that there's no membership organization for all the writer's conferences and centers in this country?"

I didn't say anything that I can recall. As I said, I was tired.

"And I'm going to start one. Here, type this up." And he handed me a tattered, Xeroxed list of pages covered with contact information for dozens of writers' conferences, centers, and festivals.

What could I say? I adored Kurt. As far as I could tell, he was a literary Houdini, again and again pulling off major events by what seemed at first to be sheer will, ambition, and desire. I sat down and started typing. I spent most of a day doing it, and at the end there was the first proposed membership roster of what became Writers' Conferences and Centers.

This is the way Kurt lived his life, and his criticism, like his poetry, grew out of that life.

3.

When Kurt died unexpectedly in 2013, I mourned in every part of my spirit. He was a gifted poet; in his final decade he became an excellent and passionate critic, as this volume attests; he was a major anthologist of contemporary poetry. I had many great teachers (including not only Walcott, but also Heaney, Czeslaw Milosz, Mark Strand, and Robert Fitzgerald), but Kurt was my only mentor. And he was my friend. All of this matters, but Kurt had another gift that is absolutely crucial and rare, one that is rarely articulated clearly enough: he was a great entrepreneur, and poetry and literature need great entrepreneurs.

In saying Kurt was a great entrepreneur, I don't mean he was a great businessman. God knows, he didn't do what he did to make money. And that's a good thing, because I can't imagine he made any. Further, there are plenty of people out there who have managed the publication, teaching, and editing of literature in ways that are effective and profitable. Kurt had something different and I believe far more important. He was institutionally creative. He could look at a community of writers and readers, whether locally or nationally, and see their unmet needs, needs that they might even hardly knew they had, then meet them. This is more than administration. It is a rare kind of creativity and it can be life-changing for those involved.

Kurt did creative entrepreneurial work when he founded the journal *Aspen Anthology* and created the Aspen Writers' Conference, now titled "Aspen Summer Words" and just one program among many run by the extraordinarily successful Aspen Writers' Foundation. As they now put it in telling the history of their organization, "In 1976, armed with little more than a lofty idea and enough charm to cajole local restaurant and lodge owners into donating food and housing, Kurt Brown, an ambitious young bartender and poet, launched the Aspen Writers' Conference." That was the Kurt I knew, the one with a sheaf of papers and a slightly maniacal look in his eye, and that was the Kurt who edited such fascinating anthologies and journals, taught and supported scores of young poets, founded a major conference, and dreamed up Writers' Conferences & Centers.

The moral is this: writing is more than writing. It does not occur in a vacuum. Now in my late 50s, several decades older than Kurt was when I first met him, I understand just what it takes to create the kinds of communities in which reading and writing thrive. And what it takes is people like Kurt, who lived almost all of his professional life outside of academe and created the possibility of poetry for thousands of people.

4.

Like many in our line of work, every year or so I find myself writhing in pain on a panel where the assembled gurus are supposed to address that apotheosis of narcissistic inquiry, "How Can I Get Published?" For years these kinds of discussions depressed me. The glazed look of the aspirants in the audience suggest nothing so much as cannibals contemplating a human sacrifice. But then it struck me that the answer of how to approach the discussion in a more productive way lay in being honest about the kinds of lives we actually live in the literary world, especially in poetry, Kurt's greatest passion. Most of us who pursue this art do more than scribble verses. We read. We write scholarship, criticism, and book reviews. We teach. We administer programs. We edit. We publish. We sit (and here it gets intense) on governing boards. We raise money. We mentor. We design curriculum. We write budgets and strategic plans. We hire and, if necessary, fire. We found programs, journals, presses, conferences, departments and even schools, and *we run them.*

As I look back, I now realize that at the time, what I thought I learned from Kurt was how to write. That's true, but I also learned much more than that, a lesson embodied in the ongoing vitality of so many other organizations he dreamed up, founded, led and supported. I learned that if we want to live in a society where the arts matter, we have to be the change we want to see in the world. Living a creative life means far more than making art. It also means doing whatever we can to make sure that it gets made and encountered by others in the first place. Approach the writing life in this spirit and you will realize that the real question is not what poetry can do for you, but what you can do for poetry.

As this book makes clear, one of the things we can do for poetry includes reading and writing criticism. It is an epistemological paradox (because it has to be true, but then we face the question of how writing began in the first place), but reading precedes writing. Criticism responds to poetry that has already been written, yet our first poetical impulse, as

Kurt understood, is tied to a critical impulse, as both involve an effort "to put the world in order." This impulse is not spiritualism. As Kurt puts it in "Poetry and the Language of Adam":

> I am at pains to avoid sounding vague and mystical.
> I am not speaking of theological revelation, the
> metaphysical visions of saints, but the direct,
> unmediated, visceral knowledge of the word—
> the world we live in every day, but almost never
> apprehend. The language of Adam is not the language
> of transcendence. It is the language of the body, the
> senses, the language of the Eden we have and not the
> ideal, abstract one we seek. It is meaning, substance,
> truth, something attainable and real the poet must
> strive for in his or her daily work. It cannot be replaced
> by mere style or technique, and it cannot be faked. It is
> not a product of intelligence, culture, sophistication, or
> literary panache. That is, it does not care to impress us.
> It overwhelms us.

The above passage suggests a criticism that takes poetry to be a foundational human activity, not merely an adornment, and again and again finds a way to bring reality, poetry, and discourse about them together by naming the subjects all must address to make sense. This is harder than it appears.

5.

The book you hold in your hands is almost entirely a work of criticism (with one major poem never before published in a book, "Abduction"), but this introduction aims to place that critical work in the rich context of its author's life. Consider this poem by Kurt:

A MOMENT

I keep returning to that moment, one
Day at your kitchen table with the sun
Slanting in through the glass above your sink.
You stood before me, brushing your long hair,
Stroke after stroke in the astonished air
While you talked of nothing, and I sipped my drink.

Then suddenly you bent your head, and threw
Your hair forward in a bright fan to show
Your beauty in a simple act, at once
Casual and contrived, while I sat there
Like some stone figure in a stone chair—
Such blatant beauty required a response.

But I did nothing, though my heart halted
In my chest, a small, numb, exalted
Animal, until you tossed that golden wrack
Of hair to settle once again upon
Your shoulders and you smiled your wan
Smile and I recalled myself, and smiled back.

This lyric is sly and unusual for Kurt, atypical in some respects. Over the
years, one of the things we debated at great length was the question of
meter, rhyme, and other aspects of prosody. Kurt was part of a generation
that could be quite fierce in its insistence that the foregrounding of such
craft was passé, whereas I and some others in my generation became more
and more convinced that his generation had thrown the baby out with the
bathwater and such elements of craft should at the very least be rigorously
taught. Kurt and I enjoyed testy epistolary exchanges about this kind of
thing, in which, going on Kurt's responses (thank God I don't have what I
wrote to him), I'm sure that I was, shall we say, a less than gracious upstart.

So imagine my astonishment when I read Kurt's last collection, 2012's *Time-Bound*, and found a number of poems like "A Moment," in which Kurt showed that he utterly knew what he was doing with meter and rhyme all along (see "For Miklós Radnóti," and "Old Howard," among others). Cunning fox. This epiphany of love uses every trick in the book, gracefully transforming the six-line "Venus and Adonis" stanza. That form goes ABABCC, whereas Kurt puts a couplet first and structures his stanza AABCCB, effectively moving the first B rhyme to the end. Kurt's poem also reverses the theme of "Venus and Adonis" itself. In the myth and in Shakespeare's poem, Adonis resists the goddess's hot overtures and goes off to get gored to death by a boar. Kurt, on the other hand, who always to my knowledge met love with love, is at first paralyzed by Laure-Anne's beauty, but soon responds: "I recalled myself, and smiled back." The meter is craggy and rich, with as many cunning twists as anything by Walcott or Heaney. A beautiful thing.

I read what I've just written, and while I think it's true, I also hear Kurt's voice castigating me from beyond the grave for a certain failure. Wait a minute, I don't have to *imagine* I hear it, I can just *quote* it, from an enormous email on another matter he sent me on June 10, 1995, at 5:52 pm Mountain Daylight Time:

> A word of caution (I can still speak like one of your
> teachers, because I'm old enough to be your Dad): don't
> approach poetry as a vast pile of work to be placed,
> according to your considerable knowledge, in its proper
> location on some vast grid. You have a tendency to do
> this, I've noticed. It's natural, I've done it too. You've
> read so much you tend to categorize things, as if that
> were the purpose of reading and thinking about poetry.
> It's not. You soon miss what's original, personal,
> new in work when you do this. ANY POEM EVER
> WRITTEN BY ANYONE, IN SOME WAY, IS LIKE
> A POEM WRITTEN BY SOMEONE ELSE. [Kurt's
> emphasis.] Once you pass through the "I know who
> that reminds me of" phase, you will begin to read

poetry again with a fresh sensibility: the way you read
it before you studied so much poetry in school (and so
much criticism, which does this ad nauseum [sic]. I do
not mean to sound condescending. But I know what
I'm talking about. The GLORY of real poetry is that it
emerges out of the legacy of all poetry, makes subtle
but sensible connections which can only deepen it, yet
feels perfectly idiosyncratic, fresh, original at the same
time. This is a lovely paradox which will keep you
coming back and back to poetry for the rest of your life.
If you approach poetry with the feeling of: "I know it
all, now I've read, studied, thought about everything"
you will soon grow weary, become jaded and hate
poetry. That would be a shame, and a real loss to your
life. And it happens to more people than not. Almost
any critic you can name, and most poets, too. Be
careful, David, you don't lose poetry and wind up with
nothing but knowledge, which is worth little in the end.

6.

Here we return to criticism, but now in a richer context of poetry, editing,
friendship, and much more, even including arts administration! Obviously
Kurt took criticism seriously from the beginning. His note to me is a con-
tentious argument from a friend who cares about life, poetry, criticism,
and other people equally. And many of its virtues find themselves worked
out in these pages. While Kurt was deeply and widely read (he seems
to have read almost every substantial book of contemporary poetry that
came out for many decades), he also managed to develop both a critical
and poetic idiom that eschewed many of the pitfalls of the contemporary
schools, always bringing his critical insights back to the poetry itself.
Again and again when reading these essays, I noted both general state-
ments and specific observations that appear to be transparent because of
the clarity of the thought, and yet which are grounded in a lifetime full of
careful reading. At one point in the essay "On the Immortality of Images,"
after carefully discussing each of the categories in his summary of what

a strong image can do, Kurt writes: "Simplicity...along with appropriateness, universality, originality, and physicality—these are some of the things that compose a memorable poetic image." Just a few pages later in the same essay, when discussing the resolutely image-free William Bronk poem, "Veni Creator Spiritus," he observes that "this is a very good poem in at least one critical way: it is intellectually complex, subtle, even brilliant in its conceptualizations," but then also observes:

> Thought, in this poem, is a construction, like a building
> or a box. It is almost palpable. Yet it is not palpable, and
> I find it difficult to hold onto the poem, line by line, as
> one abstraction slides into another.... The poem here
> has become for me an argument, and not an experience,
> and while I admire it greatly for what it does, I cannot
> react to it emotionally because my sense, my body, are
> not engaged. This is what concrete imagery can do, and
> there is no substitute for it.

This is criticism of a high order. Kurt read poems generously, at the same time as he insisted that the best ones offer an integrated sensibility, a rich, meaningful emotional coherence. He can admire Bronk's gifts at the same time as he argues for the work's shortcomings. He is a critic of negative capability. This is as rare in criticism as it is in poetry, and Kurt could write both. His ability, which grew far stronger in the last several decades of his life, to articulate this vision in prose as well as in verse, is rare.

Indeed, Kurt's criticism, which gently quarrels with itself in a number of places, is so strong because it frequently seems to build a bridge to poetry itself, acknowledging the challenges of making verse. In "Beyond Description: Poetry That Stares," he returns to the question of the specific and the abstract, and, even as he again praises the precise, also again recognizes the perennial difficulty of making it real:

> To find language for what occurs on the fringes of
> consciousness, at the border between what is speakable
> and what is not, is one of the poet's particular tasks,
> a constant wrestling with language that—even at
> its best—favors the generic over the specific, the
> approximate over the exact.

The way he phrases the question on this topic (among many others in the book) is a generous invitation to join a conversation of long standing, nothing less than the debate over how language might cleave to reality even as it cleaves from it. If criticism is rhetoric, this is highly poetic rhetoric grounded in "love of the actual," as he puts it near the end of "Beyond Description."

Kurt divided his book into two sections, one on "Analysis" (from which the examples above are taken) and a second on "Assessment," which republishes a dozen of his favorite reviews. Throughout, he reads poems closely, hundreds of them by scores of poets in the course of the book. His concerns recur: how to name things, the mysterious power of strong imagery, that contest of the abstract and the concrete, how to depict the passage of time, the importance of opening lines, the possibility of capturing experience in words, the power of narrative, the love of the actual. In the end, although Kurt did not aim to offer any new method or rhetoric of criticism, he seems to me to come close to doing so. In effect, Kurt is a close reader, but his primary concern is not New Critical construable meanings, but rather feelings and emotions.

Nowhere are Kurt's aims and gifts more clear than in his ambitious essay review, "Nature and the Poet: On the Work of Mary Oliver." Here his emotional negative capability is on view throughout. Near the beginning, after accurately characterizing Oliver's poetry of praise for the world and its roots in poets such as Whitman, he writes "Pick up any of Oliver's earlier books and browse through them at random. You will find surprises on almost every page, language so original it seems to fit—to accommodate itself—to reality," and he immediately and carefully gives a range of examples from across her work. At her best, he argues,

> Oliver does not attempt to beautify nature, to
> decorate the bare facts of reality with attractive
> anthropomorphic details, Instead, she looks deeply,
> closely, with the obsessive focus of a predator's eye,
> and the words to incarnate reality seem to come to her
> naturally, spontaneously, though we know how much
> work it takes to hone the poet's sensibility to just such
> a keen edge of vision, and how much work it takes to
> shape that vision into song.

At the same time, however, he can also write that "Part of the problem for a poet of exaltation is the exhaustion of language available for descriptive purposes." As her career drew on, he argues, "Time and again, the language blurs into hackneyed speech, cliché, easy sentiment, verbosity, a tendency towards the approximate rather than the exact," and again he provides convincing examples in the dozens. In the end of what should stand as one of the most thoughtful evaluations of a major contemporary poet's career, he observes that,

> The impulse to praise is an admirable one, even a
> necessary one. One of the oldest functions of poetry.
> But praise must come at the end of a struggle, a true
> and comprehensive assessment of reality, praise that the
> reader feels has been wrested and won out of the general
> chaos and violence of existence. It cannot proceed
> blithely out of a self-satisfied and willful solitude.

The effort required to forge a critical idiom that can contain such contradictions, such a rich internal conversation about substantial poems, is the work of a lifetime and something that few critics ever achieve. One virtue of Kurt's criticism is that he makes it seem relatively easy, pulls it off with *sprezzatura*, conveying the various and pleasurable contemplation of what it means to be a thoughtful reader as if it were as easy as a chat in a restaurant—which, for Kurt, it often could be. One gets the sense, when reading such essays, that he has merely said the obvious—yet said it so well, that his estimation of Mary Oliver, for example, articulates what many have often thought, but never expressed so well.

One way to understand Kurt's critical achievement is to revive certain words that are out of fashion but that fit here, such as "sensibility." Kurt's sensibility is clear: he has no interest in poetry that fashionably abandons making sense. As he puts it when reviewing Spencer Short's *Tremolo*,

> It's the very arbitrariness of this kind of postmodern
> poem that begins to wear one down...the lack of
> subject matter allows for interchangeable metaphors
> because true metaphor is connected, at its root, to the
> core meaning of a poem. Break that connection—or
> dispense with it—and anything goes. This is not the
> same thing as freedom. It is artistic anarchy.

Instead, Kurt is after life as it is lived, particularly the otherwise invisible existence of all things, especially sentient beings, as they express themselves, relate to each other, and inform emotion. As he writes near the end of "Poetry that Stares,"

> Poetry that stares honors reality and implies a
> valuation of its commonness, suggesting that much of
> importance—perhaps all we might finally know—can be
> found there. It is not anti-metaphysical but pro-worldly,
> devoted to the manifest, the here-and-now, as the only
> sure locus of understanding and truth. It is, perhaps
> related to...Williams's famous dictum: "no ideas, but
> in things," yet it is more than that. It involves respect,
> acceptance, even love of the actual, a curiosity and
> delight in what is, what exists, without an accompanying
> sense of judgment or degradation. It does not deny the

horrifying or the ugly, but seeks beauty in the most
unexpected places, the lowliest things.

Another useful term here might be "taste," in the sense of a judicial tem-
perament that is keen yet generous, loving yet careful, open yet precise,
and above all engaged. I do not mean by taste simply a personal or cultural
pattern of choice and preference, but rather an insistence, in Kurt's case,
that one should justify one's judgment in something like poetry by stating
it boldly, questioning it, and providing evidence: emotional close reading.
The prolific and largely forgotten Arnold Bennett described literary taste
in this way: "Literature is first and last a means of life, and that the enter-
prise of forming one's literary taste is an enterprise of learning how best to
use this means of life." That seems to be what Kurt was more or less after,
and what he succeeds in conveying with deceptive ease. In its generosity
and rigor, the union of his criticism and his poetry are a tonic for a time
when poetry is more frequently deployed as a weapon than as an art.

7.

Kurt Brown's late "A Moment" describes a memory to which he "keep[s]
returning." It is a seemingly ordinary minute in which he is so astonished
by the beauty of his wife Laure-Anne brushing her long, blond hair in
her sunny kitchen that even though he feels "such blatant beauty required
a response," he is struck dumb and paralyzed, even rendered inanimate,
"like some stone figure in a stone chair." Then, in the poem's climax, when
it seems that he will fail to respond—"But I did nothing, though my heart
halted / in my chest, a small, numb exalted / animal"—she smiles at him
and he says "I recalled myself, and smiled back." Seems simple enough.
That smile is a little triumph of ordinary life, showing us how deeply love
abides in even ephemeral gestures. But the lasting power of "A Moment"
lies not in Kurt's compelling description of Laure-Anne's beauty, in the
tender exchange of smiles, or in the sentimental moral I've suggested. It
lies in what the poem does, for like all strong poems, "A Moment" is an
action: a blessing, a promise, a vow, a declaration. Kurt's smile is one

response to Laure-Anne's beauty, but the more lasting response, the one that shows us what beauty and erotic love can be, is the carefully wrought poem itself. The true climax of the poem is the moment just before Kurt's smile, the action that caused it, when he writes "I recalled myself." For that act of recalling the self is what has led to the act of returning to and recalling the event in words, specifically in verse. It is Kurt's returning to life (from "stone") and his subsequent making of the poem that shows us some of what it means to be human when we are at our best, when in the full light of who we are our words no longer merely comment upon reality, but become it. "A Moment" is so good because it is more than a love poem, or perhaps because it is what a truly great love poem should always be. It is not just about love: it is love-making in language, a speech act, not only a depiction of life, but also living. A strong poem, tied clearly and precisely to a poetics of life as articulated in this book, it can stand as an emblem for what a poet can do who does both act and know.

Sections of this essay appeared, in slightly different form, in the following print and online journals. Grateful acknowledgment is made to the publishers for permission to reprint:

"Busy Being Born: Poems that Persist." *THINK Journal 7.1 (Fall 2016):* 5-11.

"Ask Not What Poetry Can Do for You: Remembering Kurt Brown." The Newsletter of Writers' Conferences and Centers. https://www.awpwriter. org/magazine_media/writers_chronicle_view/3600/kurt_brown_and_ what_you_can_do_for_poetry. November 10, 2014.

"On Kurt Brown's 'A Moment.'" *The Cortland Review: Special Feature Remembering Kurt Brown. Spring 2014.* http://www.cortlandreview.com/ features/14/spring/rothman.php.

PREFACE

The story of the blind man and the elephant is well known. It's a fable variously attributed to the Sufis, Jainists, Buddhists, and Hindus and is meant to teach the limits of one's own knowledge. Three blind men approach an elephant—one from the front, one from the rear, and one from the side. The one in front touches the elephant's trunk and thinks, *So this is what an elephant is—a long flexible hose-like creature.* The man in the rear touches the elephant's hind parts and thinks, *So this is what an elephant is—two high, wide, fleshy pillars with a wispy thing at the top.* The one who approaches from the side touches the elephant's belly and thinks, *An elephant is a gigantic beast—round as a barrel with a thick hide.* The lesson is simple: no one can see the entire elephant, and so must rely on partial knowledge when assessing it.

ANALYSIS

1

Poetry and the Language of Adam

The Poet is the sayer, the namer, and represents beauty.

—Ralph Waldo Emerson

What is it the poet reaches? Not mere knowledge. He
obtains entrance
Into the relationship of word and thing.

— J. Riddel

One of the things poetry can do is rename the world. It doesn't matter how many times this has already been done, how many generations rise to inherit and reinvent the language, it must be done over again. And again. In an essential and important way, each individual ever born refashions language to his or her own purposes. Each of us has a unique sense of words and how they can be strung together to communicate thoughts, experiences, and emotions. Writers, but especially poets, are people who consciously accept this fact and make an effort in their work to further the process of renaming and extending the resources of language. When we rename a thing, when we describe it anew in such a way as to almost re-*create* it, we call it forth into a fresh dimension and show it to the rest of the world as if for the first time. An old thing, a used and worn thing, about which we thought we knew all there was to know, is suddenly revitalized, brought again to life under the power of the poet's scrutiny. Of all the things poetry can do, this renewal is one of its many virtues.

Poetry is said to have begun, at least according to one theory, with Adam naming the animals. There are competing theories[1], but this is one of the most widespread and popular. It places the origins of poetry not with visions or rituals or courtly entertainments, but squarely on language—the application of word to thing—millennia before postmodernists would insist on the fallacy of this bond by instructing us that signifier and signified were forever divorced.

In the beginning, as it were, language and the world appeared together at the same primeval instant. The inner and the outer worlds, abstract and concrete, mind and body, rose out of nothingness together. By suggesting that poetry, first and foremost, is made out of language, that its primary function is description, the myth of Adam avoids at the outset the Romantic notion of poetry as a covert, magical act and places the emphasis on poetry as a practical, necessary impulse: setting the world in order through making distinctions between things by giving them their proper names. To be able to identify things, to tell one from the other, and to be able to communicate these distinctions to others is, in terms of this myth, essential. To do this, we need language. The Bible makes this assertion clear even before Adam enters the picture: "In the beginning was the Word." First there was language ("Let there be light") and out of it sprang the world.

The passage from Genesis that describes Adam naming the animals (chapter 2, verses 19 and 20) is short and seemingly straightforward. It follows immediately the episodes describing the creation of man and the planting of the Garden of Eden. Within the compass of a few short sentences, it describes the naming of the world's newly-created, though still anonymous, creatures:

> Out of the ground the Lord God formed every beast
> of the field, and every fowl of the air; and brought
> them unto Adam to see what he would call them: and
> whatsoever Adam called every living creature, that was
> the name thereof. And Adam gave names to all cattle,
> and to the fowl of the air, and to every beast of the field...

Like Adam himself, God creates the animals out of dust and clay, which makes them the progeny of earth and underscores their special affinity with human beings. The names Adam utters on that first morning are the original names, perhaps the proto-language, which Adam, as the first man, would naturally have to invent. We can imagine a language of ur-words, what the linguists call *etymons*. An etymon is the original form of a word before time and history and the vagaries of human culture combine to corrupt it, changing its meaning and thrust in largely unpredictable ways. The Greek source of the word *etymon* itself is *eteos*, meaning "true." The names Adam gives the animals are their primal names, their "true" names, by which we may know them truly if only we could somehow reclaim these words for our own.

On the surface, this passage from the Bible offers no particular difficulty. It describes in the simplest terms what appears to be the simplest of acts. But naming a thing, especially for the first time, is a more complex matter.

To begin with, naming a thing *truly* demands a knowledge of that thing, a penetrating grasp of that thing, not ordinarily required in our everyday experience of it. We must know a thing in its essence to name it properly. We must know its quintessence, its soul, not just its general qualities. This suggests an acuteness of perception, an extraordinary effort of attention to see into the nature of what is to be named.

Further, to give something its exact and proper name is to somehow bestow an identity upon it. It is *this* thing, and no other. It is now named, known, which are perhaps two aspects of the same thing, or perhaps subsequent aspects: we know first—through the act of acute attention—*then* we may name. The thing is now individuated, defined.

Finally, this kind of naming amounts to nothing less than recognition, promoting something to its full and ultimate status. To name things properly is to celebrate them in their singularity. The scene with Adam among the animals in Eden resembles a mass baptism during which the animals are sanctioned, accepted, blessed.

For poets, the task is not to name things for the first time, nor to recover the lost language of etymons in all their pristine splendor, but to describe things in the unstable language of history and culture—the corrupt, inexact, approximate language of the fallen. I am speaking not in religious terms, but in terms of metaphor and available myth. Almost every poet who has ever thought about it has testified to the faultiness, the inherent imperfections of language as a medium of expression. "What is perceived and what is said," Charles Simic wrote, "rarely match." For T. S. Eliot, every poem is "a raid on the inarticulate." Description for the poet, then, is not something florid or self-indulgent, not something to be skipped over to get to the good parts, to the action—rather, it is the very source of the action, the revelation. It is where poetry engages and grasps the world, where language, like Jacob, struggles with the mute and begrudging angel to get it to breathe out its blessing finally in a few surprising and original words.

This is the case with Walt Whitman, who has been referred to as the "new Adam" in the New World. Whitman himself honors the old literature, including the Bible, but assures the reader that "Song of Myself" will be a new source of knowledge and inspiration for human beings—at least in the United States. His brash self-confidence is not the point, but how he went about pioneering a new prosody, a new kind of language to describe a world that had never been described in poetry before. For this, paradoxically, he had to revert to ancient sources, Biblical rhythms, and Biblical forms—the long free line, the catalogs, the high rhetoric, the great resounding metaphors of nature—in order to employ words in fresh and illuminating ways. So, for instance, describing a carpenter planing a beam of wood in section 15 of "Song of Myself," Whitman explains:

> The carpenter dresses his plank... the tongue
> of his foreplane
> whistles its wild ascending lisp...

The action of the carpenter's plane as it "whistles its wild ascending lisp" has been captured—named—in such a way that we feel it has never been adequately described before, never been noticed or heard, though carpenters have been planing wood since before the time of Jesus, who was certainly familiar with the sound. The auditory imagery here is not simply functional or decorative, it is revelatory—a small rift in the fabric of time and space is opened and the world becomes sensually immediate, as if we were standing beside the carpenter hearing the sound of the plane for ourselves, not just reading about it in a book. And the effect of the passage cannot be attributed to onomatopoeia alone—that beautiful pattern of S's that, along with the assonance of two short I's, echo the sound the plane makes as it runs up the wood. It exists as well in the metaphor: the "tongue" of the fore plane whistling, like the worker himself happy at his labor. It inheres too in the word "lisp," which captures a slightly broader shade of sound than mere sibilance—the flat, curling edges of fresh wood shavings. It resides in those two crucial adjectives "wild" and "ascending," suggesting vigor, the unchecked sexual energy Whitman loved to praise. It is in each of these and all of them—the precise, surprising choice of words, and how they are placed together until language and reality, for once, seem perfectly attuned.

Whitman referred to "Song of Myself" as, in part, a "language experiment." He wanted to see what he could do in the way of inventing a language that would more directly engage reality than the older poetries whose words and metaphors had grown conventional and stale. In this effort he would enlist any and every term at his disposal, including common speech, slang, argot, and cant. So he describes the sound of shoes striking pavement as "the sluff of bootsoles." It is probable that the word "sluff"—so accurate and exact—had never been used in a poem before, and very seldom in ordinary speech as well. It is not only sonically precise—we hear shoe leather scraping pavement—but somehow existentially correct as well—we feel the foot-dragging weariness of the masses as they make their way to office or home in a never-ending routine of labor and rest. Throughout "Song of Myself" and Whitman's other poems, words and phrases crop up that seem to name reality, call it out from behind its veil of inarticulateness, and show it to us naked, immediate, whole. Like a photographer who uses his lens to frame and focus our attention, to make us really *see*, Whitman uses words to pinpoint and focus reality in poem after poem. We know the words are *not* the reality, but the illusion created is a powerful one, one that can return us to the world with greater knowledge and awareness.

It is not too much to say that for poets the world doesn't exist in some real sense until they describe it, until it has been captured and measured in words. Only then is perception confirmed. Only then is reality verified in concrete, evocative terms. This is the case with James Dickey, who has spoken about the "personal" in poetry—meaning not the intimate or confessional, but the unique, inimitable core of an individual sensibility, a diction and syntax so exact as to be almost equivalent to one's fingerprints or DNA. Dickey has hardly written a poem without this signature quality without somewhere finding the words necessary to equal and therefore body forth the world. This is true of his earliest work, poems about his experience in World War II, with its "besieging mud," the "clumsy hover" of its air transports, and the "licked, light, chalky dazzle" of the South Pacific. For Dickey, the whole project of poetry is not so much to develop and articulate psycho-socio-political themes as to match language to reality, or reality to language, until description itself is the point, the revelation which the whole poem seeks. Certainly, there are intellectual, paraphrasable themes in Dickey's work. But his poems imply something else, something more, as if each declaimed, "This is what it's like to be alive, to inhabit a body, to be conscious and aware." In a funda-mental sense, this same ambition pervades the poetry of Walt Whitman, and is one of its most important achievements. "Song of Myself" is as much a hymn to consciousness as it is to anything else, proclaiming in no uncertain terms, and proudly: "I was the man, I suffered, I was there."

The poet is still the singular, passionate observer we need to translate the world into penetrating, accurate language that somehow makes reality available to our minds in a way in which experience alone cannot thor-oughly provide. Before Adam, there was perceiving without knowing. A pre-verbal silence in which things were indistinguishable from one another, or generalized until they were finally specified. Then, like Athena from Zeus's head, things sprang into being fully themselves, startlingly pres-ent and clear. This sense of discovery, of locating and naming the distinct quality of things is immediately recognizable in Dickey's work, and easily illustrated. When, in "The Movement of Fish," for instance, we read:

No water is still, on top.
Without wind, even, it is full
Of a chill, superficial agitation... [5]

we feel that those three words—*chill, superficial, agitation*—are rigorously exact. They conform to our own perceptions of the behavior of watery surfaces. We have noticed this phenomenon before, have seen it clearly many times. Now it is acknowledged, defined. This is more than description. It is a bestowal of being, a *making-it-clear-to-the-mind*, manifesting something without robbing it of its inherent mystery and essence.

Again and again we feel Dickey making an effort to translate what he perceives into precise revelatory language. In "Diabetes,"[3] he writes of "The rotten, nervous sweetness of my blood," and we feel the disease has been characterized, diagnosed in words as seldom before. When he speaks of animals pouncing "upon the bright backs of their prey /... In a sovereign floating of joy," or the monotonously identical figures on blankets "... made by machine / From a sanctioned, unholy pattern / rigid with industry," we are convinced he has defined the essence of these actions and things, nailed them down with meticulous, unremitting care. They may be familiar, but now they are also designated clearly, accounted for to the language-requiring mind. Whatever we think of Dickey personally, his politics or behavior, his sometimes-inflated rhetoric and exaggerated stance, we cannot deny the obvious power of his best verse.

Another poet capable of translating the world into exact terms, phrases of distinct radiance and acuity, is Mary Oliver, especially in four books: *Twelve Moons, American Primitive, Dream Work*, and *House of Light*. With a profound grasp of her subjects, Oliver employs the telling adjective, the expressive term that—more than merely describing—*characterizes* creatures and things, revealing their particular nature, their sure and unmistakable "it-ness," to borrow a philosophical term. She speaks of the butterfly's "loping" flight, the "morose" movement of turtles, the ocean's "black, anonymous roar." In poem after poem, she displays what fellow-poet Hayden Carruth notes as "the depth and diversity" of her "perceptual awareness." So, we read of the "blue lung" of the Caribbean, the "muscled sleeve" of the fox, the "iron rinds" over winter ponds, and more. The list might be extended at length. Regardless of her proclivity to sentimentalize nature in her more unguarded moments, the power of her observation seldom fails. At her best, she looks at the world with a predator's eye and articulates the way things are—how creatures, plants, minerals, and weathers look, move, change, and manifest themselves to the discerning mind.

This specificity is not the *bon mot*, the "good word," which is cleverness and wit, a stroke of brilliance for the benefit of one's dinner companions. The employment of a *bon mot* involves an adept play of language in the service of entertainment, not accuracy or revelation. We are delighted by the use of a particular term in a particular context because we had never thought of it before, and because in some ways it ridicules and "fits" its object in a jocular way. In visual terms, it may be likened to caricature, which captures and exaggerates the subject's more prominent features while dispensing with other details—details that might be rendered in more exact, realistic proportions if a true representation were desired. The *bon mot* and other such linguistic pleasantries are by nature partial, superficial, and quick—deft thrusts at likeness, at portraiture.

Nor am I speaking strictly of the element of diction, the *mot juste*, or "exact word," though diction and vocabulary are certainly involved in any discussion of language and its expressive possibilities. Diction carries its own importance in writing of all kinds—especially poetry. Concerning writers, Ezra Pound notes that "when their very medium, the very essence of their work, the application of word to thing goes rotten, i.e., becomes slushy and inexact, or excessive and bloated, the whole machinery of social and individual thought and order goes to pot." This is the idea of diction as a moral responsibility, the imperative for writers to get things straight, to call a spade a spade and not some other thing. Poets, he asserts, must not give in to generalities or euphemisms, must not blur the all-important distinctions to which they are obligated as artists, as thinkers and observers. Word choice is crucial to clarity of presentation and thought. But precision and accuracy aren't all that is involved in naming, or renaming, the world.

For that, we need the kind of poetic language that lifts things into consciousness, the delicate seam of words—visionary, resonant, defining—that exists between reality and the mind, that seems to join the two in a moment of insight, until subject and object for once seem to merge, to become one. So, in the example of Oliver's poetry, she speaks of the "ocean's black, anonymous roar"—she might have written of "the ocean's loud, continuous roar" which would have been accurate enough in its way, satisfying our ordinary demands for precision and truth: the ocean *is* both continuous and loud. But the word "black" in this context suggests that the ocean is obscure, impenetrable, difficult to grasp or understand. It also refers to the beach at night, and the largely lightless depths, even at noon, which we have yet to explore. There is a hint of the crack of waves in the adjective as well—by sonic association—and the word "anonymous" suggests even more. The ocean is non-human, the not-self or *Nicht-Ich*, empty of consciousness, morality, or thought. Measured against it, our proud self-regard—our very being—is annihilated. Such is nature, most of it—a place so alien we can only stand appalled at its impersonal power. Between perceiving and describing falls the shadow.

I am not arguing that the world be abstracted into language, but that language be concretized into the world, as far as is possible. A language so visceral, so tangible, that it seems to equal and reflect in itself the concreteness of the world. Some of physicality is found in the work of Galway Kinnell. When his daughter, Maud, is born in the first section of *The Book of Nightmares*, he describes her birth with phrases like "she skids out on her face... this peck of stunned flesh / clotted with celestial cheesiness..."[4]

These phrases afford many pleasures, not the least of which is a delicate pattern of sound and a jaunty, affectionate tone balanced against a profoundly critical moment both fascinating and repellant. The word "skids" is not accurate and true, in Pound's notion of "the application of word to thing," so much as it is evocative, illuminating. It suggests ideas about birth and life somewhat different from the sentimental, pious beliefs ordinarily associated with these things. The fact that Kinnell's daughter "skids" out (and on her face to boot!) implies resistance, or at the very least an involuntary—that is to say, unintentional—action. Further, "skids" contains within it the seeds of humor, someone stepping on a banana peel, while at the same time hinting of danger, of accident—a car careening on an icy road. We do not *intend* to be born, we are ejected into the world, ready or not, leaving us "stunned" in harsh, hospital light.

The same mixture of humor and unease is picked up in the wonderful line "clotted with celestial cheesiness...." The states implied by the words "celestial" and "cheesiness" are existentially poles apart, the spirit and the flesh, and their odd connection here describes an intermediary phase in which spirit is only just beginning to cohere, or "clot," into matter, to move from the divine towards the mundane.

The passage artfully captures a father's paradoxical feelings about his daughter's birth: a brisk humor reflecting his joy at her arrival set against his anxiety about suffering and mortality, which must inevitably follow birth, and which the phrase "astral violet / of the underlife" insinuates so effectively. In fact, *underlife* is another term that simultaneously contains these polarities of thought and feeling: the seriousness of some unknown metaphysical power, and the humorous suggestion that the life of the fetus lies "under," in the womb at the lower extremities of the body, like someone living in a basement apartment under a tall building.

As with Whitman's description of the carpenter's fore plane as it "whistles its wild ascending lisp," Kinnell's description of birth goes beyond mere diction, mere clarity and responsible reporting. Such moments of heightened perception are prevalent throughout his work. In another poem, "The Fly," from *Body Rags*[5], he depicts a common housefly as it crawls over the eyelids and cheeks of a corpse, remarking, "One day I may learn to suffer / his mizzling sporadic stroll…"—language, once again, revelatory in both sound and sense in the way it reaches beyond itself to grapple with the palpable but no less mysterious facts of existence. Along with Whitman and Dickey—and clearly in kinship with Emerson and Thoreau—Kinnell's poems express a desire to realize the moment in the only way writers know how: through the agency of inspired and exacting language. "I have always intended to live forever," writes Kinnell in his poem, "The Seekonk Woods," "but even more, to live now."

To be alive, and to know it—a seemingly simple realization—is the not-so-secret program of many of our best poets. To be awake and cognizant of even a fraction of an ordinary day, which is also a fraction of eternity, cannot be so easily assumed. Poets have frittered away their lives in pursuit of far less. Thoreau asserts that he spent his time in solitude at Walden Pond because he didn't want to reach the end of his life and find he had never been alive at all. He found a language equal to the task of apprehending and articulating the world. The words of this language rely on the poet's knowledge of their inner resonances, their feel and heft and complex reverberations when placed in context with other words, the intimate associations they have forged in imagination and memory, their psychological and emotional implications, their symbolic and metaphorical potential, their particular temperature and texture and taste. This is more than the definition of connotation ordinarily allows. It is to treat words as intricate, adaptable organisms that take sustenance from what surrounds them in order to add again—to answer back with their own contributory lives—to the infinite life of their surroundings. They are their surroundings, and their surroundings are them, in the normal give-and-take of vibrant, responsive substances.

So, there is a language that is both of-and-about the world, both object and reflection in the mirror of words. In order to employ such language, delicate transactions are required between word and thing. In his essay "Romanticism and Classicism," the English Modernist poet, theorist, and critic T. E. Hulme writes:

> The great aim is accurate, precise and definite
> description. The first thing is to recognise how
> extraordinarily difficult this is. It is no mere matter of
> carefulness: you have to use language, and language
> is by its very nature a communal thing; that is, it
> expresses never the exact thing but a compromise—
> that which is common to you, me and everybody.[6]

Already, at the beginning of the twentieth century, Hulme anticipates the language theories to come. He knows that language is capable of obtruding itself, forcing its own purposes on the writer who is not careful, whose mind is already a complex network of entrenched forms, past reading experiences and second-hand concepts. As Robert Bly cautions in his little book *Leaping Poetry*, this leads to atrophy in literature. Though Bly is speaking particularly about imaginative association—how ideas and images become invariably related—the same might be said of language in general, how words are chosen automatically, almost compulsively by the mind:

> By the eighteenth century... Freedom of association
> had become drastically curtailed. The word "sylvan"
> by some psychic railway leads directly to "nymph," to

"lawns," to "dancing," so to "reason," to music, spheres, heavenly order, etc. They're all stops on some railroad.[7]

Thus, in describing the sound a brook makes as it pours over stones, we can be sure the words "purl," "bubble," "sing," and "babble" will come up as predictably as Pavlov's dog will salivate at a sound it associates with food. Here is the very crux of the matter: When stale, fossilized, pre-fabricated language overrides the poet's own consciousness and unique personal expression, the world is not revealed but obscured, dressed in borrowed rags, so that we see only the dulled reality of a socialized mind, not the rare, spontaneous glimpses—the sudden lightning strokes—of perception we expect to access in poetry. Only the best writers are capable of the "terrific struggle" it takes to precisely describe—that is, re-name—the world. As Hulme says somewhat later in the essay cited above:

There are then two things to distinguish, first the particular faculty of mind to see things as they really are, and apart from the conventional ways in which you have been trained to see them. This is itself rare enough in all consciousness. Second, the concentrated state of mind, the grip over oneself which is necessary in the actual expression of what one sees.

To see things as they really are! To "wash the gum from your eyes," as Whitman urges. Or to "cleanse the doors of perception," as Blake would have it. There are many poets, now and throughout history, who have been equal to the struggle. And the struggle has only deepened over the centuries. Gertrude Stein has said that we are in a late period of language. She means that the edges have been worn off words from constant use, that grammar has solidified in molds, like steel, that diction and syntax— the very structure of the sentence itself—has succumbed to methods of mass-production and pre-packaging that destroy any pretension towards originality of expression. She means that our language—not only the language we speak every day, but the language of poetry itself—is a fallen one and must be redeemed by poets willing to engage daily in a confrontation with words to renew, or rediscover, their lost potential.

Acknowledging this problem, poets have attempted various methods to deploy language in ways that will remind readers that poetry is made out of words—a medium about which we have many assumptions, and which can be scuffed, worn, and battered through overuse. Or, to put it another way, words can disappear through long familiarity—we no longer even see them—as we leap past them toward standard meanings and manipulated, predictable responses. Gertrude Stein herself is a good example. Her non-syntactical phrases and repetitions are meant to prevent us from easily falling into interpretation, into the referential phase of reading, by stopping us abruptly at the surface of the page itself, trying to make sense out of unfamiliar clusters of words. This practice has an effect, but is limited and empty in the end. Language *completely* devoid of referentiality is crippled language, foreshortened language, language fighting with one hand tied behind its back. "Be all you can be," the Army urges in its stirring, epic propaganda. Stein's poems, or writings, seem to exhort language to be less than it can be. The answer to renewal of language cannot reside in disposing of one of its most potent and crucial functions—the representation of meaning and thought, feeling and perception, insight and apprehension. Without these, we are left with a pile of words, inert, unrelated, mere verbiage that is interesting but ultimately mute.

Other poets like Galway Kinnell attempt to recall words back from their long exile of disuse, their historical obsolescence, in hopes that now—having been almost completely forgotten—they will appear new again, glittering with some of their former energy and significance. So, in the *Book of Nightmares*, Kinnell can imagine a moment of transcendent experience, reminiscent of Wilfred Owen's nightmarish descent into the earth below a battlefield, when he writes:

A way opens
at my feet. I go down
the night-lighted mule-steps into the earth,
the footprints behind me

> filling already with pre-sacrificial trills
> of canaries, go down
> in the unbreathable goaf
> of everything I ever craved and lost.[8]

Even in the general curiousness, the linguistic eeriness of this passage, *goaf* stands out and shimmers with unusual allure. Before we are sent to the dictionary to define it, we are struck by something that feels right, even inevitable about the word itself: the single, heavy syllable, the interesting sound, the coupling of it to a known but disturbing adjective—all in an earthy yet surreal, almost otherworldly setting. Once we find out what the word means (a mining term, referring to the hole made in the earth, the rubble taken from it, and the reservoir of gas that builds up there), we feel sure that it is right in this context and that an odd, superannuated noun has been rescued for us, given new life in a contemporary poem. This is another technique for renaming the world. However, we wouldn't want Kinnell or any poet to make a habit of filling his lines with antiquated terms or it would become mere pedantry, a lexical showing-off, as though poetry required nothing more than a good dictionary or book of synonyms. This kind of technique should be used only sparingly, and with great tact.

Other poets, like Robert Pinsky, attempt to resuscitate language by unabashedly flaunting lists of words in front of us in order to catch our attention, like a street vendor laying his wares out before us for inspection and appraisal. Some words in the list may be common, others unusual, but all are normally overlooked as we rush toward extracting only the meaning, leaving empty hulls of those words behind. The idea is to force us to stop and heft each term, as it were: to weigh it, consider it, regard it the way we might regard a vase or a picture, any object that deserves our undivided attention before advancing to the next word, then the next. For words are objects as well as abstract signs or repositories of meaning. Each has a physical presence, a linguistic body, makes a distinct sound, requires a certain effort to pronounce, and has a palpable effect on other words when put into contact with them. So, in what is arguably one of his best poems, "Shirt,"[9] Pinsky begins by listing various parts of that apparel in order to call our attention not just to the shirt, but to the language we ordinarily use to denote it. The opening line of the poem begins this process:

> The back, the yoke, the yardage. Lapped seams...

Later, he lists terms referring to the different jobs undertaken in the production of shirts, and even parts of the machines used in that production, as well as terms indicating the organization of labor:

> The Presser, the cutter,
> The wringer, the mangle. The needle, the union,
> The treadle, the bobbin. The Code...

Still later, as though it were fun, even pleasurable, to dwell on words this way, to savor them and meditate upon them the way we savor expensive and exotic foodstuffs, filling our mouths with their sumptuous textures and tastes, Pinsky give us another list, an inventory of various kinds of shirts with interesting and appealing names:

> Prints, plaids, checks,
> Houndstooth, Tattersall, Madras.

Each of these techniques represents ways in which poets strive to focus attention on words themselves, and in so doing reinvigorate language for the purpose of writing fresh and interesting lines of poetry. But as they are techniques, not revelations, each is really only a half-measure, a partial solution to the problem of actually renaming the world. They are intellectual solutions, ways of manipulating language, adding fresh ingredients to enliven an old stew. Solutions, that is, applied from the *outside*, derived from language itself; not arising from *inside*, from the wellhead of conscious experience and personal illumination which then emerge through language, finding their way out in descriptions of profound and original beauty. Technique is not enough. It lacks, in Hulme's words, "The particular faculty of mind to see things as they really are." It lacks the kind of devout attentiveness Malebranche tells us is "the natural prayer of the soul." This is the first indispensable step, the source of any true, inherent renewal of language.

I am writing at pains to avoid sounding vague and mystical. I am not speaking of theological revelation or the metaphysical visions of saints, but the direct, unmediated, visceral knowledge of the world—the world we live in every day, but rarely apprehend. The language of Adam is not the language of transcendence. It is the language of the body, the senses, the language of the Eden we have and not the ideal, abstract one we seek. It is meaning, substance, truth, something attainable and real the poets must strive for in their daily work. It cannot be replaced by mere style or technique, and it cannot be faked. It is not a product of intelligence, culture, sophistication, or literary panache. It does not care to impress us. It overwhelms us. Moreover, examples of it may be culled from the best literature of any time and place. When we encounter it, we are sure. "The hair on the backs of our hands," as Emily Dickinson has told us, "stands up. Our experience of it electrifies us, forces us to take notice, as though our own semi-conscious, half-apprehended inklings were objectified finally in words of uncanny accuracy and power." The only worthwhile question, the only real question, is how to come by it. That requires extraordinary tenacity, sacrifice, and devotion.

Writing transformative verse is not simply a gift, a matter of talent alone. The language of such poetry is inspired, primal. It arises from heightened awareness and extraordinarily acute perception, never from mere literary cunning. It is arrived at by means of Hulme's "terrific struggle with language" which may take years, even decades of apprenticeship to words and methods of focusing the mind in order to see clearly what is in front of us. All of this sounds forbidding, impossibly difficult to achieve. Yet our literature abounds in moments of revelation, penetrating descriptions of the world that make it feel freshly witnessed, glowing with the excitement of initial discovery. "It is the choice of the commodious adjective," Wallace Stevens tells us, "it comes to that in the end:

the description that makes it divinity." And the kind of description he is talking about is not confined to the genre of poetry. Exemplary passages may be found in the works of all great novelists at moments when, by virtue of an intensification of language matched to powerful insight, they lift themselves into uncommon awareness to reveal the mysterious, something half-hidden and unguessed at in the most ordinary phenomena. So, in *Moby Dick*, Melville describes a particularly languid day:

> But one transparent blue morning, when a stillness
> almost preternatural spread over the sea, however
> unattended with any stagnant calm; when the long
> burnished sunglade on the waters seemed a golden finger
> laid across them, enjoining secrecy; when the slippered
> waves whispered together as they softly ran on... 10

It is a morning before time, a paradise of tranquility devoid temporarily of suffering the burden of human knowing. Among the many other felicities in this passage, the adjective "slippered" is particularly inspired, comprehending as it does both the motion of the waves sliding off one another with liquid ease and the idea that they are hushed—as though they wore slippers—a homely but effective image. This is heightened by the seething "s" sounds and the short "i" sounds echoed in the words "slippered" and "whispered." Such sounds are woven together throughout the entire passage until it becomes a delicate tissue of meaning, expressive at every juncture and at every moment of its presentation. Moreover, Melville is describing these particular waves in this particular spot on this particular day. No other. And perhaps never to be perceived exactly this way again but caught for an instant—yet forever—in prose of uncanny accuracy and effect.

Melville fashions a proto-language, a language of ur-words and eponyms, the "true" words and phrases he needs in order to tell his daunting, colossal tale. Like Adam, he knows something intuitively, exactly as it is in its individual essence and nature. He knows the sea and is therefore able to bestow an identity upon it, to describe it for us in precise terms. In *Moby Dick*, the ocean acquires an unmistakable character, a soul. Melville stretches his hands out over "the great shroud of the sea" and blesses it, sanctifying it in language piercingly beautiful and exact.

2

Divorced Couplets

and the Evolution of a Form

The very first poems in English—starting with "Caedmon's Hymn," "Beowulf," "The Seafarer," and others in the Anglo-Saxon canon—were written in some type of meter and form. Though meters and forms have changed over the centuries, mostly through refinement, alterations of fashion, discovery, and addition, the tradition of writing in form continued virtually unbroken until the free verse revolution at the beginning of the twentieth century. Critics writing about the subject of free verse, such as H. T. Kirby-Smith in *The Origins of Free Verse* and Chris Beyers in *The History of Free Verse* have demonstrated that species of "free" verse have been with us for some time, longer than many of us might think—born under the sign of "Imagism" with its three Wisemen: Eliot, Williams and Pound—as far back as the Old Testament writings in the Hebrew Bible and in English since the Renaissance, at least. Still, free verse has never been the dominant form of English poetry as a whole until recently. As Alfred Corn, a noted formalist himself, asserts in his excellent study of traditional meter and form, *The Poem's Heartbeat: A Manual of Prosody*, "The arrival of Modernism meant for the most part a discarding of traditional metrical practice altogether in favor of various kinds of loosely metered or unmetered verse." This observation is seconded by Kevin Walzer in his study of the resurgence of traditional poetry, *The Ghost of Tradition: Expansive Poetry and Postmodernism*, in which the phrase *Expansive poetry* is substituted for the more widely circulated term *New Formalism*. "The Expansive poetry movement," Walzer writes, "reminds us of the continuing vitality of rhyme, meter, and story to poetry." But, he continues, "Those modes, while not abandoned during the twentieth century in American poetry, were marginalized for much of the time. The main line in American poetry during the twentieth century is free verse and experimentation."

Yet, a sizeable percentage of poetry written in English *before* the twentieth century—perhaps somewhere in the ninety-percent range— had been composed in traditional form. By *form* I mean traditional fixed form that uses rhyme, meter, and conventional grammar, even logic, and not the disjunctive, paratactic structures of some twentieth century experimental writing. This is not to suggest that free verse is not a form. It is. The second term, "verse," assures us of this. Free verse is not "formless verse," but measured out in lines. It is only "free" in the sense that it is void of regular meter and rhyme (except in certain temporary, localized effects). The formal aspects of lineation—and traditional stanzaic structures—remain as resources for the modern poet. Still, free verse has never been the ascendant form of poetry until now. Given this situation— the extremely high percentage of formalist verse produced in the past—it might be a good idea to examine traditional form: what it is, how it works, and what it can do. All serious and successful Western poems are in one way or another rooted firmly in the rich compost of more than a thousand years of English and American verse.

Nevertheless, the subject is impossible. It is huge, manifold, infinite. It is as daunting as the emptiness of the white page—or the blank screen—before you have conceived of the first few words of your poem. Further, the topic is contentious, irresolvable to the satisfaction of all. Poets and critics have been arguing about the nature and use of form since they began writing about it. How to begin, how to gain even a tentative purchase on such an enormous and complicated topic? The answer is as difficult and as simple as how to begin a poem, equally daunting in its prospects, but not I think, irresolvable: begin anywhere by focusing on a detail, a small part of the whole you hope your poem may eventually become. Likewise, if we can begin to understand even *one* form, even a *little bit* about the mechanics and structure of that particular form, we will have gained insight into all forms, what they are, and how they work. Each form has its own dynamics, of course, its own temper and tenor and mood. Its own personality, one might say. As Baron Wormser reminds us in his powerful meditation about form in his book, *The Road Washes Out in Spring*[1], quatrains, couplets, tercets, and such are radically diverse things. That is, as long as certain conditions are met, "For forms to live, they have to be used. For forms to be recognized, their absoluteness has to be granted its value. The world of a quatrain is a different world from that of a tercet. If such distinctions aren't recognized and cultivated, then beauty palls." Wormser is writing about the Romantic poet, Shelley, who believed that "art ministered to life" and that "the search for form that defined art as an activity was practical Platonism, a phrase that was not a contradiction in terms." Form, for Shelley (and others), was not simply the shape language makes on a page when a number of prescribed syllables and lines are deployed to fulfill an arbitrary poetic scheme. Forms were sacred vessels that existed beyond language and the poet. They had a life of their own—the way equations have for mathematicians—an essence that participated in the *essence of absolute Truth* with a capital T. So each form was unique and carried with it the possibility of reflecting a fraction of the power of Truth, if handled properly and granted its own inimitable dynamics and character.

But there are some features of form in general that seem universal, the abstract essence of what form is, and how it functions in the making of art. For one thing, all form helps the artist manage and control his vision. Vision (Imagination) is a mercurial thing. Without a container, it might spill everywhere, shatter into hundreds, even thousands of pieces. Vision is formless. It needs the strictures of art to contain it. Without the help of form, vision—no matter how passionate and intense—remains a glittering blob, reflecting light without meaning, possibility without fulfillment, thought without definition. In this way, it resembles emotion, raw emotion without context or a way of apprehending it or conveying it to another person. We need to read a Shakespearean sonnet in order to experience it, not just a second-hand prose paraphrase of the sonnet which, at best, will convey but a modicum of what the entire sonnet "means."

Another aspect of form, any form, is how it is inextricably bound up with meaning. It is the shape meaning takes, when it takes shape. Or emotion. Or thought. This is why some poets assert that the chance of writing a successful poem is greater if it is written in traditional form rather than in free verse. The claim isn't made, I think, to suggest that writing in form *guarantees* a better poem. Only that—assuming proficiency—chance favors the formalist. Why? Because pre-determined form provides us with a natural resistance to overwriting, repetition, lack of focus, and loss of direction (*Here!* form gestures helpfully at crucial moments: *This way!*).

To dictate shape and embody meaning is not trifling when faced with creating something out of nothing, which is the challenge every artist undertakes the minute she picks up a brush or a pen or wields a mallet and chisel. If you write in free verse, not only do you have to have a vision, you must create an entirely new form to embody that vision, and you must do this every time, for every new poem you write.

It's easy enough to learn "the rules" of any fixed form, the exact details of structure—meter, number of lines, rhyme scheme, and so on—but futile and senseless to follow these rules slavishly. Anyone can look up the description of a sonnet, but no one can write a good one by following that description alone. The trick is adopting and adapting the form to your own uses; the same trick advised when employing meter: set up a fixed structure, then find ways to vary meaningfully from it. The fixed forms—sonnet, villanelle, sestina, heroic couplet, terza rima, etc.—have established themselves because of certain inherent qualities in those forms (as Baron Wormser reminds us), qualities that allow the poet to exploit features of language that other poets have discovered and exploited similarly. The heroic couplet, for instance, works so efficiently and memorably because in just two lines the poet is able to posit an idea in the first line and clinch it in the second:

> True ease in writing comes from art, not chance;
> As those move easiest who have learned to dance.

Alexander Pope's often-quoted aesthetic advice takes advantage of one aspect of its meter (iambic pentameter) by placing important words and syllables in positions of stress, and at the beginning and ends of lines ("ease," "writing," "art," "chance," "dance," and so on), though it is not always true that important words, even in Pope's work, appear in positions of stress; moreover, the rhyme scheme reinforces the idea presented ("chance" and "dance" are opposites, though they rhyme); pauses are judiciously placed to emphasize what comes immediately after them (the pause following "art," and at the end of the first line); then there is the way the second line serves to illustrate, in an image, what the first line expresses abstractly as a premise; and the way each line is a complete unit of sense; finally, the feeling of closure is palpable, reinforced by the full rhyme of "chance" and "dance." These things illustrate those features of the heroic or "closed" couplet—the compact, balanced, packaged neatness of it—which has made it such a serviceable and satisfying form of verse over the centuries, though it enjoyed its real heyday during the Enlightenment in the eighteenth century, perhaps because it lends itself so easily to speculation, statement, and rational thought.

But if we were to employ this form today, at the beginning of the twenty-first century, it might be advisable not to reproduce it exactly in its eighteenth century lineaments and proportions. The lives we live, and the language we use, our attitudes, the very way we *think* have changed drastically since the age of Pope and we probably want to write in ways that reflect the truths of our time. None of the moral certitude, artistic authority, shared cultural aesthetics and beliefs, scientific and intellectual principals, historical and social structures, political realities, or literary practices of Pope's time exist today. Our age is messy, multifarious, indeterminate, unbalanced, fractured, and cynical. We are not likely to accept *any* truth, and certainly not in a form that so efficiently seems to embody it. Our couplets, then, usually allow for hesitancy, doubt, even unshapeliness, and affect little sense of completeness or snappy closure. If we encounter couplets today, they are likely to look something like this:

MASTERFUL[2]

They say you can't think and hit at the same time,
but they're wrong: you think with your body, and the whole

wave of impact surges patiently through you
into your wrists, into your bat, and meets the ball

as if this exact and violent tryst had been a fevered
secret for a week. The wrists "break," as the batting

coaches like to say, but what they do is give away
their power, spend themselves, and the ball benefits.

When Ted Williams took—we should say "gave"—
batting practice, he'd stand in and chant to himself

"My name is Ted Fucking Ballgame and I'm the best
fucking hitter in baseball," and he was, jubilantly

grim, lining them out pitch after pitch, crouching
and uncoiling from the sweet ferocity of excellence.

It's not clear why William Matthews, the author of this poem which appears in his collection *Search Party*, chose to write it in couplets instead of, say, a single block of lines. Perhaps he wanted to supply a certain amount of breathing space—which is also mental space—between stanzas so that the reader could take the poem in at a more leisurely pace. This allows the reader to think about each stanza, to let its meaning sink in, before advancing to the next stanza. At any rate, the poem is not metered, and unlike Pope the couplets do not present a single thought in a pair of matched, balanced, rhymed lines (where the rhymes served to drive the point of the couplet home, as well as make it memorable). There is a sense of closure in Matthews' poem, a sense of having said what wanted to be said in the most aesthetically pleasing way, with intelligence and a lush, sonorous vocabulary leading to that last intriguing observation: "the sweet ferocity of excellence" (which, a friend of mine has pointed out, is iambic pentameter; that is, a localized and temporary shift to regular meter in part of a line). But the poem—and the separate couplets—do not snap shut with a commanding confident click the way Pope's heroic couplets do:

Fair tresses man's imperial race ensnare,
And beauty draws us with a single hair.

Matthews is saying something he believes, of course, and saying it with an authoritative voice—with confidence and style—but what he has to say does not have that all-defining, unimpeachable air of truth, that feeling of finality one associates with the heroic couplet when a statement is being made. The statements in Matthews' poem—with perhaps the exception of that first firm assertion—are mostly observations, a description of how Ted Williams hit a baseball. Matthews is giving *his* opinion, telling *his* story of Ted Williams, not *the* story of Ted Williams, self-evident and unassailable. There is a sense of the poem moving forward without being parceled out in discrete couplets, each containing a complete thought, as with heroic couplets that have a finished, cut-and-measured, complete-in-themselves feeling. Hesitancy and doubt appear in Matthews' poem in grammatical ways, with conjunctions like "but," which qualify or dispute something just said; in phrases like "as if" and "we should say," as well as in the several oxymorons in which Matthews reveled, such as "jubilantly grim" or "ferocity of excellence." Such contradictions might not be found in Pope's pronouncements, for he believed that he was articulating universal truths that lay beyond him, while Matthews is expressing a personal truth, his particular take on Ted Williams—which is clever and elegant and entirely appealing, an artful, idiosyncratic impression of a great figure in the pantheon of baseball.

Matthews' couplets, unlike Pope's, hover and slide into each other—another mark of their hesitancy—as if to emphasize the provisional nature of truth, its momentary, not eternal, substance. The twentieth century could not be as confident or as dogmatic in its beliefs as the eighteenth century. Too many earth-shattering, mind-bending discoveries had been made, too many soul-rending events had taken place in the ensuing two centuries for the rational, systematic worldview of the eighteenth century to survive. No wonder Matthews' couplets resemble Pope's in little more than their visual aspect.

This brings up another important factor in the evolution of the couplet from the Augustan age to our own: unmetered, unrhymed free verse couplets can only be discerned as couplets when they are separated and arranged that way on the page. Without a regular pattern of end-rhymes dutifully linking pairs of contiguous lines, how would we know they were couplets at all? This has been true of other stanza forms as well—the quatrain and the tercet, for example—following the revolution of the free verse movement in the early part of the twentieth century. In order to suggest some principle of measure and order in a free verse poem, Modern and contemporary poets have adopted the *look*, if not the technical aspects, of the older forms. There is nothing wrong with this. In fact, such bluff, suggestive strategies have worked quite well in signaling to the reader that "this is a poem," and inviting, therefore, a different order of attention and expectation than a mere block of lineated type. Matthews' lines are visually, not technically, couplets in the eighteenth century sense. Not only do they not display the obligatory end-rhymes of classical couplets, but the pairs of lines in Matthews' poem are not especially linked syntactically and grammatically, not bound together semantically, fused into a meaningful whole. Instead, their sense bleeds from couplet to couplet, as Matthews' thought extends beyond the ends of lines and stanzas as it continues to unfold throughout the poem. If we were to re-lineate the poem to try to bring the pairs of lines into linked semantic conformity again, it might look something like this:

> They say you can't think and hit at the same time,
> but they're wrong.
>
> You think with your body
> And the whole wave of impact surges patiently through you.
>
> It surges into your wrists, into your bat,
> and meets the ball.

But it's impossible, really, because the habit and mode of thinking that produced "Masterful" is completely different from the modes and habits of thought that produced "The Rape of the Lock" and "An Essay on Man." If we do not believe in absolute verities anymore, it would be difficult to believe in the crisp, balanced symmetry of the couplet that traditionally contained and mirrored those verities. And if irrefutable logic has been lost, perhaps indeterminacy has taken its place. Our poetic forms, as forms have always done, strive to incarnate and reflect this fact, not deny it.

I do not mean to imply that poets in the twentieth century have not written in heroic couplets, period. Many have, but the tone, texture, and intent of those couplets are demonstrably different from the heroic couplets written by Dryden, Pope, and Johnson. This is due to changes in language and fluidities of style, but also to the cultural and aesthetic attitudes I have mentioned. Who we are and what we believe at any moment of historical time is reflected in the kind of poetry we write. The relative rigidity of eighteenth century English poetics would have no place in our own age, and the reverse is also true. It took the Romantic revolution to allow the substitution of triple meters to again be permitted in iambic pentameter lines. But it is also true that all poetic forms from all ages are perpetually available to poets no matter what age they write in as long as they are updated somehow in substance and style. Modern poets have written fine, successful poems in Old English strong stress alliterative meter. But no one, I think, would recommend a wholesale return to Old English prosody.

I am talking about the closed heroic couplet, but there is another couplet—the "open" couplet—which *The New Princeton Encyclopedia of Poetry and Poetics* describes in part this way:

> The couplet is "opened" when enjambed, i.e., when the
> syntactical and metrical frames do not close together
> at the end of the couplet, the sentence being carried
> forward into subsequent couplets to any length desired
> and ending at any point in the line. *This form of the*
> *couplet is historically older and not much less common*
> *than the closed form in English poetry* (italics mine).[3]

Still, the classical "open" couplet is rhymed and metered, so it has a more definite tone and firm sense of order, a measure and balance that is lacking in Matthews' or anyone's free verse couplets. Regardless of being enjambed, its structure signals the kind of stability and control—aesthetically, but also intellectually—that the twentieth century sought to avoid. It might be possible to describe the Matthews-like stanza as a stichic poem broken up into pairs of lines rather than a poem written directly in discrete couplets. One might be able to do this with any stichic free verse poem with an even number of lines.

If we fast-forward a generation or two, crossing the invisible boundary between Modern and postmodern in the process, we are likely to find something like this:

THE PATH TO THE ORCHARD[4]

I once was afraid of everything living.
Then I put down that old wound

and began to follow
nevertheless like a shade through the trees.

How I died then waiting in frost.
I narrowed like a great ship's wake

with all my windows glinting behind me.
The apples were falling...

which constitute the first four stanzas of a poem from Matthew Zapruder's surprising first collection, *American Linden*. I say surprising because of the poems' shifts of perspective, disjointed thought, and the elusive but dispersed meaning that keeps the reader guessing, turning in circles trying to anticipate the direction the poem might take. By this historical point in time, the coherence and compactness of the traditional couplet, its matched measured meaning, has been completely diffused (and defused). The focus on a single, verifiable subject that we found in Matthews' poem has now been blurred even further. This occurs because the narrative line in Zapruder's poem has been disrupted—meaning is everywhere and nowhere—though by the end of the poem a certain coherence reasserts itself.

A sky full of white blossoms
broke on the stones of the orchard.

I smelled sweet pungent wine.
I saw one last inflamed glorious sun

returning to set on our backs.
I came closer and shook the branches

and screamed then grew sharp-eyed.
I could hear the unloaders laughing

Back down the hill they carried baskets
of leaves burning in their arms.

Their eyes were angry.
I had found the path to the orchard.

While Matthews abandoned the self-sufficiency of Pope's epigrammatic couplets in favor of the unity of the poem as a whole, Zapruder in turn abandons the thread of development that holds Matthews' poem together, its seamless logic. No longer a terse semantic structure, the couplet has become a mere visual pattern, a measure for the eye and not the meaning-seeking mind. If we ask ourselves what Matthews is getting at in his poem, we might phrase it this way: "Excellence is something intuitive and personal, a style." But what is the theme of Zapruder's poem? Fear of life is alleviated by an experience of nature? We must find a way to escape the self if we are to be able to experience what is not the self? We would be hard pressed to express it. The poem's value lies not so much in what is said, but in how it is written—enigmatic, suggestive, multifaceted, open to more than a single interpretation, it resonates with possibility, but settles on none. We might assert that Zapruder's poem—and perhaps postmodern poetry in general—is the poetry of indeterminacy, and its father is not Pope, but Werner Heisenberg.

But even Zapruder's poem is fairly coherent, fairly narrative (it seems to adhere, more or less, to the subject of an orchard) compared to the piecemeal, scattered quality of the following poem by Jared White in an issue of the literary magazine, *Meridian*:

THE CURE IS LOVE[5]

Or diphthongs. Pronunciation
Without hopeless distances

The sky made blue not once
But every moment because

It has not changed. The mind
Conserving itself for other

Projects than blue-making.
A sound of welcome changing

In the lips. O no I. Understand
At the time of difference.

Make everything at the moment
Of transformation. Only know

When everything has changed.
There is no time, boy or digraph.

You are out. The cure is love.

If Shelley is right, that forms represent the potential for expressing truths that lie beyond language and the poet, then the putative bond between form and meaning has indeed been broken. As we move from classical to Modern to postmodern verse, meaning becomes more and more tentative and form may play less and less a part in the integral structure of the poem. By "integral structure" I mean the traditional relationship between content and form. Form is no longer functional for some, but largely decorative. A way of arranging words on a page. It would be difficult today to find many poets who still believe—along with Shelley—that absolute Truths may correspond to manmade, factitious forms of art. Far more might concede that some practical connection exists between certain poetic forms and particular kinds of content. (Wormer's argument, again, that "The world of a quatrain is a different world from that of a tercet.") Perhaps, for some, the couplet as practiced by Pope will always be married to the wit of the epigram, or the sonnet, with its roots firmly planted in the Renaissance, to the arguments of love.

In his classic treatment *Poetic Meter & Poetic Form*, Paul Fussell demonstrates over and over the suitability of certain meters and forms to certain kinds of subject matter—given certain emotional and psychological contexts.[6] I do not have the space to recap his arguments here, but a question remains: Is the sonnet, for instance, suited to romantic subjects because of inherent traits and qualities that exist in the form itself, or do we associate the sonnet with romantic subjects because historically those are the subjects that have been dealt with in the form over and over again? Can both of these statements be true without bringing the whole house-of-cards argument about the relationship between content and form crashing down? Certainly, perfectly successful sonnets have been written about hate, or war, or any other subject. It is also possible that this is only true because of the contrast such a sonnet would draw between the subject and the inherent traits and qualities historically associated with the form.

But if we tend to make every form our own and adapt it to our age, we are also engineering new forms to serve the demands of whatever new thoughts, realities, and experiences might arise. This is a challenge. What's the best form for any poem? "That form which most brings forth its content" is the classical answer. That's true, but about as helpful as Rilke's advice that we must change our lives. Yes, but how? And at what cost? What forms will best serve us in the twenty-first century as we continue to struggle with the fractured nature of existence and the scattered perceptions of the mind? What forms best serve poems whose content is either meaningless or impossible to determine with any degree of confidence? Who knows. But it's a good bet that they will be more decorative than functional; more arbitrary than integral; a way of dispersing words on a page that entertains and occupies the eye, but foregoes any pretense towards absolutism, or fitness of subject.

This decorative quality of postmodern verse might go farther than the eye, the way words are deployed in some sort of arrangement on the page. In an essay entitled "Polka Dots, Stripes, and Plaids" from *Real Sofistikashun*[7], Tony Hoagland argues that not only the eye but the mind, too, is involved in what he calls "compositional" or pattern-making poetics, a poetics that might produce poems that are "as innocent and undemanding, as purely compositional as wallpaper." But for such an aesthetic, the mind is not involved in the traditional way of interpreting and making sense of what it reads. Instead, it delights in language that presents itself in abstract patterns, and what happens when different patterns are repeated in interesting ways or placed in juxtaposition to one another—how they clash with, balance-out, negate, or emphasize one another—the way stripes and polka dots do, a principal of dressing as old as your father's advice not to wear a striped tie with a checkered shirt. He writes of "decorative aesthetics," a "compositional spirit" and a "compositional sensibility," as well as a "game-playing spirit" and "writing as a compositional game" as opposed to writing as a "pointing system." That latter concept, "writing as a pointing system," simply means writing that uses language to refer to something beyond itself—the world, if you will, experience, reality. Such language attempts to order the world, which is fundamentally chaotic, and not only itself.

Putting aside, for the sake of convenience, the whole argument about whether language *can* even refer to something beyond itself, "decorative aesthetics" may be another result of the ongoing separation of traditional form from content, one of the things—if not the elemental thing—that makes it possible. Once we wrench meaning away from language, we can proceed easily towards making patterns of words which are no longer required to "point" to anything other than themselves. We can play games with words themselves, as themselves, without worrying about the second or third dimensions that language may possess (denotation and connotation). A poem written in a solely compositional spirit might resemble a game of chess played on a conventional flat board with a limited set of rules; a Shakespearean sonnet, however, might resemble a two- or three-dimensional game played on several boards at once, with a more open set of rules, that change as the game proceeds. The one-dimensionality of "decorative aesthetics" severely limits its possibilities by narrowing the nature of language down to one thing—a level, non-referential plane. Some revel in this. Others might find it boring, restrictive, and trivial.

Among linguists, there is a process whereby a word that began by meaning one thing over centuries slowly migrates towards its opposite and eventually means something entirely different. So, a word like "nice," according to the *Concise Oxford Companion to the English Language*, "has meant foolish, stupid (13–16c), lascivious, loose (14–16c), extravagant" until today, by means of the amelioration process, has come to designate what is "pleasant, agreeable, satisfactory." The pejorative process works the other way, tipping a word with positive connotations towards a negative meaning over time. Something like this seems to have happened with respect to literary concepts and terms in the tectonic shift from Modernism to postmodernism in the last hundred years. It is difficult for me to imagine a poet feeling gratified if a critic referred to his or her work as merely "decorative" and tantamount to "wallpaper." Abstraction, so valued today, was something to be avoided for the Imagists and others in the Modernist era. Physical, concrete imagery was considered an essential component of all good poetry, no matter the genre or mode. So too, the idea that a poet would be playing "games" was not a positive thing as it seems to have become in Hoagland's idea of "writing as a compositional game."

But not all critics agree. In 1969, the critic Robert Scholes published a short pamphlet from Oxford University Press, *Elements of Poetry*, in which he claimed on the very first page of his introduction:

> When T. S. Eliot called poetry "a superior amusement"
> he said it all, so far as I am concerned. Poetry is
> essentially a game, with artificial rules, and it takes
> two—a writer and a reader—to play it. If the reader is
> reluctant, the game will not work. [8]

And to further emphasize his point, he titled the first section of his introduction "The Poetry Game" and part three of the same book, "Word Games." I wonder whether Eliot would have assented to the idea that writing is chiefly a "compositional game" and little more? In my understanding of Eliot's idea of the game poetry plays, meaning bears a central part—not only compositional structure or form, which plays ancillary roles. Still, it can hardly be argued that there is a game-like element in all poetry, especially poetry written in traditional form and meter, and that the poet's deft manipulation of language gives much pleasure to those who can attune themselves to it. Pleasure is one of the fundamental values in poetry—in all art—and without it, poetry would be far less satisfying and attractive.

There is a related aspect of form that subsumes all other considerations of it, and more than anything else, perhaps, hints back at the idea of artistic form replicating in some partial and imperfect way the possibility of Shelley's transcendental forms, the absolute shapes Truth and ultimate reality may take. That aspect, which we call structure, is sometimes also referred to as *architectonics*, and you can see right away in the first element of that word, "arch," which means to rule, or govern (as in oligarchy, or patriarchy) the comprehensive nature of what is suggested. "Arch" refers to the overall ruling or governing principal of something. And hidden in it is the shorter word, "arc," which of course means a bow or curved figure that spans and contains everything beneath it. So, one dictionary defines architectonics as first, "The science of architecture," but more importantly as "the structural design of a complex thing; the way in which the parts of a complex system fit together." The *Merriam-Webster Dictionary* defines architectonics this way: "The unifying structural design of something." A poem, or any work of art, has form in every part of it, down to the most minute, local details. And a complete poem, like a sonnet, has a complete form—of one kind. But structure is larger than form—it is the overarching form of form, if you will. Within a sonnet, you might detect the form of the quatrain, or the couplet, and the meter and rhyme scheme, but the *structure* of a sonnet involves all of these and something more: the complete unfolding shape of the thought, the intricate relations of all the parts to the whole, the balanced interconnected elements that combine to make the whole larger than its parts.

Standing under the ceiling of the Sistine Chapel and considering all of the panels above you at once (not just this one, or that one), or reading all of the prose poems in *Invisible Cities* by Italo Calvino from beginning to end, or listening to a Bach fugue in its entirety gives you some idea—a very good idea—of what structure is and what it might mean: the overall, unifying conception of a number of discrete parts. When Michelangelo conceived of the final structure that his great painting on the ceiling of the Sistine Chapel might take, he considered each panel to be a unity in itself, a part of the story of God, His creation, and the drama of humanity struggling towards redemption after the Fall. But each panel also needed to fit into the grand, integrated scheme of the whole. Here's the way it is described on the Vatican Museum's online website:

> Michelangelo places nine central stories illustrating episodes of the Genesis within a powerful painted architecture, with at their sides figures of Nudes, holding medallions with texts taken from the Book of Kings. At the base of the architectural structure twelve Prophets and Sibyls seated on monumental thrones are countered lower down by Christ's forefathers, portrayed in the Webs and in the Lunettes (north wall, south wall, entrance wall). Finally, in the four corner Pendentives, the artist illustrated some episodes of the miraculous salvation of the people of Israel.[9]

This abstract description is nothing compared to actually looking at the ceiling itself and seeing each panel as a singular work of art, while at the same time considering all of the panels taken together as a radiant, comprehensive whole whose parts reflect and build upon each other, augment each other, even transform and modify each other, until together they present the viewer with a cosmic narrative of monumental proportions. It's a story that can be read backwards and forwards, from side to side, edge to edge to edge, perhaps even diagonally in a way that accumulates and deepens meaning. But it *is* a story. Meaning makes structure and form possible, just as structure and form make meaning possible. Take that crucial relationship away and what is left? What would the ceiling of a postmodern Sistine chapel resemble? It might be fascinating, even beautiful, like a concrete wall haphazardly spray-painted with graffiti. But the integrity of comprehensive structure would be lacking, the balanced harmony of meaning and order, and that is what illuminates Michelangelo's complex series of panels, or Calvino's cities, or the great stained-glass windows of Riems and Chartres.

But to return to poetry and the humble couplet—our bellwether form adopted for the sake of this essay. It will be revealing, finally, to consider what the critic Paul Fussell, whom I've already cited, has to say about the closed couplet. Fussell's book remains one of the most compact and detailed descriptions of traditional form—filled with illustrative lines and passages of poems—which has made it a classic text for several generations of students:

> The closed couplet seems both by its nature and its
> historical associations to imply something special
> about the materials enclosed in it. It seems to imply
> a distinct isolation of those materials from related
> things, a vigorous enclosure of them into a compact
> and momentarily self-sufficient little world of
> circumscribed sense and meaning.

He could be talking about the world of the eighteenth century itself, not simply a literary form: "A self-sufficient world of circumscribed sense and meaning." In such a world, definitive poetic forms make sense—with all that phrase implies—and occupy a central place in the production of art and its enjoyment by a knowledgeable and understanding public. In our world, as we have seen, this may no longer be so. Over the centuries, form has become increasingly divorced from content, a dissociation of meaning with radical consequences for poetry. It is difficult, though, to see how it might have been otherwise. The forms poetry employs must always respond to the actualities of history and human experience. New systems of thought and social change demand new forms of art. Though poetry in traditional forms will continue to be written and contribute value to the culture, those forms will necessarily be stretched, modified, reinvented, and transformed to conform to the imperatives of the present.

3

Poetry and Restraint

He didn't teach me what to put into a poem,
but what to leave out.

—Anne Sexton on Robert Lowell

Prose is prose because of what it includes;
poetry is poetry because of what it leaves out.

—Marvin Bell

We associate the concept of restraint with classical art—the simple, fluted elegance of a Doric column, for instance, or the terse, unclouded beauty of one of Sappho's lyrics. This classical ideal of balance, symmetry, and concision was adopted and reapplied to the poetry of the neoclassical period in eighteenth century England. Though it often produced a cerebral, chilly exactness in their verses, Dryden and Pope knew the importance and use of restraint in almost every line they wrote. The word *restraint* may suggest many things: humility, decorum, tact, breeding, and good taste as well as moral, political, or ethical discretion. But I mean to infer none of those social graces except, perhaps, tangentially. Instead, I will deal only with matters of craft and aesthetic restraint in poetry—those formal, thematic, conceptual, and emotional checks on passion and self-indulgence that can overburden the reader and sink a poem.

In her essay, "Disruption, Hesitation, Silence," Louise Glück writes, "I am attracted to ellipsis, to the unsaid, to suggestion, to eloquent, deliberate silence," which pushes the idea of restraint towards obsession, an excess that goes beyond a practical principle of writing to become the basis of an extreme aesthetic. She goes on to say: "The unsaid, for me, exerts great power: often I wish an entire poem could be made in this vocabulary..."[1] This is the idea of restraint brought to the vanishing point, where the connection—the exact classical ratio—between what is said and what is unsaid is collapsed because the said is submerged in the unsaid, leaving only silence. An entire poem written in the "vocabulary" of silence would no longer be a poem. It would be an abstract, unrealized, inchoate potential existing in the mind, and nothing more. Poetry requires a balance between the said and unsaid, and in that balance lies the key to the nature of restraint.

A poem can be a barrier or a door. On first thought, most of us would choose the latter—isn't a poem supposed to be a place of liberation, a place where we can reveal what we've been thinking and feeling but have had little or no opportunity to express, a kind of coming clean that will be exhilarating for both the reader and writer? I think many of us secretly feel this way. Our ideal is even more ambitious: isn't what we love about Whitman his great prolixity, his unabashed outspokenness, that flood of images and words on which we are buoyed up and washed down a torrent of emotion, into a sea of visions, Walt's boundless fantasia of the unconscious? His most noteworthy twentieth century American disciple—Allen Ginsberg—not one to mince words himself—excerpts two lines from Whitman to append to one of his most famous poems, that outpouring of anxiety, denunciation, and sex we've come to know as "Howl"—"Unscrew the locks from the doors! Unscrew the doors themselves from their jambs!"[2] The project of writing a poem, for Ginsberg and Whitman, is to burst out of the stuffy confines of the socially-restrained self and confess everything. To fall into the arms of the reader, as it were, and win him or her over with a spate of relentless, unchecked honesty.

Certainly, there have been great poets who have mastered this approach and great poems written in this manner. No one can doubt the primitive power, the uplifting moral intensity of poems like "Song of Myself" and "Howl." They are undeniably part of our national literature, our ongoing cultural life, monuments to our famous American brashness and energy. And this impetus, this tradition of unbridled expression, is far from depleted. In fact, the idea of poetry as a door—or two big barn doors—that can be roughly and exuberantly thrown open may always be with us, is certainly still with us in the work of poets like C. K. Williams, Antler, Bridget Pegeen Kelly, Tory Dent, and many others, including most recently Campbell McGrath, a poet of breathless inclusiveness and urgency. Here is his poem, "Angels and the Bars of Manhattan," from a book appropriately titled: *American Noise*—a good example of the headlong rush of his style:

ANGELS AND THE BARS OF MANHATTAN[3]

for Bruce

What I miss most about the city are the angels
and the bars of Manhattan: faithful Cannon's and the Night Cafe;
the Corner Bistro and the infamous White Horse;
McKenna's maniacal hockey fans; the waitresses at Live Bait;
lounges and taverns, taps and pubs;
joints, dives, spots, clubs; all the Blarney
Stones and Roses full of Irish boozers eating brisket
stacked on kaiser rolls with frothing mugs of Ballantine.
How many nights we marked the stations of that cross,
axial or transverse, uptown or down to the East Village
where there's two in every block we'd stop to check,
hoisting McSorleys, shooting tequila and eight-ball
with hipsters and bikers and crazy Ukrainians,
all the black-clad chicks lined up like vodka bottles on Avenue B,
because we liked to drink and talk and argue,
and then at four or five when the whiskey soured
we'd walk the streets for breakfast at some diner,
Daisy's, the Olympia, *La Perla del Sur*,
deciphering the avenues' hazy lexicon over coffee and eggs,
snow beginning to fall, steam on the windows blurring the film
until the trussed-up sidewalk Christmas trees
resembled something out of Mandelstam,
Russian soldiers bundled in their greatcoats,
honor guard for the republic of salt. Those were the days
of revolutionary zeal. Haughty as dictators, we railed

against the formal elite, certain as Moses or Roger Williams
of our errand into the wilderness. Truly,
there was something almost noble
in the depth of our self-satisfaction, young poets in New York,
how cool. Possessors of absolute knowledge,
we willingly shared it in unmetered verse,
scavenging inspiration from Whitman and history and Husker Du,
from the very bums and benches of Broadway,
precisely the way that the homeless
who lived in the Parks Department garage at 79th Street
jacked in to the fixtures to run their appliances
off the city's live current. Volt pirates;
electrical vampires. But what I can't fully fathom
is the nature of the muse that drew us to begin with,
bound us over to those tenements of rage
as surely as the fractured words scrawled across the stoops
and shuttered windows. Whatever compelled us
to suspend the body of our dreams from poetry's slender reed
when any electric guitar would do? Who did we think was listening?
Who, as we cried out, as we shook, rattled, and rolled
would ever hear us among the blue multitudes of Christmas lights
strung as celestial hierarchies from the ceiling? Who
among the analphabetical ranks and orders
of warped records and secondhand books on our shelves,
the quarterlies and *Silver Surfer* comics, velvet Elvises,
candles burned in homage to *Las Siete Potencias Africanas*
as we sat basking in the half-blue glimmer,
tossing the torn foam basketball nigh the invisible hoop,
listening in our pitiless way to two kinds of music,
loud and louder, anarchy and roar, rock and roll
buckling the fundament with pure, delirious noise.
It welled up in us, huge as snowflakes, as manifold,
the way ice devours the reservoir in Central Park.
Like angels or the Silver Surfer we thought we could
kick free of the stars to steer by dead reckoning.
But whose stars are they? And whose angels

if not Rilke's, or Milton's, even Abraham Lincoln's,
"the better angels of our nature" he hoped would emerge,
air-swimmers descending in apple-green light.
We worshipped the anonymous neon apostles of the city,
cuchifrito cherubs, polystyrene seraphim,
thrones and dominions of linoleum and asphalt:
abandoned barges on the Hudson mud flats;
Bowery jukes oozing sepia and plum-colored light;
headless dolls and eviscerated teddy bears
chained to the grills of a thousand garbage trucks; the elms
that bear the wailing skins of plastic bags in their arms all winter,
throttled and grotesque, so that we sometimes wondered
walking Riverside Drive in February or March
why not just put up cement trees with plastic leaves
and get it over with? There was no limit to our capacity for awe
at the city's miraculous icons and instances,
the frenzied cacophony, the democratic whirlwind.
Drunk on thunder, we believed in vision
and the convocation of heavenly presences summoned
to the chorus. Are they with us still? Are they
listening? Spirit of the tiny lights, ghost beneath the words,
numinous and blue, inhaler of bourbon fumes and errant shots,
are you there? I don't know. Somehow I doubt we'll ever know
which song was ours and which the siren
call of the city. More and more, it seems our errand
is to face the music, bring the noise, scour the rocks
to salvage grace notes and fragmented harmonies,
diving for pearls in the beautiful ruins,
walking all night through the pigeon-haunted streets
as fresh snow softly fills the imprint of our steps.
O.K., I'm repeating myself, forgive me, I'm sure brevity
is a virtue. It's just this melody keeps begging to be hummed:
McCarthy's, on 14th Street, where the regulars drink
beer on the rocks and the TV shows *Police Woman*
twenty-four hours a day; the quiet, almost tender way
they let the local derelicts in to sleep it off

>   in the back booths of the Blue & Gold after closing;
>   and that sign behind the bar at the Marlin, you know
>   the one, hand-lettered, scribbled with slogans of love and abuse,
>   shop-worn but still bearing its indomitable message
>   to the thirsty, smoke-fingered, mood-enhanced masses—
>   "Ice Cold Six Packs To Go." Now that's a poem.

Clearly this poem works by addition, by an accumulation of details and perceptions building upon each other exponentially. And if that final sentence refers to the sprung rhythm of "Ice Cold Six Packs to Go," it refers just as surely to McGrath's own poem—not so much an egotistical pat on the back, as a confirmation of Whitmanesque aesthetics, its huge all-encompassing embrace. But there are counter-pressures—restraints in evidence—even here that keep the poem balanced and hold McGrath's wild rhetoric somewhat in check: the measured flexibility of his lines; the use of punctuation and whole sentences, sometimes short enough to retard the pace of the poem considerably; the cadence of his clauses piling up majestically on one another as the poem moves forward; and the high degree of selectivity employed in depicting the landscape of New York. All of this ensures that the poem will not spin out of control and fly apart under the stress of its own manic energy. Take these away and we would have a spillage of prose too nebulous and chaotic to be called a poem.

If one of our ideals, then, is to hold nothing back, to throw open the doors and windows of a poem allowing a fresh, life-giving breeze to blow through, reviving us with its oxygen of memory, experience, and emotion, can there be another approach, one which views a poem as more of a barrier—a dam holding back Whitman's pent-up sea of emotion, rather than a huge sluice of observation and confession? The idea of restraint is implicit, of course, in formal verse. And condensation has long been held as an ideal in Modernist poetics. "Condense," says Pound, from the Latin root: CONDENSARE, which Pound yells at us in capital letters. Of course, he goes on to write a vast tome of his own, called *The Cantos*, but that's another story. To begin with, it's a good idea to remember that one of the first qualities of poetry we value is condensation, compression of thought and feeling. This is the haiku-nugget of immense implication, a universe compacted into a few resonant syllables whose significance rings and rings into a vast surrounding silence. "Poetry consists of gists and piths," says Ezra Pound—quoting a Chinese student. This impulse, too, has found a home in our poetry. Consider the following poem by John Haines, "Marigold," from his book *The Stone Harp*:

> This is the plaza of paradise.
> It is always noon,
> and the dusty bees are dozing
> like pardoned sinners.[4]

In four short lines and a particularly apt metaphor, Haines manages to imbue his poem with meanings far beyond those of conventional nature poetry. Instead of sentiment and a mere appreciation of the beauty of flowers, Haines is able to suggest the theological debate that has engaged some of the best minds in the Judeo-Christian West for centuries: The Fall of Man and man's relation to Nature since that defining event. In a strict Calvinist sense, all of nature was dragged down into a sinful condition along with Adam and Eve. Both Man and Nature are corrupt. But Haines suggests something else: that Nature is *not* corrupt—or is at least unaffected by any belief in corruption—because plants and creatures have no knowledge, no consciousness of human morality. They exist outside the drama of Sin and Redemption. Hence, the bright gold face of a flower becomes "the plaza of Paradise" where it is "always noon," which is to say nature and its creatures exist outside human concept of Time as well. That is why the bees can doze peacefully, unagonized by thoughts of hell, death, and damnation. They are "pardoned," in their ignorance, their exemption from the mental torment humans suffer for their beliefs.

Whether you agree with Haines and his metaphysical ideas is not the point. The point is how deftly he can compress the complexities of theology into a few simple details. But is compression really the same thing as restraint? Somewhere between the volubility of Whitman and the reticence of Haines lies a vast territory of restraint—more or less—which most poems inhabit, attempting to say all they have to say without saying too much, both releasing and withholding emotion; revealing much, but leaving much to the reader's imagination at the same time—a balancing act that necessitates the finest instincts on the part of the poet. If the poet says too much, the reader will feel coddled, patronized; if he says too little, the reader will feel frustrated and confused. Saying too little is, perhaps, another issue. Today we are concerned with saying too much: how can we avoid it? If we think of the poem as a barrier to hold back—to restrain—much of what the poet is thinking and feeling, by giving just the right details, the right number of them but no more, we may begin to understand the concept of restraint in poetry and see how it differs from classical ideas of compression. Compression is economy of means. Restraint, economy of emotion and speech, something akin to discretion and tact—two qualities that are indispensable to the idea of restraint in poetry.

Let's look closely at the following poem by Robert Hayden, "Those Winter Days." Here is a poem that virtually defines in its manner, method, and form the ideal of restraint I am trying to identify:

THOSE WINTER SUNDAYS[5]

> Sundays too my father got up early
> and put his clothes on in the blueblack cold,
> then with cracked hands that ached
> from labor in the weekday weather made
> banked fires blaze. No one ever thanked him.
>
> I'd wake and hear the cold splintering, breaking.
> When the rooms were warm, he'd call,
> and slowly I would rise and dress,
> fearing the chronic angers of that house,
>
> speaking indifferently to him,
> who had driven out the cold
> and polished my good shoes as well.
> What did I know, what did I know
> of love's austere and lonely offices?

Much else, besides restraint, might be praised with respect to this poem. Its music, for instance, the crackling sounds those variations on the vowel "a" make throughout the first two stanzas, allow us to hear the fire blazing which the father has so dutifully made. The precise diction, too, that compels the use of adjectives such as "blueblack" and "chronic" over less suggestive ones—or none at all. But restraint is evident from the very opening of the poem, the first two words, which let us know that Hayden's father performed his loving ritual every day of the week, not just on Sundays. That the father stokes the fire on Sundays as well is an affecting detail, for the father is obviously a working man, and Sunday is normally the day reserved for rest. Yet the father gets up to perform his self-imposed task, which is largely ignored by the rest of the family, certainly by his son, who is probably the main recipient of the father's beneficence. The family's ignorance of the father's devotion is acknowledged in the simple sentence: "No one ever thanked him," and in the adverb "indifferently" in the third stanza. That is all. But it's enough to inform us of the situation, enough to engage our sympathy, balanced as it is against the father's lonely, ceremonious care.

If, as some poet has averred, every lyric poem represents a fragment of a larger, unspoken narrative, the whole history of this family, with its self-absorptions and "chronic angers" is beautifully suggested in a few telling details. This is a poem whose floodgates are shut. It's a poem we might think of as a barrier, rather than a door. Yet it's as powerful as a poem that bursts uncontrollably forth, inundating us in a flood of words. There is a vast reservoir of emotion here that is unexpressed, but you can feel the weight and pressure of that emotion informing every word, every line, held in check by the poet's faith in the power of restraint. This is what makes the final two lines—which might otherwise court sentimentality—possible. The cry here, when it comes, is also artfully restrained. Not many poets can get away with repeating phrases for emotional effect. But here, because so much restraint has been exercised in the rest of the poem, we feel the full impact of that repetition: "What did I know, what did I know..." In every respect, Robert Hayden's poem is an example of the effective use of restraint in poetry.

In a review of Elizabeth Bishop in the April 2, 2006 issue of the *New York Times Book Review*, critic David Orr says something similar about

Bishop's poetry. He even uses the same imagery to make his point about Bishop's famous restraint:

> The more one reads a Bishop poem, the greater the
> sense of huge forces being held barely but precisely
> in check—like currents pressing heavily on the glass
> walls of some delicate undersea installation. It doesn't
> seem as if the glass will break, but if it were to do so,
> we'd find ourselves engulfed by what Frost (her truest
> predecessor) called "black and utter chaos."[6]

Orr stresses the containment of dark forces here, emotions that—if let loose—might overcome the poet's ability to control them and so become frightening and self-destructive: the "savage god," perhaps, that A. Alvarez wrote about with respect to the poetry of Sylvia Plath. But what is restrained can just as easily be what is trivial or superfluous, from padding and fat to unnecessary editorializing.

We can learn a great deal about how to write with restraint by studying "Those Winter Days." The poet places just the right details, the right amount of information, in front of us on the page—and no more. Think of the poem as a complex of hints, suggestions, and innuendoes that point toward an overall meaning we want the reader to grasp. By using the words "hints" and "innuendoes" I don't mean to imply that poetry is a game, a mere pastime for the intellectual enjoyment of the bored. The reader must feel a sense of participation in the poem, a feeling of discovery and satisfaction in his or her own ability to interpret what is given to them, and not to be spoon-fed explanations along with the substance of the poem. A certain amount of trust is involved: *Will the reader be able to infer what I've left out from the details I've included?* And a certain amount of respect for the reader's intelligence: *I don't have to explain this, it's self-evident.* The words and the details they embody must resonate with precision and clarity. They must be the right details, in the right order, delivered at the right time, for the reader to respond correctly. There is no surefire way of explaining how to write with restraint, no formula for determining how much to put into a poem and how much to withhold. Only a great deal of reading and study of exemplary poems—like the ones above—may begin to instill in us a proper sense of balance and restraint.

By now, you might have begun to suspect that restraint on the part of the writer is one thing; on the part of the reader, something else. The reader's restraint has to do with reading between the lines, reading that which is not present, but forcefully implied. Let's examine a poem by William Stafford, "Traveling Through the Dark." Here is the real, "restrained" version, the one which leaves out all that can be inferred tactfully between the lines:

TRAVELING THROUGH THE DARK[7]

Traveling through the dark I found a deer
dead on the edge of the Wilson River road.
It is usually best to roll them into the canyon:
that road is narrow; to swerve might make more dead.

By glow of the tail-light I stumbled back of the car
and stood by the heap, a doe, a recent killing;
she had stiffened already, almost cold.
I dragged her off; she was large in the belly.

My fingers touching her side brought me the reason—
her side was warm; her fawn lay there waiting,
alive, still, never to be born.
Beside that mountain road I hesitated.

The car aimed ahead its lowered parking lights;
under the hood purred the steady engine.
I stood in the glare of the warm exhaust turning red;
around our group I could hear the wilderness listen.

I thought hard for us all—my only swerving—,
then pushed her over the edge into the river.

In contrast to the real poem, consider now the following bloated, "unrestrained" version of "Traveling Through the Dark," which leaves almost nothing to your imagination. It fills in everything that you have just read—i.e. *understood* —between the lines:

TRAVELING THROUGH THE DARK II

Traveling through the Dark I found a deer
dead on the edge of the Wilson River road.
These poor animals are always getting hit,
and we stop and wonder what to do with them.
It is usually best to roll them into the canyon
as the road is narrow and to swerve might cause accidents
and then not only an animal, but people will be dead as well,
and that would be truly horrible.

It was so dark I only had the tail-light by which to see
so I stumbled to the back of the car
and stood by the body, a doe, recently hit and killed
by another car, probably one just a few minutes
before I got there. But she was already stiff, almost cold.
I dragged her off towards the edge of the road
to push her into the canyon when I noticed
she was large in the belly. That was odd.

My fingers touching her side brought me the reason—
her side was still warm. Oh my god! She was pregnant!
Her fawn lay inside her, alive, in danger of dying too.
Beside that mountain road I hesitated: what should I do?
Should I throw her mother's carcass into the canyon anyway,
because it was more humane to let the fawn die that way
then to bring her up in captivity without her parents?
Or should I cut her open and save the fawn and bring her up
myself in my own backyard where it would be safe
and she'd be fed each day and at least be able to survive?

So many philosophical questions!
The car aimed its lowered parking lights; it was no help,
just a machine, so I was left to make this big decision myself.
Under the hood purred the steady engine, as if impatient,
pressuring me to get on with it and get out of there,
back on the road towards home where I had things to do.
I stood in the glare of the warm exhaust turning red.
Around our group—the dead deer, the car, and I—
it seemed I could hear the wilderness listen to see what I would do.
I felt that whatever action I took would have cosmic consequences!

I thought hard for us all—the animal kingdom and the human race,
nature, history, civilization—my only swerving a mental one,
(not a physical one with my car) as I pondered what to do.
Finally, I thought it would be better to let the fawn die with the mother
rather than have to live among humans and never know
the love of her mother and the freedom of the forest.
So I pushed the carcass over the edge into the river
and drove away satisfied that I had done the right thing. Or had I?
We just can't ever know that our decisions are the right ones.
Such is the human condition, and it will always be that way.

Though much of this is humorous, of course, *I do not mean it as a parody
of Stafford's poem.* What I have filled in between the lines is a somewhat
messy account of the unspoken matter of the poem, its actual sugges-
tiveness made clear. We laugh because we are uncomfortable with being
spoon-fed so much obvious information. You may have inferred more
or less from the poem, but I'm betting that you interpolated something
like this in your first reading and hearing of the "official" version of the
poem. A poem that explains itself this way is highly undesirable, even lu-
dicrous. How can we participate in a poem that so thoroughly exhausts its
own possible meanings? There's nothing left for us to do, no imaginative
space to stretch out in and enjoy the pleasure of our own well-drawn con-
clusions. Restraint in poetry, then, is related to this idea of imaginative

space, of allowing the reader room to exercise his or her own interpretive capabilities. Restraint in this sense is also related to good manners, allowing readers to do for themselves, not treating them like children. A poem, as Stephen Dobyns reminds us in his book of essays about writing, *Best Words, Best Order*[8], is something that is made by both the writer and the reader working together through the text on the page. The reader plays a part in the fulfillment of the poem. A writer's restraint makes this possible. Without it, the poem becomes a lecture, relentless and definitive, not something we can experience.

We resist the concept of restraint in poetry, I think, because—as Americans—we associate it with Victorian ideals of decorum and refinement, even self-repression. Any Martian dropped into our midst and placed before a television set would be able to conclude that restraint is not one of our cherished ideals. But if we think of restraint less as a chastity belt and more as an element of discipline and control, a matter of *craft*, without which no real work of art can be produced, we might see it as desirable, even crucial to our efforts as writers, engaged in the daunting struggle to write lasting and successful poems. Restraint is more, to paraphrase an old saw. With a certain amount of judiciousness and restraint we can leave a powerful impression. We can affect our reader with a deep sense of emotion beyond words, beyond even the words we choose to place upon the page. A sense of empathy, of connection and communication, is what we seek, often more obtainable through restraint than outspoken frankness and confrontation.

4

On the Immortality of Images

> That the world is ultimately unknowable makes images
> so complexly evocative.
>
> —Campbell McGrath

My wife, also a poet, came into my office and asked, "Do you have two examples of images that have stuck with you for years; images that you have never forgotten no matter how much time has passed?" I thought of an image by the Midwestern poet John Woods, from his wonderful poem "The Deaths at Paragon, Indiana." The poem is about a terrible car crash in which five people die, and is divided into four parts—allowing us to see the horrific event from the perspectives of a waitress who witnesses the crash, an ambulance driver who rushes the victims to the hospital, a junkman who hauls the wreck away, and the doctor who tries—but fails— to save those who were barely alive. It is packed with powerful imagery and written in a language so condensed and spare it practically transforms itself into poetry in the mere recording of the event. The image I recall— the image that lodged itself into my memory so ineradicably almost half a lifetime ago—appears in the final section, entitled "Doctor Sweet."

> Yesterday I fished for bass,
> But now I fish for breath in bones
> Clasped as bottom roots. The pulse
> Nibbled like a chub but got
> Away. All five of you are dead.[1]

The image that opens this section ("I fish for breath in bones / Clasped as bottom roots") is remarkable, as is the image that opens the entire poem sequence—"Sun streaked the coffee urn / And wrote AL'S LUNCH across the cups"—which is spoken by the waitress just before the crash occurs outside the diner where she works. But imagining the body as a lake in which bones are like underwater vegetation—marvelous as it is—and where breaths are like fish requires intellectual effort, some time spent in interpreting the comparison to make it work. And the second image, though curious and beautiful in its Hopper-esque starkness, is entirely visual, which is not bad in and of itself and certainly memorable. What I remember of these two images, once I re-read them, is how wonderful they are—but I did not remember them *specifically* in the same way I remember "The pulse / Nibbled like a chub but got / Away." Why? Why did this image have an almost imperishable afterlife for me when the other images faded into what I remember as a general excellence of the poem's other imagery? I cannot be certain, but I can make a few guesses about why some images seem to imprint themselves indelibly on our imaginations while others do not—no matter how good they are. To be clear, I am talking about images from literature here, images someone has contrived and written down as part of a novel or a poem, and not recurring memories from actual life. Those are something for which only a psychologist or neurologist might be able to account.

The sheer simplicity of Woods's image has to do with its memorability. It is a homely image, taken directly from ordinary life in the Midwest (or anywhere rural). It is not intellectual or complex, not abstract in any way. In fact, it seems plausible that a person might say such a thing naturally—a country doctor, for instance, who loves to fish—when trying to describe what it feels like to take someone's pulse as they are dying. I spent a lot of time fishing when I was young and that I know what a "chub" is (a very common species, sometimes called *whitefish*, that inhabits our rivers and lakes). That may have something to do with my personal connection and fondness for this image. I know what it feels like to hold onto a line while a fish in the depths nibbles my bait once or twice tentatively, then vanishes. And, of course, I have felt my own pulse, and others', many times. So, I know from first-hand experience what Woods—or Doctor Sweet—is describing. It is clear to me how this comparison was made, though I might never have thought of it myself. It seems perfect, exact, beautifully imagined and made.

Another thing that makes this a memorable image is its universality. Who hasn't gone fishing at some point and had a nibble—perhaps even caught a fish? The excitement of feeling something invisible, unknown, tugging softly at the end of the line down in the depths is the reason fishing is such a popular sport. For that moment, you can imagine you have caught anything—a bass or trout or pike or any other kind of fish, and that it might be three inches or three feet long. It might be a lunker or a minnow. The suspense is wonderful as you fight your unknown quarry up from the depths into the light of day where you can finally see what you've caught. But first, there is only that nibble. It is the beginning of everything and once you have experienced it, you never forget. You could spend a lifetime waiting for it to happen again.

Appropriateness, then, is another feature of the image that allowed it to remain precisely branded in my mind. Its appropriateness to Dr. Sweet and his life. The image emerges naturally out of his immediate experience. It's a homely image, but one that does not seem forced. Often, we read images in a poem that give us the sense they have been artificially contrived. While all images in literature are contrived, the trick is in presenting images that seem as though they flourished effortlessly out of a line of poetry the way they might appear during the course of someone's conversation. With an inept image, we feel that the poet has taken a long time to find it, groping around in his or her stockpile of images until one is found—and self-consciously chosen—that will be startling and impressive. We can feel the poet reaching for the exotic, something arresting and obviously calculated. Mostly, I think, we do not like it when a poet shows off. Certain critics have talked about the concept of inevitability in the greatest poems, the idea that a phrase or a line or an image seems inevitable, that nothing else would suffice at that particular moment in the poem, that out of all possibilities only this one would do—perfect, incontestable, mysteriously fit to the exclusion of all else. While not as grand, my idea of appropriateness is related to the idea of inevitability. A good image feels like no other image would do. It feels right, completely satisfying—inevitable! At the same time, it feels original, fresh, surprising. A good trick if you can pull it off.

So originality is a feature of good imagery, as well. We have all read poems that describe someone's cheeks as being like apples. That red, that bright. Utterly predictable. Cheeks have been burnished apples since the dawn of poetry, it would seem. And the moon! A friend of mine once began his poem: "The moon, tired of its literary career… " The moon is always a piece of ice floating in the blue sky, or a skull half buried in a desert, or a streetlamp at midnight, and the crescent moon invariably reminds us of a scythe or the paring of a fingernail. No wonder the moon is tired! It's like hearing the same joke told about you over and over again. But poets are resourceful, and the good ones can always find a way to "make it new," to come up with something pristine and surprising. I do not recall the poem or poet, but one image for the moon I remember describes the moon drifting out of a cloud one night as a doddering old lady, tottering forth from her chamber, white-haired, gray-faced, fragile, the flesh on her bony face translucent and taut. I think this image might occur in a poem by Byron, but whether I remember the author or poem containing the image, the image has stuck in my mind for almost forty years, ineffaceable, almost eternal. That's what a good image can do. It may seem not like something read in a poem, but something experienced, witnessed, something that occurred in actual life.

But there is another aspect to Woods's image comparing the thready heartbeat of a dying patient to a chub nibbling on the end of a fishing line that undoubtedly encoded it directly into my body-memory: its physicality. Most imagery in poems is visual. This is understandable, because eyesight is one of our most important senses. Much of what we need to know to survive on a daily basis comes to us through the organs of sight: our eyes. But we have four other senses out of which poetic imagery might stem. Auditory imagery might vie with sight for the second major category of poetic imagery. Poems are full of sounds—hammer blows, trains, gulls screeching, kisses—and poetic devices such as assonance, consonance, alliteration, and onomatopoeia reflect and, one might say, incarnate this presence. Taste, touch, and smell account for the production of less poetic imagery than sight or hearing, but they play their parts in any body of work that will represent a full range of human activity and experience. Physical imagery situates us in the world (even in imaginary worlds) and orients us to our surroundings. Without concrete imagery, poetry would be closer to philosophy, with its powerful but ultimately anemic intellectual formulations. It would be constructed out of airy thoughts and abstract assertions. That this is not the case with poetry is one of its advantages, and the source of its particular attraction.

When I think of Woods's image of a pulse as a fish nibbling on the end of a line, I do not really *think* of it at all. I experience it as a soft but insistent tugging in the crook of my right index finger, and I remember that it indicates the presence of something unseen, something in the depths that for a moment is communicating with me, a few tentative taps that I must interpret and "read" correctly. That is, I remember viscerally, with my body, and interpret the metaphor with my mind. But the image appeals to my body first, where it is physically recreated as an experience I've never forgotten. Tactile imagery is surprisingly rare in poetry, though if one surveyed the entire range of English and American poetry many noteworthy examples might be found. Think of Keats's rabbit on the Eve of St. Agnes, which occurs on January 20th each year, the dead of winter. A master of imagery of all kinds, Keats starts out by simply saying it was cold: "St. Agnes' Eve— Ah, bitter chill it was!" But before long he is serving up telling images that make us understand how cold it was, and to which our bodies instinctively respond: "The hare limp'd trembling through the frozen grass... " Though the speaker doesn't actually touch the hare, the image appeals directly to us in a tactile way (and not only in a visual one)—we, too, have felt our limbs stiffen in gelid weather. And we have felt the frozen grass on evenings after the temperature has plunged well below freezing. Everything about Keats's line recalls such body knowledge and we shiver.

One of the most dramatic examples of tactile imagery occurs in Hart Crane's epic poem, "The Bridge," at the end of the section IV, "Cape Hatteras." In ecstatic verses aligning himself with Whitman and Whitman's vision of America's future, Crane ends by presenting us with a picture of the two of them forging ahead on the open road:

> My hand
> in yours
> Walt Whitman—
> so—[2]

When has that relatively insignificant English word *so* borne the weight of so much dramatic tension? Two hands, two small letters, isolated at the end of a wildly ascending poem, strophe after dithyrambic strophe, two significant figures in American poetry striding off into the white infinity of the page. The locked fingers of those two hands, the muscularity of that grip, felt in a single syllable. You feel that clasp in your own hand—the strength and solidarity of it. The aesthetic, political, and homoerotic implications are obvious, but what's important here is how that simple word trembles with the tension of so much tactile energy. Poetry is abstract, of course, only printed letters on a page that elicit thought and feeling, or sung syllables in the air, but every so often—through a particularly deft physical image—we are teased into believing that we are touching the material substance of the world.

Simplicity, then, along with appropriateness, universality, originality, and physicality—these are some of the things that compose a memorable poetic image. But in truth, in poetry there are no such things as rules or absolute formulations. There is no recipe for a memorable image and all I have done is point out some of the characteristics which go into making effective imagery, though there may be more, and other characteristics, or none of these at all if the poet can find a way to construct arresting imagery using other ingredients and other ways of combining them.

Each of us has our own bank of imagery into which we have made deposits over the years of reading and writing poetry. I try to keep my senses alert and open when reading a poem. I want to enter its world through my senses and if I can do that, I can respond in the way the poet intended. But I cannot respond emotionally or intellectually without first experiencing the poem through its imagery. Once I have entered the world of the poem and fooled myself into believing I am actually *there*, my mind and emotions become engaged and I experience the poem as if I were truly experiencing something in reality. This is why Emily Dickinson said that she knew a great poem if the hair stood up on the back of her neck and the top of her head felt like it had come off. Once the reader is squarely in the center of the world of the poem, whatever is happening in the poem (so it seems) is happening to *her*, immediately and directly.

And it's not only beautiful or agreeable imagery that attracts our attention, etching aesthetically pleasing shapes or events somewhere into the cortical hinterland of our brains. The repugnant, the unsettling, the horrific, even the disgusting might make an ineradicable mark on our minds as well. This is the case for me with a poem in J. D. Reed's remarkable first volume, *Expressways*, published long ago in 1969. Once again, Reed's poem involves a car wreck on a highway somewhere in the vast prairie lands of the Midwest:

THE WEATHER IS BROUGHT TO YOU[3]

It is 64° in Devereaux,
and a volunteer pumper
hoses gas from the expressway.

Troopers with the faces of mandrills
hobnail over crushed metal,
using big flashlights like pointers
in a planetarium.

Sprockets dangle in the weeds,
torn radiators gurgle,

and the dead wait under wool blankets,
expiring
like tungsten filament
in a hissing, broken headlight.

This short poem is all imagery, without a word of speculation or commentary. As the Imagists pointed out to us at the very dawn of Modernism, if you get the image right there is no need for explanation of any kind. The image that has burned itself into my memory occurs in the first line of the second stanza. I have never been able to rid myself of the faces of those troopers. I have never been able to see them as anything but marauding, ominous monkeys prowling over the wreckage of cars in the dark looking, perhaps, for the bloody remains of victims who—here, at least—"wait under woolen blankets," like sleepers groggy with the shock of impact, waiting to be roused. But we know they will never wake again. In an eerily apt auditory image, Reed has them "expiring / like tungsten filament / in a hissing, broken headlight." The soul escaping? Perhaps. Whatever the case, the bodies here have been reduced to the senseless, inanimate state of metal, inert, unfeeling, no longer sensate or alive. The horror here need not be supplemented by even a syllable of explanation.

How is it that Reed so effectively associates the sober expressions of troopers with the primitive faces of old-world primates? We have all witnessed the dispassionate expressions on the faces of police officers as they go about their work. That official detachment—professionally necessary or not—is associated with the hard-boiled desk sergeant, the wary cop on the beat, the state trooper on the side of the road suspiciously edging up to a car he has stopped to ask for the driver's license and registration. Objectivity and suspicion are approaches endemic to the policeman's job. It is just that cold, impersonal look that Reed remembered when he came to make his image of troopers "hobnailing" over the detritus of an automobile accident that brought to his mind the stoic, impassive faces of mandrills he must have seen in books about wildlife in Africa. The intense, beady-eyed, slightly menacing glare of a mandrill is something you never forget once you've seen it in photographs or observed first-hand in a zoo. Characterized this way, the troopers too suggest something machine-like, something robotic and not altogether human in their behavior around the site of such a disaster.

Is it possible to write a poem that is entirely abstract, a poem composed of propositions and statements, concepts, and notions? Yes. However, with such a poem we do not enter the world, but the author's mind—and there we discover ideas about the world, not the world itself. Meditative poems may be compelling, even fascinating, yet even expository poems usually rely on imagery and metaphor to anchor their insights in the tangible world. Otherwise, they risk vapidity, even if the thoughts they contain are grand. Not many intellectual poems remain rooted in memory, except as the gist of their arguments or theories. But the poems themselves, the very language of which they are made, may be overlooked or forgotten. Consider the following poem by William Bronk:

VENI CREATOR SPIRITUS[4]

If one were all, there were still the want to be
something. The wanting something. One says all
or nothing; something is in between but not
halfway. All and nothing meet, conjoin,
speak of the same, as circumference and area
speak of the same circle. Something across
from there, something besides, as if besides
one, there were numbers besides. One wishes there were.

I would argue that this is a very good poem in at least one critical way: it is intellectually complex, subtle, even brilliant in its conceptualizations. It would not be easy to write a poem as successful as this one in its deft handling of abstractions, its way of unfolding a thought *as if* it were physical, something material the mind can grasp (though it leans towards the physical when it imagines that "all" and "nothing" can meet, as if they were two people, as well as employing the idea of a circle). Thought, in this poem, is a construction, like a building or a box. It is almost palpable. Yet I find it difficult to hold onto the poem, line by line, as one abstraction slides into another. It is like trying to grasp a wet bar of soap in the shower. It keeps slipping away from me, and I have to go back and start over, trying to hold onto the idea in each sentence and remember it as the next sentence, and the next, unfold. Finally, if I read it enough, I begin to grasp—not its concrete particulars, for there are none—but its essence, its general drift, the idea that is at its core. And this is what I will take away with me while I forget its words, its language, what the poem actually says phrase by phrase and line by line. The poem here has become for me an argument, not an experience, and while I admire it greatly for what it does, I cannot react to it emotionally because my senses are not engaged. This is what concrete imagery can do, and there is no substitute for it.

To be fair to Bronk, who is a first-rate poet by anyone's standards, most of his poems make use of concrete imagery as a way of making the abstract concrete, of drawing thought into sense, into form, so that it can be apprehended by the senses and experienced that way:

THE TORMENT[5]

I am that bull they bait, this way, that way,
head down, stupid, off to the side of the ring.
Who are they? They fade to the fence whenever I charge.
Let them watch out! I think I am in disguise.
There may be nothing more if I am gone.

This is as good a place as any to admit that I also revere poems that have nothing to do with physical imagery of any kind, even metaphor. Poems that rely solely on statement without a concrete detail in sight. The trick is to compose statements of such directness, such simple but accurate straightforwardness, that abstractions themselves will have the heft and clarity of physical detail, exemplified in this short poem by Patrick Phillips from his second book, *Boy*:

HEAVEN[6]

It will be the past
and we'll live there together.

Not as it was to *live*
but as it is remembered.

It will be the past.
We'll all go back together.

Everyone we ever loved,
and lost, and must remember.

It will be the past.
And it will last forever.

Much might be said about the poise and balance, the shapeliness of this short poem, about its rhymes and repetitions, its syntactical cadences, its ability to pack so much emotion into so small a space. One might even fault it for flirting so openly with sentimentality. But the point here is that it manages to succeed without imagery, without a single object in view. People, and perhaps even a place, are implied. But they are not represented. It is a poem of concept and feeling only, the dream of a place that is not a place and is therefore furnished with no imagery whatsoever.

A cogent argument can be made—and has been made, originally by the Imagists—that a poem might be composed of nothing *but* imagery, sans abstract statement of any kind. That would be poetry based on nothing but description, nothing but things, the very opposite of Bronk's poem, "Veni Creator Spiritus," or Phillips poem, "Heaven," above. Such an extreme represents the ideal of objectivism, in which William Carlos Williams's famous dictum "no ideas but in things" is given full reign, and in which any abstract content remains thoroughly embedded—one might say buried—in a radical reliance on things alone to bear meaning:

NANTUCKET[7]

Flowers through the window
lavender and yellow

changed by white curtains—
Smell of cleanliness—

Sunshine of late afternoon—
On the glass tray

a glass pitcher, the tumbler
turned down, by which

a key is lying— And the
immaculate white bed.

No ideas, with a vengeance, but feelings implicit in an observer who stands in the doorway of a room noticing and selecting details and arranging them in such a way as to clearly evoke an atmosphere and a mood. But what is the "meaning" of such a poem? What is its content in terms of thought? Simplicity is elegant? Cleanliness is a homely virtue? New England is uncomplicated and rustic? Such interpretations are trivial in comparison to the gravity of objects, their particular dignity and weight, the very power of their muteness. Williams desires only that we look at the world without interpreting it, without turning everything we see into an idea or a metaphor for something else. Not mind, but not-mind, is here all important. What exists *outside* our consciousness and beyond the self, with no urgency to appropriate it, is what Williams is after, and where the ultimate value of imagery may rest.

But, ironically, this use of imagery turns on relating it to complicated intellectual theories about what an image is and what it does. Thought returns through the back door and imbues concrete images with an abstract purpose making them somewhat dependent upon the reader's knowledge and aesthetics. I prefer to return to the simplistic love of images with which I began this essay: Why do some images stick and what makes them so effective and memorable? What keeps an image tugging on our imaginations even after years of first reading them? The answers are ultimately mysterious. Imagery appeals not so much to our minds as to our bodies through the senses. This much has been known for centuries, perhaps. In life, one might say that where the mind goes the body will follow. In poetry, the opposite may be true: where the body goes, the mind and heart will follow.

The world of poetry is the world reflected through imagery. But that reflection can sometimes be more vivid than the world from which it emanates because of the poet's ability to add something—it's been called Imagination, with a capital "I"—the original does not possess.

5

Beyond Description: Poetry That Stares

[Gerard Manley Hopkins had] a capacity to look at
things as though time did not exist: as though he and
that flower, that leaf, that formation of ice on a pond,
that sunset or that drift of cloud were the only things in
existence: as though he and the object were both placed
in the world exclusively to meet and understand each
other's essences.

—James Dickey

It's commonplace to assert that contemporary experience has been broken
up into fifteen second ads, rapid cinematic cross-cuts, bewildering lan-
guage collages, and ephemeral soundbites. Consciousness, we agree, has
been fractured—perhaps beyond repair. It's as though the whole culture
were suffering from attention deficit disorder, unable to sustain collective
thought. This frazzling of attention might be welcomed by experimental
artists and merchandizing outfits of all kinds. Such shattering of aware-
ness is relatively new, as recent as a half-century ago—certainly stretch-
ing back through preceding millennia—the human mind was capable of
extended periods of concentration, of focusing itself on objects and events
that moved relatively slowly, and which therefore yielded up more about
themselves the longer the observer stayed put. A Zen-like meditative state
might not have been widespread in the Middle Ages, but attention spans
during that historical epoch were probably more durable than ours, and
distraction—at least rapid immediate distraction—less a problem.

As one of the oldest human activities, poetry is still capable of evok-
ing the meditative state, of recording an almost trance-like attachment to

people, places, objects and events and allowing even ordinary experience to reveal depth and dimension, significance and substance, lastingness and solidity. Of yielding up, that is, the secret qualities of things—the deeper meaning of phenomena, the unseen reality that might begin to emanate from each object if only we could stay fixed and focused on it long and faithfully enough for such subtle details to be revealed. The modern mind, skating swiftly over the surface of things, making rapid surveys of all it sees, bouncing from perception to perception, cannot know—cannot *get* at—the secret life of things, to borrow a concept from Rilke. We might notice the gleaming torso of Apollo while we sprint through the museum, but we can no longer experience the fact that it is also noticing us. That kind of dawning, radical awareness may now have been rendered passé.

Traditionally, poems represent acts of attention, though postmodernism delights in reversing conventional approaches to writing by favoring interruption, disjunction, floating pronouns, shifting grammar, fractured sentences, and so on over what Tony Hoagland calls "the poetries of continuity." The postmodern poem, then, seeks to imitate the fractured nature of contemporary experience, to mirror it in formal strategies and scattered syntax, rather than trying to reconstruct wholeness—to re-member the scattered corpse of the Muse—the dead Horus of all poetries leading up to Modernism which was the first to introduce fragment and collage into the mainstream of Western literature. What I call "staring" poems, then, is naturally inimical to the whole project of postmodernism. This is not necessarily a judgment, but an essential feature that excludes postmodernism from the possibility of producing poems of extended focus and attention, separating it from the centuries of poetry that preceded it. Whatever virtues it may have gained by attempting to replicate contemporary experience, it can no longer partake in the qualities and discoveries of prolonged meditation.

A distinction has to be made, too, between poems of observation and poems that stare—though of course they are related, the latter being essentially a noticeable magnification of the former, a particular species of descriptive poetry that, by its sheer persistence, represents a higher degree of attention. The poem of observation has been with us for a long time, perhaps from the very first. One of the glories of Homer, we are told, is the precision of his imagery—the physical, concrete nature of what he presents to our senses—which critics have praised with such terms as "visceral" and "alive." The wine-dark sea and the rosy fingers of dawn have come down to us almost undiminished in their imaginative rightness and surprising beauty. When Dante escorts us through hell, we shrink from the rippling tapestry of flames and the acrid smell of sulfur. Milton, too, allows us to see the massive body of Satan sprawled out in a lake of fire with the other fallen angels scattered around him "thick as leaves that strow the brooks in Valambrosa." Modernism itself is founded on the idea of observation and representational aesthetics. Imagism, the movement that began it all, was fundamentally an effort to restore clarity and precision to poetry after the emotional fuzziness and haze of Victorian emoting.

More recently, Francis Ponge's poems have received admiration for the painstaking effort they make to focus attention on a single object—an orange, an oyster, a pebble, even roadside dung—though in Ponge's treatment of things the mind travels side by side with the object, informing it, imbuing it with meaning, probing it and commenting on it at every step. The objects in Ponge's poems are infused throughout with a fine, delicate subjectivity that heightens and illuminates them even further. One feels Ponge's mind suffusing each article with an interior light, the dim light of partial understanding, an inkling as we say, even as the power of his attention surrounds each object with the fierce halo of his gaze. We are as aware of Ponge the observer as we are of whatever it is he is observing. That is to say, the presence of the observer is felt in every word of the poem; we are never allowed to forget he is there.

But this is true of most poems of observation, whether immediately or at some point later in the poem. Take, for example, the following poem by Francine Sterle, a very fine poem of close description that appears in her book *Every Bird is One Bird* from Tupelo Press in 2001. Here's the poem in its entirety, because it will be necessary to talk about it at some length in order to note the qualities of observation that may be found in most poems of this kind:

SNAKE[1]

Saw it hatch from an egg
like a bird, saw it surge
months later from a mud hole,
glide across a log, wave upon wave,
into a dark crevice in the rocks,
saw its feathery tongue flicker
as its eyes went cold,
and it swelled thick-bodied
until it burst from its skin
in one luminous stroke, saw
the undulating string of chevrons
shiver down its back,
saw it slip into the world
in roots and umbilical cords,
wheels and smoke and curling hair,
saw it in the whip-tailed wind
hissing behind me, in the uterine earth,
the Great Serpent writhing under my feet
when I walked. Saw it coil
into a wreath, and still it stirred
without arms or legs or wings, slithered forward,
unlocked its jaws over a mouse, unlocked
something in me: Lord of this world,
Lord who delights in blood,
and my shovel crushed its head,
and this is how I yielded.

The first thing to notice about the poem is how Sterle seeks to detach
herself from what she is observing, to direct the reader's attention, not to
herself, but to the snake she wants us to observe with her, something she
partially achieves by dropping the subject of these sentences—the "I"—
which would normally stand in front of those anaphorically migrating
verbs: *saw*. "Don't pay attention to me," she implies, "look only at what I

have to show you." The observing consciousness doesn't enter the poem until after line twelve, which ends a long list of details about the snake's physical attributes and behavior. After that point, however, the observer's presence is detectable in the metaphorical forays she makes into snakiness itself, the curling and writhing of other things—smoke, roots, hair—that resemble the creature she has just described. But metaphor, we know, takes place only in the mind of the speaker and not out there in the world. Line by line, she comes forward until, finally, she steps completely into the poem by revealing herself—for the first time—with the pronoun "I." And that is where the poem, for the first time as well, comes to rest before pushing on towards its inevitable disclosure, the revelation towards which it has been tending. Observation has done its work and can now be left behind. Statement—the framing of an idea—is in order and takes its place: "unlocked something in me... and this is how I yielded."

More might be said about this poem, about its prosodic features—those anapests that advance trippingly after the clogged spondees of lines two and three: "saw it surge / months later from a mud hole, / glide across a log, wave upon wave, / into a dark crevice in the rocks"—its numerous enjambments and positional vagaries of the verb "saw," which enact or at least underscore the sinuous movement of the snake, and the single long line that describes how the snake "slithered forward," even as the line slithers forward to tell us so. It is an adept performance, in almost every way.

And of course it reminds us of other poems about snakes: Dickinson's great poem that ends in "zero at the bone," and Lawrence's wonderful meditation about "one of the Lords of Life." It hardly needs mentioning that the whole myth of Eden lurks behind the words and images of "Snake," contextualizing it even further to give it resonances and meanings not necessarily present in the poet's actual experience of her particular snake. When she yields, it is to that urge towards violence that we associate with snakes, especially snakes that represent the Devil. This is a strong poem that uses observation skillfully and for a very definite purpose. What I'm looking for, though, is something more radical than this. Poems or passages of poems in which the observer all but vanishes into the background of the text while we, its readers, are left alone completely absorbed in what we are seeing, hearing, and experiencing, albeit imaginary, as art. In poems that stare so hard we become, in Emerson's memorable phrase, "translucent eyeballs," no longer aware of ourselves, much less the observer who is describing what we see.

Let's begin with Elizabeth Bishop's poem, "At the Fishhouses,"[2] which describes one of the coastal fishing villages of her youthful Nova Scotia. It is not necessary to cite every line of "At the Fishhouses," as Bishop *does* appear—memorably—at various places in the poem, but not until thirty-one lines have been spent painstakingly and beautifully observing the details of the fishhouses and the interesting terrain surrounding them. The staring here is selective but intense, unwavering. From an old man working on his nets in the evening, we move to the "steeply peaked roofs" of the fishhouses, to "the heavy surface of the sea, / swelling slowly as if considering spilling over," to "the benches, / the lobster pots, and masts, scattered / among the wild jagged rocks," to "The big fish tubs... completely lined / with layers of beautiful herring scales," and so on, so that when Bishop finally enters the poem at line thirty-two by handing the old man a Lucky Strike, we are startled, shocked, as if she had just emerged from the twilight at our elbow to break the spell cast by the powerful manifestation of the landscape she has just been observing for us. The scene has been so potently depicted, and we have been so deeply drawn into it, that we had forgotten she was even there. Even brief moments of subjectivity—such as that suggested by the word "considering" above (who has this idea?), and the lines "The air smells strong of codfish / it makes one's nose run and one's eyes water"—fail to destroy the sense of detachment, the impersonal feeling built up over so many lines of painterly description, that we pass over them almost without notice, without considering how they might imply an observer, a speaker standing nearby in the gloaming with us.

Staring poems resist the temptation to turn the object(s) of their observation into metaphor. At least, not at first, often not until the very last lines of the poem. Though she is present at various places from line thirty-three on, Bishop continues to observe the landscape and the creatures in it until she finally gets to the revelation she's been seeking—the master metaphor that will deepen and enlarge the significance of all that has come before. The sea, finally, is figured as something other than itself, something abstract and uncontained:

It is like what we imagine knowledge to be:
dark, salt, clear, moving, utterly free,
drawn from the cold hard mouth
of the world, derived from the rocky breasts
forever, flowing and drawn, and since
our knowledge is historical, flowing, and flown.

This feels rather operatic and self-conscious—worked over—in comparison to the acute observations with which the poem began ("from the rocky breasts / forever" seems particularly forced). What we remember about the poem, I believe, is not this final rhetorical summation, but "the small old buildings with an emerald moss / growing on their shoreward walls" and the old man with "sequins on his vest and on his thumb" who "has scraped the scales, the principal beauty, / from unnumbered fish with that black old knife, / the blade of which is almost worn away."

Perhaps the weakest moment in Bishop's famous staring poem, "The Fish,"[3] is its ending, which many critics denounce for its note of sentimentality, a predictable gesture of sympathy at the last moment which feels tacked on, moralizing at the culmination of a much more interesting and powerfully obsessive description of the fish. Though Bishop is present in "The Fish" in first-person pronouns scattered throughout the poem, here again the force of observation is so intense it tends to overwhelm the sense of an observer by aggressively directing our attention to the object itself. Who really cares about those intersecting, oily rainbows and the notion of fishly victory when we are presented with such astonishing detail, such minutely observed specifics, as in the magnificent passage describing the fish's skin:

Here and there
his brown skin hung in strips
like ancient wallpaper,
and its pattern of darker brown
was like wallpaper:
shapes like full-blown roses
stained and lost through age.

And she continues:

> He was speckled with barnacles,
> fine rosettes of lime,
> and infested
> with tiny white sea-lice,
> and underneath two or three
> rags of green weed hung down.

As if her obsession with describing the fish cannot stop at a presentation of its exterior details alone, Bishop now enters the fish's body and describes what she can only imagine, but most surely has seen many times while cleaning fish—that is to say, her depiction of these things is not fanciful, but literal. She speaks of:

> ... the coarse white flesh
> packed in like feathers,
> the big bones and the little bones
> the dramatic reds and blacks
> of his shiny entrails,
> and the pink swim-bladder
> like a big peony.

The description is riveting. Bishop's gaze is so clear, so particular, that we again enter a kind of observational trance, an absorption in the object of contemplation so complete we forget about her and ourselves and perhaps even the fact that we are reading a poem, a representation of the thing, and not seeing the thing itself. After this interior survey of the fish's principal organs, Bishop imaginatively exits the fish to take note of its eyes:

> the irises backed and packed
> with tarnished tinfoil
> seen through the lenses
> of old scratched isinglass.

The notations here are so fresh and surprising that we feel we could linger with her over every feature of the fish—lovingly, completely—until the creature has been thoroughly limned, thoroughly illuminated in words and images that possess the inevitableness Harold Bloom touts in his little book *The Art of Reading Poetry*[4] as one of the most important values a poem might exhibit: the conviction that what is stated and presented could have been stated and presented in no other way. Nothing about the poem feels arbitrary. Everything about it feels determined, fated, having that exactly-this-and-nothing-else quality that satisfies our deepest sense of fitness and artistic achievement.

In what I feel is one of Bishop's most successful poems, "The Moose,"[5] she retreats even further into the background to allow the landscape, other lives, and the moose itself to take center stage. In this poem, she is little more than a camera eye—perhaps a video camera—dutifully recording what happens during a bus trip through the Nova Scotia countryside at night. When she does enter the poem, it is not as a singular "I," but submerged in a group, an indistinguishable member of the pronouns "us" and "we." All her attention is directed outward, a mere amanuensis of what transpires, which is filled with both ordinariness and mystery, capped off with the appearance of the moose. Bishop is both voyeur and eavesdropper submerged in the all-encompassing darkness—and even at the ultimate moment, when the moose steps out of the woods, sniffs the bus, and is left behind, she avoids drawing a moral conclusion or turning the beast into a metaphor for primal nature, the unconscious, a pagan god or totem of any kind, or imagination's awkward ambassador. All of these might exist as layers beneath the literal events of the poem, but Bishop remains an objective reporter throughout. She has been staring into the night for twenty-eight stanzas and is willing to let whatever emerges from it speak for itself. It is one of the great poems of prolonged attention we have, written somewhat before the fracturing of our postmodern sensibilities had taken place.

One of our most notable "staring" poets is C. K. Williams who, through a number of remarkable volumes since *Tar*, has given us poems that are disciplined, alert, marvelously detailed, and unique for the way in which they can parse not only physical actions and things, but abstract concepts, thoughts, and feelings as though they were as solid and visible as any object. Like Ponge, whom he has translated, Williams is capable of an obsessive, determined gaze. But unlike Ponge, Williams is almost exclusively interested in people—what they say and do, how they interact with each other, what they think, and feel. A poem like "Waking Jed"[6] will serve to illustrate the sheer hypnotic nature of his attention, a patience and dedication to *getting it right* that is almost preternatural in its power.

Deep asleep, perfect immobility, no apparent evidence of consciousness
  or of dream.

Elbow cocked, fist on pillow lightly curled to the tension of the partially
  relaxing sinew.

Head angled off, just so: the jaw's projection exaggerated slightly, almost
  to prognathous: why?

The features express nothing whatsoever and seem to call up no response
  in me.

Though I say nothing, don't move, gradually, far down within, he, or
  rather not *he* yet,

something, a presence, an element of being, becomes aware of me: there
  begins a subtle,

very gentle alteration in the structure of his face, or maybe less than that,
  more elusive,

as though the soft distortions of sleep-warmth radiating from his face and
  flesh,

those essentially unreal mirages in the air between us, were
   modifying, dissipating.

The face now is more his, Jed's—its participation in the almost Ro-
   manesque generality.

I wouldn't a moment ago have been quite able to specify, not having its
   contrary, diminishes.

Particularly on the cheekbones and chin, the skin is thinning, growing
   denser, harder,

the molecules on the points of bone coming to attention, the eyelids
   finer, brighter, foil-like:

capillaries, veins; though nothing moves, there are goings to and fro
   behind now.

One hand opens, closes down more tightly, the arm extends suddenly
   full length,

jerks once at the end, again, holds: there's a more pronounced elonga-
   tion of the skull—

the infant pudginess, whatever atavism it represented, or reversion, has
   been called back.

Now I sense, although I can't say how, his awareness of me: I can feel
   him begin to *think*,

I even know that he's thinking—or thinking in a dream perhaps—of me
   here watching him.

Now I'm aware—again, with no notion how, nothing indicates it—that if
   there was a dream,

it's gone, and, yes, his eyes abruptly open although his gaze, straight before him,

seems not to register just yet, the mental operations still independent of his vision.

I say his name, the way we do it, softly, calling one another from a cove or cave,

as though something else were there with us, not to be disturbed, to be crept along beside.

The lids come down again, he yawns, widely, very consciously manifesting intentionality.

Great, if rudimentary, pleasure now: a sort of primitive, peculiarly mammalian luxury—

to know, to know wonderfully that lying here, warm, protected, eyes closed, one can,

for a moment anyway, a precious instant, put off the lower specie onsets, duties, debts.

Sleeker, somehow, slyer, more aggressive now, he is suddenly more awake, all awake,

already plotting, scheming, fending off: nothing said but there is mild rebellion, conflict:

I insist, he resists, and then, with abrupt, wriggling grace, he otters down from sight,

just his brow and crown, his shining rumpled hair, left ineptly showing from the sheet.

> Which I pull back to find him in what he must believe a parody of sleep,
> himself asleep:

> fetal, rigid, his arms clamped to his sides, eyes screwed shut, mouth
> clenched, grinning.

Anyone familiar with technical manuals might recognize the affinity this work has to process analysis, whereby engineers or chemical workers might learn, step by step, how a particular sequence of mechanical or chemical events might unfold. With a crucial difference: no engineer would be expected to have to read, much less understand, the complex abstractions presented here. Even most poets might be satisfied to note that "a very gentle alternation in the structure of Jed's face" takes place without fine tuning this observation by pushing it farther, to include something "more elusive": "the soft distortions of sleep-warmth radiating from his face / and flesh, / those essentially unreal mirages in the air between us, were modify- / ing, dissipating." To be aware of such subtleties, much less finding the language to articulate them, is one of Williams's gifts, and what sets his observations apart from many other poets engaged in describing the spectral or ephemeral qualities of things. Compare this, for instance, to Bishop's beautiful evocation of the sea at dusk, in "At the Fishhouses":

> All is silver: the heavy surface of the sea,
> swelling slowly as if considering spilling over,
> is opaque...

and later, again:

> I have seen it over and over, the same sea, the same,
> slightly, indifferently swinging above the stones,
> icily free above the stones,
> above the stones and then the world.

The point isn't that Williams is a better poet, or a more careful observer. It is just that he is after more liminal, elusive phenomena, states of awareness almost impossible to portray because of their frail, shimmering brevity, their almost-not-hereness, that only the most refined sensibility can detect. Williams is one of the poets who have made it possible again to partake of the widest array of terms the English language has to offer. His poetry is a far cry from the primitive "stone," "wind," "ice," and "star" vocabulary, mostly symbolic, favored in the 1960s when he began to write poetry.

In fact, it might be argued that Williams clutters his lines with too many heavy, abstract Latinate words, too many hesitations, second-guessings, and qualifications, and that these distract from the object of his attention rather than bringing it into sharper focus. But if we look closely at Williams's sentence structure, the wide array of adjectives and adverbs employed, and his use of what I call "triadic focusing" (which I will define shortly), we might understand how the apparent complexity of his style actually helps, not hinders, the exactness of his descriptions. In "Waking Jed," the observer is patient, fastidious in the details he selects for us to regard, and rigorously fixed on an object that is essentially still, or changing but slightly over a short period of time. The drama here is provided almost completely by the force of the observer's gaze. The language is lavish, intricate, sometimes concrete, sometimes attempting to make the abstract concrete and, therefore, graspable. The long lines allow, even encourage, the observer to inch over his material with no pressure to hurry because he has plenty of room to do so. Roominess is a quality, a condition of long lines and almost guarantees a slower pace than shorter lines would provide.

There is an imperative to keep qualifying and revising himself in the interests of getting it right, of nailing it down, of finally capturing those aspects of what he sees in words and phrases that will serve when no language, really, will serve in the face of such transitory, gossamer-like phenomena. So, his doubts and self-interruptions are scattered throughout—"or maybe," "or perhaps," "although," "or rather"—and are reflected in provisional words like "seem," "as though," "somehow," as well as in the periodic sentences that appear here and there in his examination of Jed, marked by suspended clauses that clarify, *en passant*, the main body of his sentence. We are often told that a poet's style mirrors his or her thought processes. This is surely the case here, with the caveat that Williams's poems, like any poet's, present the *illusion* of the thought processes that made them—not the actual process itself, which is messy, imprecise, halting, and unavoidably incomplete. Williams's chief technique, however, the mechanism with which he most strenuously tries to "get it right," is provided by what I have called "triadic focusing." When Williams employs this technique, he is not stumbling. He is allowing the reader to move with him from the most generalized expression of a thought to a clearer, more pointed formulization of that thought which is probably the closest he will ever get to actually articulating what he observes.

So at the very beginning of the poem, Williams moves from "Deep asleep" (most general), to "perfect immobility" (more specific), to "no apparent evidence of consciousness or of dream" (most specific) in the course of a single line, adjusting the lens, as it were—until he is satisfied that he has found the best way to embody his thought, to clarify it as far as it is possible to do so with the clunky, imprecise apparatus of language. Not much later, concerned with what he senses is taking place "far down within" the remote being of the sleeper, he does it again—how to describe this? He starts by saying "something," (most general), then decides he will call it "a presence," (more specific), and finally settles on "an element of being" as the most precise way he can articulate the insubstantial, vapory half-life of whatever it is that begins to stir deep in Jed's slumbering brain. In fact, the word "something" occurs twice in the poem and the word "nothing" five times. It is how Williams gets from "something" or almost "nothing" to "what will suffice," as Wallace Stevens put it—some final compromise in words—that provides the poem with its raison d'etre, its challenge, which Williams keeps asking of himself, and meeting, and going on, and which is a measure of the poem's ultimate value and success. To find language for what occurs on the fringes of consciousness, at the border between what can be spoken and what cannot, is one of the poet's particular tasks, a constant wrestling with language that—even at its best—favors the generic over the specific, the approximate over the exact. That is why language has so many modifiers. Adjectives and adverbs are specifiers, various choke-holds for grappling with the generality of nouns and verbs in an attempt to pin them to the mat.

So the list of modifiers in Williams's poem is impressive, and it flies in the face of Pound's generally accepted advice to avoid adjectives as much as possible in poetry. Williams employs the following in his struggle with the ineffable: *deep, perfect, apparent, partially relaxing, exaggerated, subtle, gentle, elusive, soft, essentially unreal, almost Romanesque, denser, harder, finer, brighter, foil-like, infant, mental, great, rudimentary, primitive, peculiar, mammalian, precious, lower, sleeker, slyer, mild, abrupt, wriggling, shining, rumpled, fetal, rigid, shut, clenched,* and *grinning.* The comparative (*denser, harder, finer, brighter*) is often used by the poet in his attempt to narrow things down to the particular. Woven in with this array of adjectives is an equally impressive array of adverbs: *lightly, partially, slightly, gradually, tightly, suddenly* (twice), *abruptly, softly, widely, consciously, wonderfully, ineptly,* and *almost.* Taken together, then, this dense web of modifiers helps Williams clarify his subject—what Jed looks like and what he does. Strip away these modifiers, and the poem presents only the archetype of a boy asleep in a bed, waking up. Any boy doing what any boy might. What Williams gives us is not a portrait, but an account of a particular boy in a particular moment, without preventing us from seeing some of the universal, as well. I believe the urgency to pay more than usual attention goes beyond a father's natural interest in his child, but suggests the artist's obsession with a subject—any subject—so long as it piques his interest and engages his imagination.

If, as Malebranche asserts, "Attention is the natural prayer of the soul," then each of these poems is a prayerful response to some aspect of the world, quotidian though it may be, on which the poet freely lavishes attention. Poems that stare honor reality and imply a valuation of their commonness, suggesting that importance—perhaps all we might finally know—can be found there. It is not anti-metaphysical, but pro-world-ly, devoted to the manifest, the here-and-now, as the only sure locus of understanding and truth. It is, perhaps, related to another of Williams's famous dictums: "no ideas, but in things," yet it is more than that. It involves respect, acceptance, even love of the actual, a curiosity and delight in what is, what exists, without an accompanying sense of judgment or degradation. It does not deny the horrifying or the ugly, but seeks beauty in the most unexpected places, the lowliest things—in gray, weathered fish tubs spangled with herring scales; in the cocked jaw of a loved one's face misshapen by sleep. Considered as a noun, the venerable O. E. D. defines *stare* as "the power of seeing" and "a condition of amazement, horror, admiration, etc." ("Why stand you," writes Shakespeare in *The Tempest*, "in this strange stare?"). As a verb, its definition is even more explicit: "to gaze fixedly and with eyes wide open." Is this so different than what we normally think of as being enraptured by something that stops us in our tracks and compels us to attend? In the poetry we've been considering, that something is the ordinary world.

6

Time and the Lyric

In a recent round of panel discussions on the lyric, several leading American poets have reminded us that, contrary to popular belief, the lyric poem does not "stop time," but rather preserves the course of a moment conditioned by time. It does this with lines which have to be read left to right, one by one down the page, until the poem ends; with grammar and syntax, which take time to unfold; even with the spaces between words and stanzas; and with thought development and narrative or associative logic. These remind us that poetry is a temporal art. Time is part of the essential fabric of a poem, as it is of the novel, dance, theatre, and music. It is not a spatial art, to be taken in all at once in an instant—or at least all *there* in a single moment—like painting, photography, and sculpture. The lyric preserves a moment—the process of a moment—but can't actually halt that moment or make it static. It has dimension, duration, periodicity, a beginning, middle, and end.

What the lyric can do is control time by managing to speed it up or slow it down, stretch it or make it contract, treat it like so much abstract silly putty that might be meted out in different ways according to the needs of the poet and the poem. Time, that is—literary time—is elastic. Novelists know this and control time through retarding it in a scene, speeding it up in summaries, leaping forward by foreshadowing or retroactively in a flashback. Poets, on the other hand, are not so conscious of time as an element in what they do because poems (except the epic) are usually short, and take up little of it—time, that is—stuffing it back into itself by condensing it in a phrase or an image that a novelist might spend many pages explicating. The poet leaps, foreshortens, collates, and conflates experience as much as possible, so that whole sweep of time and the actions that unfold there might be packed into as few words as possible, as in Dylan Thomas's telescoping of events in a line from "Ballad of the Long-Legged Bait":

And the hawk in the egg kills the wren.[1]

Much that can be said about instinct, inevitability, and fate is contained in the rapid succession of images Thomas presents to us in nine brief words—a complete philosophy of life and the workings of the natural world. Poets labor, as Lorine Neidecker suggests, in the "condensary." Pondering this notion, visions of poets like Emily Dickinson appear in their respective garrets, brilliantly stuffing hawks back into eggs, oaks into acorns, universes into homely metaphors that will explode later in our minds as our imaginations grasp what has been done and, in a real sense, reverse the process by reading the universe back out of those metaphors, unfolding and examining every suggestion, listening hard to the reverberations of what the words connote, not only what they literally mean. Poems burst open and unfold in our minds like those bathtub toys that turn into recognizable shapes the minute they touch water.

Condensation, of course, may result in both speeding up and slowing down a poem—contradictory forces whose tension creates some interesting effects and not a few real difficulties. The poem speeds up because the poet constructs it to be as brief as possible while simultaneously slowing it down because the pressure on every word, phrase, and line to carry the maximum possible meaning prevents hasty reading, forcing the mind to exercise a high degree of attention and interpretive skill. This cannot be done quickly. The clearer and less dense the metaphor(s), the quicker the poem might be read and grasped, but this does not imply anything about the value of the poem, only about its strategies and the amount of material it compresses. In the following haiku by Wendell Berry, a single metaphor supplies a great deal of meaning and emotion:

The evening after
the dog died his tracks are still
fresh on the wet path.

The relative speed with which we assimilate and interpret this haiku is not only a function of its brevity, but its clarity as well, its "simplicity," so to speak: a single resonant metaphor presented in uncomplicated language. We know, almost in the instant we read it, what it means: the dead leave physical traces of themselves in the world for a while after they're gone. It's important to recognize that the *implications* of this meaning continue to ripple outward after we have read the poem. It is not simple-minded, only brief.

Compare this to a poem, almost as concise, by John Haines from his book, *The Stone Harp*—not a haiku, but surely haiku-like in its compression of much matter and substance:

MARIGOLD[2]

This is the plaza of Paradise.
It is always noon,
and the dusty bees are dozing
like pardoned sinners.

The language here isn't demonstrably more complex than the language in the first poem, though words like "Paradise" and "pardoned" carry higher degrees of association—symbolic freight—than anything in Berry's haiku. That means that it will take a bit longer to interpret them, a bit more time to figure out what they might mean in this context. Moreover, the poem presents us with two metaphors, not one: a flower (marigold) as "the plaza of Paradise" and ordinary honeybees as "pardoned sinners." That is, the central idea of the poem develops in two steps rather than being contained in a single image. More *time* is needed to move from one contributing idea to the next until the larger overarching idea is grasped. The complexity of that central idea, moreover, is more wide-ranging in its implications than the one presented in Berry's haiku. The idea involves age-old Christian beliefs about the myth of Eden and the Fall—both of man and nature—and doctrines concerning sin and morality which would take pages and pages of explanation to document adequately. Haines has perhaps packed more into the space of his lines than Berry has into the space of his.

Density and complication, though, are no assurance of profundity, while clarity and straightforwardness by no means signify shallowness or simplicity of mind. Both Berry's and Haines's poems contain a high degree of emotional and imaginative depth. But density and complication do effect speed, the pace at which the content of a poem might be taken in and assimilated, and since speed is a factor of poetry that most interests me here, I would like to look at Kim Addonizio's poem, "Rain," for what it reveals to us about the way a poem moves forward with relatively unhindered ease.

RAIN[3]

is what I can't bear going on & not
easing all day hitting the windows like someone
throwing shovelfuls of dirt onto a
coffin keeping me in bed sick but not physically only
reading a poet's lines about Vietnam thinking of
Harry & Danny & Ron how long ago it was now
I don't know them or only my body remembers
lying beneath Harry on the hard
ground of the field frozen with little stars
of frost his hands holding an M16 or a woman
with black hair or my shoulders as he
came inside me crying & Danny strapping on
his wooden leg to teach me karate saying Don't
be afraid to maim his naked thigh scarred
& oddly beautiful & his one foot the divot of flesh gouged
out or Ron talking bitterly about America & the night
I pushed his wheelchair too fast ran it
off the sidewalk into a tree & we laughed &
how I'd grow so tired of listening to him & never
knowing if he cared what I thought all of it
gone into my history of loss a litany I need

> to sing I don't know why today it's just the rain
> keeps up & I feel so cold inside I can't get out
> of bed or understand why these ghosts
> of men come back to press me down I couldn't
> help them or I did maybe a little tenderness a
> breast or kiss what I could offer not knowing I was
> so young believing I could heal them the rain
> relentless against the windows when will it stop oh when

The poem is pitched forward, a headlong rush, as it tumbles from image to image, idea to idea, its characters displacing each other as they appear suddenly and disappear like portraits in a slide show. For those who still believe in the functionality of form—that form reflects content—the form of "Rain" seems entirely appropriate to the situation here: a sick person (not physically, but in spirit) lying in bed alone on a gloomy day is likely to hallucinate (or free-associate) this way. The slight delirium produced by relentless weather may cause the mind to enter a hypnotic state where thoughts and memories run into other thoughts and memories seamlessly, as they do in the poem. We've all experienced this state where perceptions are not so well-defined, orderly, or neat, so *punctuated* and complete as they might be in more ordinary states of consciousness. Even the fact that the speaker is reading poetry adds to the likelihood of the mind becoming acutely receptive to various suggestions, sudden shifts, and rapid stimuli, the mind acted upon and prepared to float more freely from thought to thought without impediment.

If we ask how the impression of speed is created technically in the poem, we might begin with punctuation—that is, the lack of it—which has become practically a convention in modern poetry, one a poet might employ if he or she wishes the poem to be "less pinned down to the page," as W. S. Merwin defined it when explaining how he came to discard punctuation in his own poetry. Other conventions include doing away with capital letters at the beginning of every line, the use of ampersands as substitutes for the conjunction "and," and the way the title runs into the first line of the poem so that the reader is off to a flying start from the beginning. Add to these the avoidance of complex grammar and diction to help clear the way for the mind's dash through an historical and personal minefield and you have a poem that is contradictorily racing at the same time it is accumulating more and more depth, gathering emotional weight even as it plunges forward.

And there's more: constant enjambment ushers us quickly from line to line, while the poem itself is one long sentence, eschewing periods or even semicolons, though there are at least four likely spots the poem might halt for breath before hurrying on (at the end of line six, for instance, and later after the phrases "need to sing," "press me down," and "against the windows"). Even at the very last the poem has no final period, no punctuational closure, like a song that fades while the musicians continue to play on and on forever. The lack of a period at the end also implies an answer to the speaker's question "when will it stop oh when" which is *never*, a violence that is as relentless and disturbing as the rain itself.

We can track the metaphorical and associative movement of the poem beginning with the endless rain of the title, a meteorological gloom that works on the speaker's own interior weather to produce a gloomy mood and therefore gloomy thoughts. The image of dirt thrown on a coffin occurs early in the poem, a result of this moodiness and because the speaker has been reading poems about Vietnam. This leads to memories of three war vets—boys at the time—who are dead or maimed, and therefore "ghosts" of their former selves. Rain keeps pounding the windows, so by the end of the poem the downpour has taken on the symbolic meaning of relentless violence. The dark rainy day is associated with dark evil times, while relentless rain is associated with the continuous violence of history. Three elements are posed to counter these negative, threatening influences—sexual pleasure, an "odd" beauty, and laughter—which correspond to the three men, characteristics of their nature the speaker fondly recalls. But these gestures seem small and weak compared to the thundering power of the storm, so the idea of helplessness emerges which in turn creates a sense of poignancy, or sorrow, almost despair.

An important conflation of time occurs when the speaker recalls making love to one of the boys in a field:

... my body remembers
lying beneath Harry on the hard
ground of the field frozen with little stars
of frost his hands holding an M16 or a woman
with black hair or my shoulders as he
came inside me crying...

The shift in thought from an M16, to a (Vietnamese?) woman, to the speaker takes place with astonishing speed as we imagine Harry first holding his rifle, which turns into a woman with black hair, then quickly into the shoulders of the speaker—a sequence in which one thing morphs into another with all the fluidity of technical effects in a modern movie. A similar acceleration of time and imagery takes place shortly thereafter when the speaker remembers pushing one of the boys in his wheelchair:

I pushed his wheelchair too fast ran it
off the sidewalk into a tree & we laughed &
how I'd grow so tired of listening to him & never
knowing if he cared what I thought all of it
gone into my history of loss...

Here it is not rapidly morphing images, but thoughts, none of which are developed past a simple mention as one dissolves into another. And at the very end of the poem, time seems to collapse altogether as the speaker melds memories of the past with images of the present as if they were occurring at the same moment.

In these ways, Addonizio creates a rapid cross-cutting phantasmagoria that works on us imaginatively and emotionally, and perhaps more efficiently, than a measured, punctuated, completely grammatical account of the same material might. The stripping away of all but the barest language, the starkest imagery, allows the poem to work directly and immediately on our feelings because we are unguarded and have little time to pause and reflect upon what we've just read. We are as open as the speaker to what is rushing at us, and as helpless to stop it. And stopping it would be difficult because the poem makes it so easy for us to continue, having removed all stumbling blocks, all hindrances to assimilating the poem's psychological and emotional burden.

A second example, taken from *Charles Simic: Selected Poems 1963-2003*, illustrates how the lengths of lines themselves and how they are disposed on the page work to expedite our reading of the poem, setting up an effect that perhaps could have worked no other way.

ELEGY[4]

Note
as it gets darker
that little
can be ascertained
of the particulars
and of their true
magnitudes

Note
the increasing
unreliability
of vision
though one thing may appear
more or less
familiar
than another

Disengaged
from reference
as they are
in the deepening
gloom

nothing to do
but sit
  and abide
depending on memory
to provide
  the vague outline
the theory
of where we are
tonight
  and why
we can see
so little
  of each other
and soon
  will be
even less
  able

  in this starless
summer night
  windy and cold

  at the table
brought out
  hours ago
under a huge ash tree
  two chairs
two ambiguous figures
  each one relying
on the other
to remain faithful
  now
that one can leave
  without the other one
  knowing

> this late
> in what only recently was
>   a garden
> a festive occasion
>   elaborately planned
> for two lovers
>   in the open air
> at the end
>   of a dead-end
> road
>   rarely traveled
>
> o love

Opposing forces are at work here: Simic wants to get to the revelation at the end of the poem as soon as he can, yet at the same time hold it off for as long as possible. Timing is everything. If he arrives at those two little words "o love" too early, the poem will feel sappy, contrived. If he arrives too late, the poem will have run its course and the effect will be anticlimactic, tacked on. Suppose, for instance that the poem ended after the lines "windy and cold"—

> in this starless
> summer night
>   windy and cold
>
> o love

It *could* end there, but the effect would be entirely different, the maneuvering more blatant, as though the poet were indicating that he had only brought up the idea of the encroaching dark in order to express the sentiment with which the poem concludes. But Simic doesn't want the true subject of the poem to emerge yet (if he even knew what it was himself at this stage of writing the poem). He wants to continue to exploit the subtle hints provided by words and phrases like "deepening gloom" and "memory," the slower the better. He wants the "two ambiguous figures" who "remain faithful" to resonate with the suggestiveness of the early phrases, and to find their way only later to that "dead-end road" before he pronounces the affecting address to whoever else is there with him in the darkness: "o love."

Yet the slow emergence of the subject of the poem directly contradicts the ways in which Simic formally hurries the poem along, being careful not to linger too long on any one detail that might sidetrack the main thrust—which is to get to that simple declaration, that pathos-heavy recognition to which everything in the poem will add up. So, to speed up the progress of the poem, the actual experience of reading it, Simic employs much that Addonizio employed in her poem: no punctuation, clarity of thought through mostly simple diction, continual enjambments, no capital letters at the beginnings of lines, and so on. What he adds to this panoply of techniques is important: extremely short lines and a shifting series of indentations which somehow heighten and reflect the speed of the poem. How? By not returning us to the left-hand margin after every line, the poem seems to thwart any sense of stopping and starting, hesitating and beginning again, that conventional lineation supplies. The indented lines seem to hover and suspend our halting sense of a justified left-hand margin, allowing us easier passage to the next line, and the next, so the poem seems to glide rather than march forward. Or perhaps downward would be a better way of putting it. The shifting margins of the poem track us down the page vertically, not horizontally. More like a leaf falling than a shuttle weaving back and forth. The indentations suggest that the poem is laid out on a vertical axis (though it is not, not exactly) and that impression is what draws our eyes—and our sensibilities—toward the foot of each page.

Even the choice of separating the poem into stanzas does not detract from this descending movement. The white space between stanzas seems like another easy passage, a place to fall through, rather than a place that traditionally suggests a pause, an interruption, before moving on. This is partly due to there being no punctuation, no finalizing period at the end of each stanza, but it is also because the poem is one long, smooth, uninterrupted thought—no leaps to a new subject, no digressions, no sidebars or suspended clauses to complicate matters. We are happy to float down the page with the poem, buoyantly picking up those hints and clues as we go.

It is only at the last moment, the ultimate moment, when the poem leaps forward to a new subject, "o love," transfiguring all that went before. Now we know the poem is not merely about the oncoming night, but about the approach of death, and how no matter how hard the two people try to "remain faithful" to one another, one of them will soon get up and leave without the other even knowing, or, at least, knowing where the other went. If where the two people are at present is only a "theory," then where they are going is even murkier, a place where they "soon will be even less able" to see or find one another.

This explanation, this summation, is provided nicely in the penultimate phrases "at the end / of a dead-end / road". The repetition of the word "end" at the ends of two contiguous lines prepares us for how to interpret the two words which suddenly confront us at the extremity of that single, long, smooth thought: "o love". All along, then, the speaker has been talking—not about the night—but about himself and his companion, whom he had objectified briefly in an earlier stanza as "two ambiguous figures." The poem comes to rest here, it's true, but without the little lock of a period to shut it tight, the poem seems to drift into inarticulateness, into a vast unbounded space, "this starless summer night windy and cold."

"Elegy" seems altogether porous, fluid, allowing as little resistance as possible to the reader as she moves from word to word, line to line. There are words here like "ascertained," "magnitudes," "unreliability," and "disengaged" around which, like small stones in a stream, the poem may eddy for a moment. But they don't offer any real drag on the flow of feeling and thought. The relative simplicity of grammar and syntax sees to that, allowing for the quick apprehension of everything that is read.

Verticality as an aesthetic is not new, of course. E. E. Cummings and William Carlos Williams make use of it, each in his own way. Perhaps its foremost proponent in American poetry is Robert Lax, who built his entire career—if that is not too odd a word to describe Lax's sporadic poetic activity for nearly eighty years—on the thinnest lineation possible, sometimes consisting of a single word, part of a word, or even a letter. As Paul J. Spaeth asserts in his fine introduction to Lax's collection, *A Thing That Is*[5], which was published by Overlook Press in 1997,

The effect of this kind of display on the page is that the reader is forced to slow the pace of his reading and in so doing finds himself concentrating more than is usual on each phrase, word, syllable, and letter.

Spaeth goes on to describe Lax's work as "contemplative" in "that it causes one to focus in a direct way on the image itself. Both the content of the poems and the visual display of the words on the page call the reader away from the rush of the world to a state of reflection." Another critic has said that "the poems are laid out in a way that invites the eye to linger."

It is ironic, then, that Spaeth is claiming the opposite of what I claimed for Simic's poem, "Elegy"—that short lines effectively accelerate the reading of a poem, allowing it to be taken in at a quicker pace. Certainly, Lax's poetics appeal to the eye and "invites it to linger" on the uniqueness of this strange aesthetic.

What
is
be
ing

what
is

ex
is
tence

can
the
rab
bit

be
said

to
be

if
it
is
dead

?

We
say
it

Is
dead

What
is

Is
that

?

By breaking up the words, Lax is able to isolate some key concepts in the
poem and show how language is often snuggled within language, like a
set of Chinese boxes. He can separate the word ex-is-tence into its basic
parts so that the second syllable, "is," reveals itself to be the present tense
of the verb "to be"—to be alive, to exist in the world. At the same time,
he can suggest the reverse: "ex-is" hints at being out of "is," of having

once been "is," but no more. He does the same thing by parsing the word "be-ing," so the first syllable again indicates the verb "to be." By breaking up the word "rab-bit," he can indicate the tininess of the creature—it is only a little "bit" of a thing. But whether the poem reads more slowly this way, or more quickly, remains a question for each reader. In my opinion, shorter lines generally allow the reader to move through a poem more quickly than long, luxurious lines filled with language, imagery, and metaphor, even if the poem is relatively long (more than a page or two). Even if it's a thin epic, shorter lines facilitate speed, and speed sometimes is what it's all about.

7

Six Bullets Ripped Into My Chest:

How Poems Begin

Many years ago, a friend of mine was praising a poem by Charles Simic, particularly admiring the way it began:

> Seems like a long time
> Since the waiter took my order.[1]

He looked at me and shook his head, "How could you resist reading a poem that begins like *that*!" At the time, I wasn't sure I knew what he meant. I was pretty naïve for someone who wanted to be a poet. I thought Simic's opening lines were too muted, too mundane. Shouldn't the opening lines of a poem be thunderous and dramatic, rhetorical and grand? Not something so ordinary? Shouldn't the first words grab you by the throat and yank you into the poem, the way opening sentences in detective novels sometimes do: "Six bullets ripped into my chest…" *That's more like it*, I thought then. I wanted to overwhelm the reader, to dazzle him from the outset, and Simic's humble lines seemed too ordinary, too unambitious to me. "O for a Muse of fire!" Subsequently, I have come to realize the truth of what my friend noticed: an opening line, to be effective, has to engage the reader's interest, stir or delight her, in some way draw her in without sounding flashy or trying too hard, not overtly dazzling, but balanced, plausible, appealing.

The first lines of poems are like pickup lines in a bar—you've got one chance, so the words you choose had better be right. You must consider them carefully, but at the same time they have to sound completely natural and sincere. What a quandary. Subtle humor might help—too serious, and you'll be left in the lurch, unsmiling and dull. Too silly and you'll be left smirking to yourself. A measured combination of elements is needed.

In ancient times, epic poems began with an invocation to the Muse, goddess of memory and the arts. There was no other way to start, and so invoking the Muse was prescribed. The poet might be called upon to frame the words in his own way, but the fact of beginning with an invocation was *de rigueur*. "Sing in me, Muse, and through me tell the story," Homer propitiates the goddess at the opening of *The Odyssey*. "Arms and the Man I sing," echoes Virgil at the beginning of *The Aeneid* many years later, though by that time the invocation had become a mere convention, no longer the heartfelt prayer it had once been. In later centuries, the classical invocation to the Muse is replaced by an apostrophe to various persons, animals, and things that represent divine afflatus and the Romantic Imagination (with a capital "I"). "O wild West Wind, thou breath of Autumn's being!" Shelley fulminates at the beginning of his "Ode to the West Wind," while Byron personifies liberty, addressing it in lofty terms: "Eternal Spirit of the chainless Mind!" Wordsworth directs his words to one of his English predecessors, asking for help—both artistic and political: "Milton! thou should'st be living at this hour: England hath need of thee." Later still, in an even more secular age during the height of the Modern, invocations lose all pretense of the divine and become instead sonorous secular statements, thunderous and dramatic, rhetorical and grand: "I think continually of those who are truly great," Spender intones at the beginning of his poem by the same title, while Allen Ginsberg elevates his voice to make his famous American pronouncement, "I saw the best minds of my generation destroyed by madness" (highbrow equivalent of "Six bullets ripped into my chest"). Once the opening of a poem is prescribed, at least some of the anxiety of how and where to begin is alleviated.

But no such convention exists in contemporary poetry, so we must return to the question of beginnings—each poem a separate challenge— and the question of how best to commence writing, a question that looks more naïve the further we pursue it. If we return to Simic's opening line and look at it closely, we can see some of the features that make a certain kind of opening line appealing. To begin with, it presents the situation of the poem in *medias res*—always a fine way to draw the reader in. No need to preface, no place for preambles or fancy preludes. Get right down to it. "Seems like a long time / since the waiter took my order." The situation has both comic and potentially serious implications: We've all been kept waiting for our food, so we identify with the speaker's plight instantly and perhaps even smile to ourselves in sympathy. And we've all felt uncomfortable in an empty restaurant if we are left alone too long, as if we've been forgotten or something dire has happened of which we are yet unaware. Which is it going to be? We don't know yet, and that is one of the reasons we want to keep reading, to see how the situation will resolve itself. The tone of the speaker is measured, completely unaffected. We trust him, and share his complex emotional reaction—impatience, curiosity, mild alarm. Such an ordinary situation, yet so full of possibility! All of this held in delicate balance, all of it plausible, and therefore appealing. The poem allows us to enter it on our own, not dunned like a barker at a circus, herding customers in with wild and exotic claims, and certainly not lured by the glamorous extravagant suggestions of a movie poster. Simic's opening line is inviting, unaggressive, even friendly. "Come in," it proposes, "sit here with me; let's see what happens."

Another kind of opening, one radically different from the subtle effects offered by Simic, may be found in the work of his friend and contemporary, Russell Edson. Edson's strategy is to present the reader with some absurd situation, an astonishing proposition of one sort or another, so skewed it will grip us by the power of its imaginative logic—or illogic. "What!" we think, "what's this?" We are shocked into attention, and our interest is engaged. So Edson begins a poem with the line, "A man has just married an automobile."[2] Excuse me? Did we read that right: a man married an automobile? We read it again. What in god's name could that mean? We read on. And with Edson, we are almost never disappointed. His poems work by this device again and again, because once he has posed such an absurdity, he is obliged to make good on his claim. He has to follow the thread of his illogical opening wherever it might lead, and it is this journey through the world of the irrational—which, if the poet is good enough, makes an absurd kind of logic—that charms by satisfying something in us as primitive and childlike as a fairy tale.

Other opening lines by Edson confirm the way he arrests our attention by unveiling such absurdities: "My father by some strange conjunction had mice for sons," or "A woman has killed her parakeet with an axe."

Sometimes the initiating line can be so bizarre we might wonder how he can unravel anything of interest from it at all: "A man had just delivered a toad from his wife's armpit." Skittish readers might turn away, but many will follow Edson into the twists and turns of the unconscious that produce a brief treatise on how we love our children, no matter how ugly or deformed, and how vanity often brings us to name them after ourselves.

Shock treatment is effective, but the poet has a tremendous challenge when employing this technique. Will the rest of the poem bear out the level of imagination contained in its opening, and result in something marvelous—even oddly serious—rather than something just plain silly? Many poems that begin with bizarrely creative opening lines slip into mere gibberish as the poet's imagination flags and cannot fulfill the promise of the poem's beginning. It's as though the poet, happy with himself for imagining such a catchy start, soon settles for something more superficial: inane social banter. We feel the abatement of imagination's force and stop reading, perhaps a bit disgruntled at the failure of the poem to deliver on its captivating opening.

Another poet who works by broaching some curious opening gambit and then exploiting it is Thomas Lux. The temperament here is less jarring but equally effective in spurring the reader's interest and encouraging her to read on. So, the opening lines of "Traveling Exhibit of Torture Instruments"[3] draws us in to see what the poet will have to say about such an odd event: "What man has done to woman and man / and the tools he built to do it with / is pure genius in its pain." We nod, sadly, but also with some fascination at the way Lux expresses this first thought. The word "genius," for instance, is not what one would expect in a sentence whose main subject is torture. But even that seems appropriate, the idea that human genius is as often perverted as put to beautiful or virtuous ends. This contradiction energizes the lines—pure genius associated with pain—a contradiction fused alliteratively by the plosives of "pure" and "pain."

While it is often true that Lux's titles contribute greatly to positing some curious metaphor or idea and that these are more spread out in his poems than in Edson's, Lux's opening lines contain more of interest than many poets who write about similar subjects and aspire to similar ends. A brief survey of some of his first lines illustrate this:

All the slaves within me
are tired or nearly dead
                                    —"All the Slaves"

Sometime around dusk moose lifts
his heavy, primordial jaw, dripping, from pondwater
and, without psychic struggle,
decides the day, for him, is done
                                    —"Wife Hits Moose"

You love your dog and carve his steaks
(marbled, tender, aged) in the shape of hearts.

                                    —"So You Put the Dog to Sleep"

This valley: as if a huge, dull primordial axe
once slammed into the earth
and then withdrew, innumerable millennia ago.

                            —"Grim Town in a Steep Valley"

Lux's sensibility is ironic, fierce, tender. What he makes of these inaugural
ideas seldom disappoints and is often affecting in the best sense of the word.
    One of the most famous opening lines in English poetry, T. S. Eliot's
"The Wasteland," makes use of contradiction as well, but is interesting not
for the metaphorical possibilities it offers but for the intellectual problem
it immediately poses:

    April is the cruelest month...

April, cruel? Normally, we think of December, January, or February as being "cruel" because they are frigid, the very deadest time of the year. April, on the other hand, marks the beginning of spring, when flowers first show buds and birds return from winter sojourns. Eliot turns nature on its head and gives us an intriguing first line that leads us to investigate further. Such seemingly outlandish statements are enticements to which we respond as a sort of challenge, the way we are challenged by a puzzle or a brain teaser. *Let's see if the poet can get out of this*, we think, *and let's see if I can figure this out and come up with an answer myself.*

Beginning with an enigmatic statement, then, is another way to induce the reader to make a commitment to the poem, then push on. Because expecting a reader—any reader—to take time out of her busy day, to drop whatever else she may be doing and pay attention, to take her precious time to read, absorb, and interpret a poem, is asking a great deal. No one, with the exception of school children or graduate students, is required to read your poem—and even *that* is a highly unlikely occurrence with so much else from which the teacher has to choose. That is exactly why opening lines are so crucial: You either set the hook immediately or the reader gets away.

Another poem that falls into the category of contradictory openings is Theodore Roethke's famous work, "In a dark time, the eye begins to see."[4] This is the best kind of paradox in poetry because it almost immediately resolves itself. We seize upon the contradiction and interpret it in one stroke: yes, our eyes are suddenly, if painfully opened when we confront corruption and evil. Revelation is the flip-side of complacency. And because Roethke's poem is written in traditional form, each line is a complete unit of thought and we can take it all in at once. It is focused, balanced, complete. If the paradox presented in Roethke's first line were more obtuse, more logically gnarled and difficult to unravel, the reader might be brought up short and not able to continue reading, forced to ponder the opening line that has now become a bolt on a door, not a key. If the opening line is so difficult to analyze, what might be expected of the rest of the poem? Will the reader have to pick the lock of paradox after paradox, exerting so much effort that finally he will give up after having decided it is not worth the struggle? We have all read poems in which we have gotten lost from line one, and so have never been able to find our way to the right path, the thematic thread that will lead us through the poem and out the other side like Theseus in his labyrinth. But I do not mean to imply that Roethke's opening line is superficial because it is quickly absorbed and readily interpreted. In fact, the line is full of suggestive depths and resounding meaning. It is a near perfect mixture of profundity and accessibility, a recognition that strikes us the way a good epigram strikes us, a short poem by Porchia or one of W. S. Merwin's "Asian Figures." What seems illogical for a split second suddenly unfolds and makes the greatest sense in the world.

This is as good a place as any to stop and admit that I'm being a bit disingenuous about first lines and how they work—as if there were good opening lines and bad ones and the two categories were easy to tell apart and therefore easy to learn to write and apply to one's work. This just isn't so. We read, mostly, poems that begin rather blandly but slowly accumulate emotional power and imaginative force so that, by the end, we are aware of how successful the poems are. The opening lines play very little part in that success and serve only as ports of entry, access to the greater substance of the poem that awaits us as we read on. If I make a quick survey of opening lines from a pile of books on my desk, I find the following:

I dig into a patch of curbside grass: my little urban yard.

—Mike Dockins,
from *Slouching in the Path of a Comet*

You strolled whistling
through the front door, ...

—Jim Peterson,
from *The Bob & Weave*

First thing in the morning the phone rings

—Steve Kowit,
from *The Dumbbell Nebula*

"Your train departs in ten minutes"

—Julianne Buchsbaum,
from *Slowly, Slowly, Horses*

As we cross the square, she remarks that it has been
a warm December...

—Eleanor Lerman,
from *Our Post-Soviet History Unfolds*

today mom comes outside

—Cammy Thomas,
from *Cathedral of Wish*

They were sitting on the thin mattress
he'd once rolled and carried up the four floors
to his room

—David St. John,
from *Study for the World's Body*

The poems begin modestly, not with a bang but a whisper. Rather than try
to intrigue the reader from the outset, pose some intellectual challenge, or
present some wildly imaginative situation, they quietly open a door and
invite the reader to walk in, but with this understanding: soon, something
intriguing or challenging or imaginative will happen. And it does. In
each of these poems, the poet holds his or her best lines in abeyance, but
not for long. This unstated promise, "If you follow me for a few minutes,
if you trust me, I will lead you to something interesting, even fabulous,
but you must have patience," is probably the norm, and for a good reason.

The other ways of beginning a poem that I have examined are perilous. If they are not handled well, they will seem merely gimmicky, self-conscious, contrived. Safer, most times, to induce the reader to come in and trust you—trust a voice that sounds reasonable and true—a calm, level address—before upping the ante with formal pyrotechnics or a wild surmise.

And there is another factor to consider. The more lyrical the poem, the more condensed it is, the more likely its opening will be polished, chiseled, highly wrought, not as casual as the opening of a longer, more narrative poem. This is a generalization, but a poem that has more room to operate has more time to prepare its strategies and accomplish its effects. So, the opening line of Roethke's lyric is already concentrated, refined. It begins if not eventfully, at least formally in *medias res*. By the opening line of a lyric, the engine of technique is already running.

In the same pile of books I mention above, the volume *After The Others* by Bruce Weigl[5] illustrates this point. Unlike many of the other books, I was hard pressed to find a poem in *After the Others* that began in a relaxed manner. The openings of Weigl's poems are tersely to the point:

> I dread those lace doilies
> lonely women stitch
> for the ill…
>
> > —"The Happy Land"

> They thought the sun was a wheel
> turning…
>
> > —"Prologue in Minor Key,
> > For the Ancestors"

> Not the hummed vibration
> through her body's
> trailing silk…
>
> > —"The Latin for Black Window"

> She wanted to make the violins
> playing over the blue water
> go away
> —"For the Anthropologist, Merging"

The texture of this language is palpably different than that of the first lines of poems cited above. Weigl knows he only has so much space in which to work, so he goes to work right away. He is striving for condensation, the measured, stark particular syllables of Tu Fu or Wang Wei. A few exact brushstrokes, and no more. Not haiku, not *that* radically compressed, but a polished reticence nevertheless. His poems give the impression that every word has been held up and considered carefully before being delicately, but firmly set into place next to other words—until the language stands out from the page as though it were embossed there. We are as aware of the language as we are of what it finally expresses. But not stopped at the language, or distracted by it, as in poetry that seeks to arrest us at the level of the word—a superficial level—without allowing us to pass through it to the depths of meaning and emotion which it signifies. Weigl's poetry allows for the double pleasure of savoring both language and meaning at once, without either usurping the other.

It is equally true, however, that much formal poetry commences without feeling formal at all, without the tension we associate with lines written in regular meter and rhyme. Some formal poems have a loose, colloquial feel as they begin, a more conversational tone that we recognize immediately as closer to speech:

> Whose woods these are I think I know,
> His house is in the village though;
> He will not see me stopping here
> To watch his woods fill up with snow.[6]

"Whose woods these are I think I know" is a far cry from "In a dark time, the eye begins to see," or even "I dread those lace doilies lonely women stitch." In Frost's famous poem, he tries to approximate—paradoxically in metered lines—the lax, swinging insouciance of much free verse, the formal equivalent of poems that begin rather blandly but slowly accumulate emotional power and imaginative force. Here, Frost is asking us to be patient, to trust that if we stay with the poem, something important will emerge. And, of course, it does in those two powerfully repeated last lines, "And miles to go before I sleep." Frost based his career on writing meticulous formal verse that created the illusion of being composed in the vernacular, the natural clipped rhythms of New England speech. This is one of his greatest accomplishments—not only for his region, but for Modern poetry in general. His lead has been followed by most successful contemporary poets writing in strict form. It is now the lingua franca of formal poetry, though some formal verse continues to be written in a higher rhetorical mode from time to time. Roethke came *after* Frost, as did Lowell, Berryman, and other formalists whose work retains some of the elevated qualities of the older verse practice.

Some poems present us with openings meant to charm, to disarm our natural skepticism at the outset with a statement or image that is anti-poetic in its sardonic or light-hearted way. Jeffrey Harrison's poem, "My Worst Job Interview," runs into the first line: "had to be the one where I was naked."[7] The strategy here is similar to Simic's, if a bit more self-consciously contrived: Who could resist reading a poem that begins like *that*? Contrivance does not necessarily carry a pejorative meaning when it comes to poetry. All poems are contrived because they are works of art—sleights of artifice—calculated to affect the reader in one way or another. How well they do that is the only measure of value that applies, and the only way we can rightly judge them. Harrison draws us in because we are pleased by the whimsy of the situation and we want to know how it might be possible that someone could find himself in such a situation.

Charm is not necessarily a shallow or an empty trait, as it may sometimes be when encountered in certain people. Charm, in poetry, may be a positive poetic virtue, a useful tool when counterbalanced by a serious purpose. Its first cousin, wit, has been with us for centuries and was especially prized in the eighteenth century in the work of Dryden, Pope, and Johnson. The century prior to that relished the drollery of Donne, Shakespeare, and that fast-quipping company gathered in the legendary Mermaid Tavern—

a Palace of Wit, if there ever was one. Wit is a way of making often bitter truth somehow palatable, a socially acceptable way of skewering someone—acceptable if you were clever enough to make the thrust not only lethal, but delightfully apt at the same time. Otherwise, you were just being nasty and no matter how much truth there might be in what you said, no one wanted to hear it. Charm works in a similar way. The reader might allow herself to be drawn to certain features of your work—luscious imagery, fantastical metaphors, sonorous phrases—as long as she senses there is substance, real insight couched beneath such superficial allure.

A poet who likes to charm us is Tony Hoagland, whose opening statements often beguile us with notions that seem oddly innocent and sophisticated at once:

> I should walk up the stairs right now
> and make slow love to the woman I live with
>
> —from *Sweet Ruin*[8]

> I thought I saw my mother
> in the lesbian bar
> —from *Donkey Gospel*[9]

> To whoever taught me the word *dickhead*
> I owe a debt of thanks
> —from *Donkey Gospel*

> That was the day we swam in a river, a lake, and an ocean.
>
> —from *What Narcissism Means to Me*[10]

Just as often, his opening gambit employs a highly inventive metaphor:

What was the name of that bronze-headed stud
of a Greek deity
in charge of the Temple of Distraction?

—from *Sweet Ruin*

I'm driving on the dark highway
when the opera singer on the radio
opens his great mouth
and the whole car plunges down the canyon of his throat

—from *Donkey Gospel*

A forlorn guy with a guitar
issues bulletins from the coast of Melancholia

—from *What Narcissism Means to Me*

Sometimes Hoagland likes to shock us into attention by making a remark
that is nothing if not *outré*:

I wanted to punch her right in the mouth and that's the truth.

—from *Donkey Gospel*

Along with poets like Charles Simic, Stephen Dobyns, Charles Harper
Webb, and Billy Collins, Hoagland is one of our most engaging alchemists
of metaphor, and like them, his wacky and surprising comparisons yield
depths of emotion and thought that redeem any notion of mere silliness,
of cute but superficial kibitzing. His charm has an edge, dark interiors
where anything from guilt to anger, grief, existential nausea, doubt, and

regret might hide and from which they inevitably emerge at one point in the poem or another.

But not all poems commence with flashy metaphors or startling, attention-grabbing remarks. One of the most effective ways to begin a poem is with the description of a landscape or a place. In this respect, such poems allude to narrative prose fiction again with their initial exposition, locating the reader in time and space, and conjuring atmosphere and tone before proceeding to the main action of the story. "Just before it rains, the lilacs / thrash weakly, / storm light heightening / the clusters drooping / at their peak of scent, / wind running / through them like slow water" writes Chase Twichell in her poem, "A Lamb by Its Ma," [11] and we are oriented in a landscape at a particular time and place (though not yet specified) before the slightest hint of subjectivity has entered the scene. That will come, but at first we are simply *put* somewhere, alert and observing, all our senses awake. The same thing happens at the beginning of Sebastian Matthews' poem, "Coming to Flood" [12] :

> The fields, just the other day lost to water,
> have emerged saturated in green, decked-out
>
> in the new day, the only sign of the flood's
> accidental profusion in a few skewed mud tracks,
>
> branches wedged into a fence, a propane tank
> placed daintily in the fork of a tree

Soon, the real action will begin—the author or some other character will enter the scene and begin interacting, or a thought will insinuate itself into the description and reveal it for the context it ultimately is. All description in literature is context—sometimes backdrop, sometimes symbolic, sometimes exhibiting features and traits as to almost become a character itself. To allow your reader to enter a scene and acclimate himself to his surroundings before presenting him with your ideas is only good manners, akin to relaxing over dinner and drinks before asking

someone to donate money for your good cause. "Time enough," the sce-
nic impulse implies, "we'll get to the real order of business soon—but
first, how about those lilacs, what about those fields?"

Good description is crucial, and we should not take it for granted. It
is not easy to write, and it is anything but irrelevant, not if it is employed
skillfully. When someone says, "I skip over the descriptive parts," they
either mean they don't understand imaginative literature, or the text they
are reading is poorly written. Good description—vivid, scrupulously
selective, and powerfully evoked—*is* action as far as the imagination is
concerned, an epic to the senses. Keats's "Ode to Autumn" or "The Eve
of St. Agnes," or really any of his poems, are riots of color, sound, taste,
smell. The scene is interfused with meaning, as meaning is interfused
with the scene. Description is raised to the level of philosophy, or at least
meditation, and no understanding of the text can occur devoid of the
imagery, the physical facts of the poem's terrain. Description is not décor.
It is at the heart of the matter. The *world* is important, not our ideas about
it, not at the outset. The way to the reader's heart is through her senses.
What is presented, and in what tone, may win the reader's trust before
launching into ideas, no matter how interesting and profound. It is not im-
possible to begin a successful poem with a discursive statement—good
poets do it all the time. But a less tricky, safer tack is to begin by portray-
ing a place, or depicting a scene into which the reader might settle and in
which she might ultimately feel more receptive to thoughts, propositions,
or schemes. Unless you are a rhetorician of the first order (think Auden,
think Thomas), or shrewd enough to couch your initial declamation in
a way that obviates the reader's need for assurance by first establishing
your "voice" and therefore your authority, you might find it difficult start-
ing with a declaration, no matter how earnest or "true." Description is a
calming technique, a deep breath before plunging into the matter at hand.

Though I have explored a number of interesting and effective ways
to initiate poems, it is clear that they may begin in infinite forms, none
intrinsically superior to any other as long as the overall poem is suc-
cessful, balanced, and complete. Still, a generalization may apply: good
openings have about them the sense that the poet is beginning at just that
point where utterance becomes necessary, where the pressure to speak
has overcome the natural inclination to reticence, just as good closure has

about it a sense of finality and fulfillment, that all that had to be said has been said, and it is time to return to silence. So how and when we break the silence becomes the question, the great uninterrupted silence that precedes the poem and out of which the voice of the poem first speaks, drawing our attention from the white space—the surrounding oblivion— of the page. A good opening conveys to us a sense of these accumulated pressures—thoughts, feelings, dreams—that only *now*, with the poem's first few words, have gathered enough force to break through the mind's muteness into speech—the inchoate, unspoken abstractions that find their embodiment in language, grammar, syntax, and word. It is the critical moment when we feel "the pale cast of thought" and emotion tipping over into coherence and articulation; the fulcrum between remaining fluid or embryonic and finding form in the integral relations between sentence and phrase. There is simply no prescription for this. It is an instinct, a writer's intuition, and it applies to any genre—fiction or nonfiction—as well as poetry.

So, the question remains: how and where to begin? "Begin at the beginning," advises Dylan Thomas with characteristic archness and a jeering wink. *Begin at the beginning.* But where is that? Out of myriads of potential starting points, all equally possible, all intriguing doorways through which imagination might step deftly into the dream realm of the poem—where is that?

Let's suppose you've been traveling all day by train, and you finally arrive at a small city where you plan to rest for the night. You gather your bags and find a suitable hotel not too far from the train station, in a decent part of town. After obtaining a room, you go out for a walk to stretch your legs after a long day of sitting. The inhabitants of this city hustle past on the sidewalks—happy and excited, solemn and glum. You don't know where you're going, but that doesn't matter. You are content to wander, to let the streets guide you from corner to corner, place to place. Eventually you feel tired and a bit hungry. You look around for a good restaurant, someplace comfortable and cheap, with local color and a homey atmosphere. When you enter, you know you've found the right place. There is almost no one else inside and you take a booth at the far end by the window so you can still observe the city as you eat. Which is what you do after ordering—gaze out half-dreaming in the dusty light that alters even as you watch the trees a block away in the park, and the buildings that turn gold, then gray, and a few stars tremble above as the evening bells begin to peal in a large church you passed on your way here—wherever "here" might be. Now streetlamps begin to emerge from the gathering dark, each expanding in its own halo of light so slowly, so subtly, you are hardly aware that your situation has altered, until finally you wake up: "How odd," you think. "I must have been sitting here for a while." And then you think:

>Seems like a long time
>Since the waiter took my order...

8

Writing Habits and How to Kick Them

> You fight what you've got.
>
> —Anne Sexton

Writers, like everyone else, fall easily into habits. And like everyone else, this is understandable. We are human beings and we like to find the easiest way around obstacles so that we can get to our goals by the quickest route. We know our strengths and weaknesses, and naturally play to the former while avoiding the latter. Habits may be nothing more than strengths calcified, anxiety minimized, success assured. Habits serve us, comfort us, define in a sense even who we are, how we appear to others. And habits allow us to be as efficient as possible. We can get more done, and get it done well, if we rely on our habits to avoid the pitfalls of unknown paths. It's hard enough to reach any goal; why make the struggle even harder? Take the well-worn path. Gratification and profit lie at its end. What lies at the ends of other paths? Who knows. Wilderness. Confusion. Perhaps even failure.

But habits also limit us. They encompass the known world and reduce it to drudgery. They turn us into automatons, trudging from A to B to C and back, assuring that we will never discover anything different about the world, much less ourselves. Comfort may become monotony. Efficiency the hardest route of all. Why go by a more uncertain, hazardous route? The answer is simple: Discovery and surprise may lurk there. Habit reduces us, and discovery enlarges us. Surprise waits to pounce and carry us off to a place where we will have to reassess ourselves, adapt ourselves, for habit is also a mode of slavery and bondage. A soporific drug. "Lie back," whispers habit. "No need to struggle or make much of an effort. I will do most of it for you. You can rely on me. Relax. You're not going anywhere you haven't been before."

So, as writers, we discover our strengths fairly quickly, early in our careers. One writer finds that he is good at the deftness and structural ability it takes to produce good formal verse. The game-playing, architectural faculty of the mind is strong and can manipulate language into various shapes and relationships with relative ease—or at least, without the agony of effort that more often results in a stiff, lifeless poem than a fluid, living one. While those who write strong, convincing free verse, or even prose poems, revel in the sense that they are doing something revolutionary and liberating, that formal verse is a straightjacket from which they have thankfully slipped. They have learned, the free verse poets, how to make organic verse sing, how to bend it and sculpt it into unexpected patterns, unpredictable configurations. Or have they? So often, we detect habitual patterns, certain regular moves a free verse poet makes in poem after poem, book after book. If they are *good* poets, they are good moves, but they are habitual nonetheless and the reader might feel a lessening of the true delight he or she felt when first encountering such work. The strength of a free verse poet may eventually become a weakness if repeated too often.

I have to make a distinction here between habit and style. Style, when it is real, is deeper, more essential than habit. It is closer to voice, to who we are, a fundamental way of engaging the world. Style inheres in character, and issues from it. It is behavior moving toward instinct, rather than something conscious and socially—or artistically—calculated. I speak of style "when it is real" because style can be aped—that is, imitated to some degree. But when this happens, it is immediately detectable. We say someone is writing like so-and-so, or someone belongs to such-and-such school of poetry, or someone sounds like someone else. But this kind of similarity can never be fully realized or complete. We cannot literally be someone else. This is another way of saying that style is who you are, unduplicatable by anyone else.

Habits, on the other hand, are arbitrary. Our habits come to us by a process of trial and error, chance, even something like whimsy. We pick them out of experience and adopt them one day and they settle in for good. They become so familiar to us, and to all who know us, we begin to confuse habits with style. We think they indicate who we are. But habits may be changed with less effort than you might think, even exchanged with a little effort for other habits. Style is more concrete. Who can change who they basically are without the deepest, longest struggle imaginable? "You must change your life," Rilke says, but very few of us will ever accomplish such a thing. To do so would mean overhauling our hearts, our minds, the fundamental self we have so painstakingly and mysteriously constructed over the course of a lifetime.

When you change your writing habits, you will not really change your style of thinking or of expressing yourself and living in the world. If anything, changing habits will provide you with new and interesting material to investigate and exploit. New habits are new routes or paths into the old self, but new paths lead to new territory, facets of yourself you may not have been able to reveal, or even acknowledge before. Perhaps it is less dramatic than that. But at least these new paths will lead to places in yourself with which you have not yet dealt because you were busy walking the old paths of habit, which led inevitably to the same destinations, conclusions, gestures, and notions you've dealt with hundreds of times before. I think we all know when this occurs. We begin writing a poem, we make a turn, another, then we feel the old obsessions fall into place, the old certainties to which we cling, towards which we tend with the single-mindedness of a bloodhound once it has caught the scent. We know where we are going, and we know how the poem will end. And we do end: cleanly, brilliantly, beautifully once again. But after a while, perhaps after years of writing, we lose some of that quality of satisfaction we once felt at reaching such conclusions. We think, "I am writing the same poem over and over again." When this happens, some of the truest joy we can experience as writers drains from our work, that of discovery and surprise. At the very least, that of exploring new territory.

In an interview with Jeff Clark, whose book *Music and Suicide* won the 2005 James Laughlin Award, the interviewer remarks: "Michael Palmer once said that he tried to 'write against himself,' referring to the effort to resist his most immediate poetic inclinations... are you also working to disrupt your *default tendencies*?" I love that phrase, "default tendencies," because it indicates how thoroughly we have assimilated computer jargon not only into our everyday speech, but into the vocabulary of poetry, a development that would make Whitman and other champions of everyday American English proud. Poetry is, and ought to be, an omnivorous consumer of all modes and levels of speech, no matter where they are found. I like the reverberations of the word "default" as well for its moral overtones and what they suggest about habitual gestures as flawed, or defective behavior, and the insinuation of how automatic and mechanical habits are, in distinction to free and open thought—how habits snap us back into the same old ruts the minute we relax our vigilance and give less than our full attention to what we are writing. There is a certain amount of self-doubt, of suspicion and skepticism necessary to keep on the path of originality and surprise, a quality of objective evaluation needed to assess one's own work effectively.

What can we do, then, to help us break free, assist us in discovering new territory, new subjects and ideas? First, as I've stated above, we must stay alert. We want to write out of our subconscious, yes, but that is where old habits lurk as well. This is a paradox we can overcome by simply paying attention to the landscape of the poem we are writing. As soon as we recognize some feature of the terrain through which we are moving, we must let our habits go that way, and steer our imaginations another. This takes trust, which is the second thing that can help us on our trip into the unknown. We must have faith that by rejecting the expected routes, we will wind up someplace rich with unforeseen possibilities. The new place might even be a little frightening, which is bad in reality, but not necessarily bad for art. That is why there is a fallen tree blocking the road in most horror movies on a rainy night. We cannot continue on our proposed journey to Cleveland or Forest Hills where safety and the most ordinary comforts await us. We are forced, instead, to leave the car and climb a slippery hill to that curious looking house where something is flickering in the windows, we know not what. Except that it will be an adventure finding out, a place we might have passed without noticing if that damn tree hadn't made it necessary to abandon our plans and participate in the unusual.

There are many things we can do to block the known paths of our writing, to divert us into discovery and surprise, so that—like the protagonist in that horror film—we will have to wake up and summon the best that is within us, our unknown strengths and capabilities, in order to deal with the new situation effectively. Here are a few obstacles you might throw in your path to set yourself spinning in a new direction, suggested to me by poet Martha Rhodes:

- If you write poems with short lines, try writing poems with lines as long as Whitman or C. K. Williams; if you write long-lined poems already, try limiting your lines to a few words or phrases, or parts of sentences, so that you will be forced to chop up your thoughts and deal with an unusual amount of enjambment.

- Change your stanza structures—if you find that most of your poems are written in quatrains, try tercets, or even couplets, or try writing one-line poems, like William Matthews, to see if you can compress what you are thinking and feeling at the moment into a single verse.

- If you always write in the past tense, try writing in the present tense, or even the future tense, write about things as if they *will* occur at some later date; and if you always write about the past, try writing about the present.

- If you write mostly in the first person, try second person, or third person, or even *plural* so that you won't have to investigate that creepy looking house alone.

- If you are prone to punctuation, take it out, sweep away all those commas and periods and semicolons as if they were so many partitions that keep your thoughts from communicating with one another (note: W. S. Merwin used to say that once he began writing without punctuation his poems seemed less pinned down to the page, hence freer, more likely to drift and explore); on the other hand, if you already write without punctuation, try putting it in, and see if this gives your poems a new clarity and pacing.

- Examine your line breaks, then try breaking them at unaccustomed places, places you would normally not stop to take a short breath before moving on.

- Take a poem you think is finished, then start a new poem using your last stanza (i.e., begin where you think you have finished, and see if you truly have more to say).

- Remove all of your adjectives, then reinsert only the ones that are vital to keep the poem alive; then try this with your adverbs and move your adjectives around—if you always put them directly in front of nouns, see what happens if you place them in some other position (several words before the noun, or after the noun) or turn them into verbs ("The woman's hair got browner overnight" or "The woman's hair browned overnight").

- Do you always put weather into your poems, clouds and rain and lightning that stand in for emotion? Get rid of that storm! Get rid of the moon, the sea, any image or figure that recurs in your work, in hopes of finding new metaphors for what you have to say.

For those who like to take a more radical approach, who want to jolt themselves into change, try packing everything you own and moving abruptly to another country; or even better—go to a hypnotist and experience a full regression and see what *that* does to your writing process! One writer told me that after hypnosis, material he'd suppressed in his earlier books flowed more easily into the book he wrote directly following his regression. Most of us are not prepared for such drastic measures, however, so it's a good idea to find less dramatic ways of combating our habits.

This might be a good place to mention another tool useful in combating habit and striking out on the path of newness and discovery: The Poet's Stylistic Personality Indicator! Or PSPI, for those who prefer acronyms, no matter how unappealing. Here's how it works. Make a list of your most prominent features as a poet:

- Begin with subject: What do you usually write about—the past, death, identity, guilt, war? Put them down.

- Move on to form: What forms do you usually write in—columns, quatrains, tercets, a scattering of words across the page? Note them.

- Now consider your lines: What is the usual length of your lines—
  short, mid-length, long, a mixture of all three? Consider your
  general practice here, not exceptions.

- And what about image: Are there images that recur in your work—
  rivers, shadows, darkness, trees? Surely, you've noticed how often
  the image of hands or knives or stars crop up in your work. Note
  them all.

- Next look at metaphor: Are there metaphors you exploit again and
  again—roads, oceans, staircases, sports? List them.

- Think about tone: Does every poem you write seem to have the
  same tone—ironic, sarcastic, bouncy, conversational, solemn? How
  often, really, do you vary your voice according to subject, situation,
  and speaker?

The result will be a list of things that reoccur in your work. You now have
an up-to-date stylistic portrait of yourself as a poet. The point is to try
to avoid these repetitive elements when writing future poems. You can
begin by writing a poem that starts with the words: "I'm tired of… " and
then go on to embellish your list of recurring features. When you finish
the list, take a break, then begin a new stanza by writing: "I want to… "
and continue from there. This won't result in one of your best poems, no
doubt, but it will at least make clear what you must do to write more orig-
inally in the future. Tape your self-portrait above your desk and glance
at it before writing your next poem. Vow that you won't explore the same
old subjects again; promise that you won't employ the same old forms,
images, metaphors, in the same old tone of indignation or regret.

These, and any number of other technical devices, will serve to deflect
your writing and force you to set out in a new direction. They will allow
you to approach material you haven't been able to reach before. I can give
you an example from my own experience. One day, for no good reason,
I started to write in very long lines, which freed me to explore certain
ideas and experiences I hadn't been able to write about in any other form.

I needed a longer line to write more narratively, more autobiographically, about things I thought I could only deal with in short stories or a novel. Poetry simply seemed too compressed to me, too chronically constipated for the stories I had to tell. This was the case until I found I could stretch out in longer lines and loosen my tone of voice to be more conversational and inclusive, more direct and rangier. Soon, I had opened up a wide area of my past which had resisted expression in poetry until then. It was like breaking into a rich vein of ore when you thought the lode you had been mining was all played out. I needed that new formal impulse and tone to escape the labyrinth of my habits, to allow previously remote material to flow into my poems and find expression in more flexible, extended lines. This new vein was soon played out, and then I had to go looking for new ground to break. But at least I was able to produce a number of poems about important (to me) subjects, and I can always return to longer lines if I feel the need to adopt them for any purpose again.

The poet Stephen Dunn devised a way of breaking free of habits involving the way his poems ended. He looked back at his books and noticed how almost all of his poems seemed to be the same length: a page-and-a-half. "I had become the 'page-and-a-half man,'" he told me, with a chuckle. When I asked him what he did about it, he said he had come up with a good method of escaping this habit: "It is essentially this: Resisting a move toward closure that has become somewhat habitual by introducing an idea or image that might be tangential to the concerns of the poem, or entirely foreign to them, at the moment you would normally start moving toward closure." I think we all know what he is talking about—that moment when, like happy horses, tired and satisfied with the work we've done, we smell the barn and begin heading straight for home. If you've been writing long enough, you begin to feel this turn in yourself, an almost physical sensation, about the same point in almost every poem you write. Dunn continues: "Then the imagination must stretch to accommodate the new detail, and probably the beginning of the poem will need to be altered to give yourself permission to go where you have gone. Always some re-stitching will be necessary. The trick is finally to make the poem's new inclusiveness feel seamless, inevitable. But this can only occur if you're not overly wedded to the poem's initial impulse." This good advice will almost certainly result in the revelation, the epiphanic surprise, that most good poems embody somewhere during their development, which is to say: somewhere in the process of their unfolding.

This new idea or image "tangential to the concerns of the poem, or entirely foreign to them" is the log Dunn throws across his path that forces him to get out of his car and wander off blindly into the night looking for a solution to his dilemma. But Dunn doesn't stop there: "The corollary to this," he says, "is revision by expansion, as opposed to the more common impulse, which is revision by paring." If we are unsatisfied with the poem we have written, we usually return to it to see if there are things we can change or strike out. This is a common form of revision, so common it is almost habitual. But Dunn is suggesting a new way of re- vising—keep the poem you have and expand upon its events or assertions, delving even deeper into their possibilities, or—*a la* Martha Rhodes— simply continue from the place you left off, the place you thought you were done, the last line, using what you have written so far as an inroad to further explorations into the interior of your original idea. Perhaps there is another idea behind that one, or another subject entirely beyond the one you thought you were addressing. We never know until we push further into the material we have already put down.

Formally or thematically, then, we may find ways to break the mold of our personal writing habits. There are other ways you can devise to throw an obstacle across your path in order to move in a new direction. One of the traditional methods poets have been using for many centuries, and reasserted by Ezra Pound and others at the beginning of the Modern era, is the adoption of a persona or mask. One of the best reasons is that such a strategy allows us to escape—to an extent, and for a brief time—the confines of our own personality. And this includes our habits of thought and speech, the area of human activity we normally explore. If, through a powerful effort of imagination, we can become someone else, perhaps we can discover something alien and strange, something outside the pale of our usual experience. The trick is to choose a persona as re- mote as possible from ourselves, someone with whom we would normally have little or no contact, and about whom we feel almost no affinity at all. This may mean masquerading as people you might even dislike, or even renounce, in normal life. Think of Frank Bidart's poem, "Herbert White," which presents the monologue of a rapist and murderer who has sex with a young girl's corpse. Or James Dickey's poem about a peeping Tom, "The Fiend." Though it is written in third person, Dickey has to imagine what it is like to be a voyeur in a tree observing a woman through a window at night. He was so successful at doing this that once the poem was published, a police officer on the vice squad wrote to Dickey and said that he (the officer) dealt with such people all the time and that he sympathized with Dickey, that he felt sorry for him! Dickey thought this was one of the best compliments he had ever received as a poet: he had succeeded in convincing an ordinary reader that he was something he was not. The illusion of art had worked perfectly.

We read many persona poems about people from other historical eras and cultures, poems ostensibly spoken by Antony or Cleopatra, George Washington, Genghis Kahn, Marco Polo, Columbus, Joan of Arc, even Ptolemy or Augustus Caesar. But almost never about people from contemporary life unless, like Herbert White, or James Dickey's voyeur, they are highly unusual characters who come to us from the shadows of ordinary life. Often, poets change genders, or races, or both, in order to open up new fields of subject matter. Sometimes, we might exchange ages with someone greatly younger or older than ourselves—or even speak from a coma or beyond the grave. Often, the choice of a persona will come from literature, not life, and we may adopt the mask of Ulysses or Madam Bovary, Achilles or Huckleberry Finn. The point is to get an angle on experience, to liberate yourself from the strictures of your own personality and normal ways of seeing things. In persona poems, you may still use the same forms and diction as you do in your own first-person poems, but you will probably go places you would never go as yourself, which is the same dark and rainy night mentioned above, fraught with the unknown.

If human beings fail you, try animals, vegetables, minerals, even abstractions to see if you can inhabit their consciousness, or create one for them. This, too, will provide you with an unexpected perspective on your usual subject matter. Or take any mundane household object and re-imagine it in the most preposterous terms. By de-familiarizing an object in this way, we make the quotidian world interesting and strange. When Charles Simic begins describing a fork by saying,

> This thing must have crept
> Right out of hell.

we are galvanized, ready to lavish our attention on one of the most common objects in the world. And he doesn't stop there. In a few short lines, Simic's fork becomes a bird's foot from a truly grotesque bird:

> Its head which like your fist
> Is large, bald, beakless, and blind.[1]

Now we're getting somewhere! The everyday world we thought we knew so well is fascinating transformed, even a little scary. The transformation is all the more effective for having begun with such a dull subject: a fork. Who would have thought such a primitive creature existed in our own house, on our very own table, right before our eyes? Something we use every day, and hardly notice. "There *is* another world," said the poet Paul Eluard, "but it is in this one."

Let me end by telling you a story, something I suspect that many of you are guilty of as well: When I get into my car to drive somewhere, or leave my house on foot heading for some unaccustomed destination—perhaps a location I've never been before—I often wind up daydreaming along the way and, before I know it, I've arrived at a place I have been many times. While I was daydreaming, another part of my mind which has been trained by habit to follow particular grooves and unseen ruts and tracks in the highway, takes over and simply moves me along, steering me by "automatic pilot," the programmed routes my subconscious knows well. So inculcated are these routes that they are imprinted on my muscles and nerves, they are mapped in my unconscious mind and I become a robot—wound up and pointed once again in the old directions. I don't know how many times I've come to myself with a jolt, realizing that I am once again plodding an old path, and I feel, foolishly, like one of those mules harnessed to the post of a millwheel, trotting mindlessly in a circle. To quote Charles Simic again, this time from an essay: "It is worth emphasizing that the poet is not in control of his poems. He is like someone who imagines he is driving from New York to Boston only to find himself in Tuscaloosa, Alabama."[2] This is fine, as long as you've never been to Tuscaloosa. In order to get there, you will have to toss some sizeable object in your path. You will have to veer off course, divert your intentions, career off into the unknown.

This will not be easy, of course, though I may have made it sound simple in this essay. It is not. Nothing about poetry is simple. Changing your habits as a writer will take more than a few tricks and a pep talk about how to go about such a transformation. It will take discipline. Yet isn't writing hard enough already? Why make it doubly difficult by trying to reinvent yourself along the way? Besides, friends and a few editors like your work as it is. Wouldn't it be easier to simply settle into the poetic self you've painstakingly constructed over years of writing? Yes. But if you want to push yourself to another level of accomplishment, if you want to enlarge yourself as a writer, you will have to circumvent your old moves and gestures, you will have to find your way around what you have already done to continue to develop and grow as a writer. Go ahead. Barricade your old habits; thwart thyself!

9

Long Story Short:

Techniques of Fiction in Poetry

In Jonathan Holden's wide-ranging and intelligent survey of American poetry published in 1991, *The Fate of American Poetry*[1], he argues that much of the blame for poetry's dwindling audience during the twentieth century lies principally with Modernism's wholesale commitment to erudition, elitism, arcane allusion, and complicated theories about subject matter. At least part of his prescription for winning back an audience for contemporary verse lies in a return to narrative forms. "Moral wisdom," he claims, "is, like most of our accumulated human knowledge, inherently narrative." The supremacy of the Bible in Western literature and thought is one proof of this, he explains, along with the development, in the eighteenth century, of the novel with all its subsequent ramifications and styles.

The point was made in the 1960s by James Dickey, who wrote in favor of the return of narrative as a means of countering the overwhelming popularity of the crabbed, associative, complex Modernist lyric which seemed at that time to have won the day. Poets were writing lyrics almost exclusively, and when they wrote longer poems it was usually some form of meditation or discursive verse that confounded many readers and critics who accused such work of being "obscure." Dickey made a plea for "reclaiming some of the narrative ground that had been ceded to the novel," whether he took his advice with regard to his own work or not. But a growing number of poets have come to believe that abdication of narrative to prose fiction has not been altogether healthy for poetry, and it may be time to turn things around.

There have been a number of straightforward narrative poems produced in recent times, but most of them do not extend further than a few pages and the stories they unfold are of a single incident, not a series of linked incidents with many characters as in an expanded prose fiction.

A poem like John Logan's "The Picnic," published in 1960, or the darkly humorous prose poems of James Tate's most recent books certainly tell a story, but are brief in comparison to traditional narrative poems, even those written as recently as the nineteenth century, like Longfellow's "The Song of Hiawatha," "Evangeline," or "The Courtship of Miles Standish." Longfellow is a good example of a poet writing during a time when narrative poetry held a place in the popular imagination and could be read and appreciated by many people. Prior to Modernism and the institutionalization of the lyric, extended narrative poetry was still thriving as a literary form before it "ceded its narrative ground to the novel." The novel and the long narrative poem existed side-by-side for a time and flourished. This was possible, perhaps, because other popular sources of narrative—radio, television, and movies—had yet to be invented or perfected.

In the early twentieth century, poets such as Stephen Vincent Benét and Edward Arlington Robinson, who failed or declined to Modernize themselves, struggled to continue the tradition of book-length narrative poetry, and their days were numbered. Mostly, they established their careers on shorter, more lyrical work. Some readers might remember Robinson's "Richard Corey" and "Eben Flood," but who remembers his book-length narratives *Amaranth*, *Tristram*, or *Matthias at the Door*? Perhaps Robinson Jeffers, too, is remembered more for "To the Stonecutter's" and "Shine, Perishing Republic" than *Cawdor* or *The Double-Headed Axe*. As late as 1958, Winfield Townley Scott attempted to revive narrative poetry with his book-length poem, *The Dark Sister*, about which James Dickey offered these glowing words:

> *The Dark Sister* is a very good narrative poem indeed…
> had this poem come down to us from the time it treats, it
> would have been reckoned a masterpiece, and dutifully
> enregistered as such in many a textbook and anthology.

And yet it went nowhere, as far as sales and the reading public are concerned. It now belongs to that oblivion where so many other once-noteworthy American poems are entombed. This is not *entirely* due to its having been written in narrative form, of course, but that must surely have had a great deal to do with it. The reading public, however large or small it may have been in 1958, was simply not up to reading and appreciating a long narrative poem, one that was surely as good or better than many of the contemporary novels that were written at that time, and which that same reading public bought and read in the tens of thousands. Not narrative, but narrative *poetry*, was decidedly out.

A number of book-length narratives have been written and published as late as 1985 and 1988 by Frederick Turner. His first, *The New World: An Epic Poem*, followed by *Genesis*, are attempts to restore the book-length narrative—indeed the epic poem—to prominence and win back readers of the novel and enthusiasts of movie and television drama. The idea of resuscitating the epic, with its historical associations and forms, may or may not have been a good idea, however. A science fiction that occurs in the future, *Genesis* alludes heavily to *Beowulf* and begins with a rhetorically heightened sense of grandeur that must have made more than a few potential readers nervous (*uh oh, this is a poem, not a novel*):

> Listen! I must tell of the beginnings,
> Of corpses buried in the walls of worlds,
> Of how those men and women worth a story
> Burn and consume the powers they're kindled by;
> And how their acts, mortal and cast away,
> Are crystallized in the melt of history,
> But their live selves are lost and gone forever
> To leave a safer and a duller age ... "[2]

It's possible to believe that readers of novels might accept (or not even notice) the formal aspects of a loose iambic pentameter, blank verse line, punctuated by the alliterative effects of Anglo-Saxon verse, but not perhaps the tone and manner of epic poetry which create a density and tension more demanding than that of most contemporary prose fiction. The oracular lines above are good poetry, but taxing as a medium for the kind of story to which readers are accustomed in the season's latest best sellers. Readers of novels, memoirs, biographies, and protracted volumes of nonfiction might be expected to pay attention to sound, rhythm, diction, form, metaphor, and other poetic elements for a short while (i.e. the lyric), but they might find the prospect of reading a book-length volume of such language a bit daunting.

More recently, Derek Walcott has attempted to revive the epic with his sweeping and challenging book, *Omeros*[3], which not only borrows something of the epic tone and form, but alludes to one of the greatest epic poets of all time in its very title: blind Homer chanting his thousands of lines near the sea in the ancient Hellenic world. But Walcott's poem—divided into seven longish "books," which are further divided into "chapters," each of which are again divided into three sections—is intimidating in its weight and density. And, as if that weren't enough, it is written in terza rima, a form that allies it with Dante and his *Divine Comedy* as well. Homer and Dante both, in one poem! It's a breathtakingly ambitious work, and one with which most readers of novels would be cowed. Even readers of poetry might shiver a little when confronted with such a grandiose scheme—a 325-page poem whose lines scintillate with the compacted density of a lyric. Walcott's habitual sense of metaphor and other time-tested figures of speech combine to slow the reader down and, as with a lyric poem, force him to pay attention to every syllable, every word, while keeping the overarching sense of the story in mind as well as all the characters who are near namesake-stand-ins for characters in Homer's original *Iliad* and *Odyssey*. Only a reader with the requisite knowledge and experience would be able to make his way through the thicket of words, images, and allusions comprised by the narrative of *Omeros*. A much easier and more accessible—though by no means less interesting or powerful poem—is Walcott's "The Schooner *Flight*" from *The Star-Apple Kingdom*[4], an eighteen-page narrative poem in eleven sections that displays all of Walcott's considerable gifts while remaining assimilable to anyone who will take the time to read it with interest and attention.

Another noteworthy attempt at a contemporary epic was made by John Barr in his book-length poem, *Grace*[5], published in 1999, in which a Caribbean poet, Ibn Opcit—condemned to die—disburdens himself from jail like a latter-day Chidiock Tichborne, singing the soul's wisdom at the brink of death. Opcit's grandiloquent monologue covers a wide range of subjects from politics, marriage, ontology, sex (always sex), death, and religion, to economics, creationism, and diet, all delivered in a tongue-in-cheek style that compounds high rhetoric with Caribbean patois to produce something that might better be described as an expository epic, with mock overtones. Each of Opcit's "Eclogues" is a foray into *la condition humane* with humor and pungent wit.

Besides the seamless narrative of epic length, there is a second type of poem that takes a different tack, breaking the narrative into more digestible bits. The reader of this essay will no doubt be able to supply any number of book-length poems—or "novels-in-verse"—produced within the second half of the twentieth century (David Mason's fine *Ludlow* is noteworthy). I list only a few of the most prominent works here that attempt to affect the kind of return to narrative poetry envisioned by Dickey and Holden, but by a different route. This second category, to which Walcott's "The Schooner *Flight*" properly belongs, has been more successful in finding readers both within and beyond the community of poets—poems that might be described as episodic or serial, a sequence of vignettes that suggest a longer, more complete narrative, but present that backstory in fragments rather than reveal it in its entirety. These include Rosellen Brown's *Cora Fry*, Ellen Bryant Voigt's *Kyrie*, Philip Dacey's *The Mystery of Max Schmidt*, Kim Addonizio's *Jimmy and Rita*, Dan Tobin's *The Narrows*, Martha Collins' *Blue Front*, and many others. These poems share a similar strategy: to suggest a novel's sweep in snapshots, a long episodic work that fills a book and tells a single, but discontinuous story.

But there is a third way which preserves and combines both aspects of narrative and lyric. A hybrid form that might be called *lyrical-narrative*, or more accurately *narrative-lyric*, exemplified by Stanley Kunitz's visionary poem, "The Wellfleet Whale."[6] The poem uses narrative devices customarily employed by fiction writers: The narrative begins quietly with an exposition of the setting; each section is a "chapter" and ends at a moment of drama, creating suspense and leading the reader on to the next section; there is an upward trend in the first sections, then a catastrophe that leads to a darker, downward trend in the later sections; events occur in sequences (sections two, three, four), depicting a day and a night followed by another day and night—the first day and night are given over to a rising action (hopeful, exciting, positive), while the second day and night describe a vigil and are given over to a falling action (despair, sorrow, and death). Finally, the "story" is framed by a "prologue" (section one) and an "epilogue" (section five). This scheme is only approximate, of course, not absolute, and requires reading the poem with the elements of fiction in mind. But if it is read as a story, the elements will emerge more clearly. Some of the sections even have a cinematic aspect and might be imagined as scenes in a film.

Section one, which I am calling a "prologue," opens the poem with a consideration of the sounds whales make, a description of their calls to each other as they migrate from place to place in the ocean, exemplified by this brief sample from the text:

> You have your language too,
>   an eerie medley of clicks
>   and hoots and trills,
>   location-notes and love calls,
>   whistles and grunts. Occasionally,
>   it's like furniture being smashed,
>   or the creaking of a mossy door,
>   sounds that all melt into a liquid
>   song with endless variations,
>   as if to compensate
>   for the vast loneliness of the sea.

The purpose of this prologue is to establish an identity for the whale that will soon appear, to establish, that is, a sympathy between the whale and humans which will be exploited so powerfully in the final section. We are told that whales have language—a particularly human quality—and that they call to one another in the depths of the sea. We might imagine this "language" to be much like our own—expressing danger, sorrow, love, or joy. Kunitz heightens this identification with whales by referring to "love calls" and "grunts," of which human beings are capable, and to things associated with the human world: smashed furniture and a "mossy door."

Kunitz also establishes the form the poem will take section by section: two or three stress lines, with a variable iambic rhythm, and shifting tercets that shuttle back and forth, like waves, or swimming fish.

The poet also makes use of some conventional metrical effects—in line fifteen, for instance, he refers to the whale's "long mournful cry," which presents us with three stressed syllables in close proximity, thereby elongating the phrase so that it mimics the thing it describes. Throughout the poem, Kunitz will be mindful of exploiting such musical and expressive effects even though the poem is not written in strict meter. It is interesting to note, too, that the final line of this section is a half line. Only two words appear—"running down"—even as the line itself runs down. This contraction is followed by a sense of finality, a stoppage followed by a silence. It prepares us for something else to begin, a commencement that will shortly follow.

Section two, then, begins the narrative of a specific whale, the Wellfleet whale, and introduces a new tone, one that is more factual and objective—at least at first—in the sense that it is slightly less lyrical. Punchy sentences at the beginning of the section set the tone and distinguish the feeling of this section from the one preceding it. The purpose of section two is to set the scene—an exposition of sorts—in three iambic fragments: "No wind. No waves. No clouds." Those three iambic negatives, "No," set up an atmosphere of expectation. There is only "the whisper of the tide, stroking the shore." As with most fictions—film and drama as well—a state of equilibrium exists before the first events of the story take place. In this state of equilibrium, the scene might be set, but it will be broken only when the first players appear on the page (or stage) to initiate the action. Kunitz also tells us that gulls drift overhead, describes the light on the water, and lets us know the time—the very end of summer.

The languor of the scene is disrupted suddenly by an extraordinary occurrence:

> From the harbor's mouth
> you coasted into sight,
> flashing news of your advent,
> the crescent of your dorsal fin

clipping the diamonded surface.
We cheered at the sign of your greatness
when the black barrel of your head
erupted, ramming the water,
and you flowered for us
in the jet of your spouting.

This description of the whale's arrival, and the expected hymn of praise to its awesome power and "eerie" beauty (to borrow a word from section one) remind us of heroic scenes from other stories when something or someone magnificent appears to create a sense of hope and to rally people to action. The word "advent" is of special interest here. Capitalized, *Advent* is a biblical term that refers specifically to the coming of Christ at the Incarnation. Uncapitalized, it generally means "a coming into being" or use. The whale itself, its appearance in the humdrum hours of a late summer day is a kind of annunciation, a coming into being of something almost otherworldly, or at least from a very different world than the one in which the spectators on the beach are living.

Section three continues, or extends the praise, the celebratory tone of being visited by something beyond the ordinary, something almost talismanic or totemic in its symbolic presence. The language in this section changes back to something like the opening section—a higher level of rhetoric and a greater sense of abstraction, of interpretation and thought:

And when you bounded into air,
slapping your flukes,
we thrilled to look upon
pure energy incarnate
as nobility of form.

With the exception of "diamonded," the diction in section two is spare, even common. But in section three, words of Latinate origin appear more regularly: "imperceptible," "undulation," "incarnate," "nobility." The observations are more subjective, more complex: "you seemed to marry grace with power," "we thrilled to look upon pure energy incarnate as nobility of form."

In the last six lines of the section, the physical whale becomes almost ghostly, or spiritual, as it swims by moonlight, leaving a trail of phosphorescence in its wake:

> That night we watched you
> swimming in the moon.
> Your back was molten silver.
> We guessed your silent passage
> by the phosphorescence in your wake.
> At dawn we found you stranded on the rocks.

Now it becomes mysterious, a visitor from the unknown who exists half in shadow, half in light. The scene is dreamlike, visionary. We have reached the apex of the rising action—the exciting, hopeful, positive part of the poem.

But the shock of the last line of section three sets up a change in the narrative, from praise to dirge. The catastrophe has occurred and from now on the action will fall off from the rising excitement of the first three sections. This downturn, from positive to negative, is introduced linguistically by an ominous, or more objective tone in section four. Once more the language becomes ordinary, and the observations more concrete. The focus of the opening lines expands so that it resembles a wide-angle shot taken from a position somewhat above the beach: We see the whale stranded on the sand, then people arriving from various spots outside the frame of the shot to gather around the body of the huge mammal like filings drawn to a magnet. Quickly, the focus narrows again and we return to the whale's side so that we can see and hear details of the creature's death agony—the hulking size, flippers and flukes, its "roaring" blowhole. When Kunitz describes the various cruelties perpetrated on the whale by thoughtless onlookers—initials carved in the belly, strips of skin peeled off for souvenirs—he resists moral outrage. Like any good writer, he lets the facts speak for themselves:

Somebody had carved his initials
in your flank. Hunters of souvenirs
had peeled off strips of your skin,
a membrane thin as paper.
You were blistered and cracked by the sun.
The gulls had been pecking at you.
The sound you made was a hoarse and fitful bleating.

A stanza break occurs to mark not only a passage of time (from day to night), but a change in perspective too, from objective to subjective, from description to meditation. On this second evening, the poet-narrator responds more personally to what he has witnessed: "What drew us to the magnet of your dying?" Even the diction and imagery of these lines are more emotionally charged:

Toward dawn we shared with you
your hour of desolation,
the huge lingering passion
of your unearthly outcry,
as you swung your blind head
toward us and laboriously opened
a bloodshot, glistening eye,
in which we swam with terror and recognition.

The "unearthly cry" here parallels but transforms the "long mournful cry" of section one. It is a death cry, a cry of despair, not the lonely, life-asserting cry of a whale far at sea searching for its comrades. And, too, the identification we experience here is a tragic reversal of what we felt in section one. In the first section, our sympathy was based on shared positive traits: language, loneliness, sorrow. In section four, our identification with the whale is with its dying. We observe its "bloodshot, glistening eye" and feel the "terror" of "recognition." We too will suffer and die. Perhaps we will even be tormented, if not physically, then psychically, at our deaths.

Section five begins what I have called the epilogue, in which the poet will reflect upon the events of the narrative he has just related. Kunitz addresses the whale directly, but in a more general way apart from the events that took place in Wellfleet harbor. Whaleness itself is the subject, not only this particular whale and its circumstances. The section begins with another change of tone—back to a higher rhetoric, richer diction, and a change of address, an apostrophe that is more like a public speech than the descriptive language of the previous sections. In fact, it is a funeral oration where—like all funeral orations—the whale will be praised and admired for its character and exemplary life. The scope will widen again to become planetary, even cosmic, as great sweeps of time—eons and epochs—will come into play, restoring some of the creature's grandeur from the opening section. The whale here becomes mythic, a symbolic creature:

> Voyager, chief of the pelagic world,
>   you brought with you the myth
>   of another country, dimly remembered,
> where flying reptiles
>   lumbered over the steaming marshes
>   and trumpeting thunder lizards
> wallowed in the reeds.
>   While empires rose and fell on land,
>   your nation breasted the open main,
> rocked in the consoling rhythm
>   of the tides.

By addressing the whale at first as "Voyager," Kunitz distances himself (and us) from the whale and adds an element of respect that did not exist in the earlier—and more personal—pronoun, "you." For the remainder of this section, "you" will take on a greater weight of esteem, of reverence even, each time it is used. Later in the section, Kunitz will refer to the whale as "Master," another distancing sobriquet, as it introduces the idea of hierarchy, placing the speaker (and all human beings) in a subordinate position to this now mythic being.

The whale becomes an emissary from the primeval world, an incarnation of Nature itself and its mysterious sources. It is "both more and less than human," a "god in exile," like Christ who became mortal to suffer and die like us. The identification of the whale with Christ—or any god who takes on human characteristics and becomes mortal—is not far-fetched. Like Christ, this "god in exile" chooses to enter the human world where he becomes vulnerable, is discovered, then crucified and reviled (instead of a crown of thorns, whips, and spears, initials are carved into his belly and strips of his skin peeled off as souvenirs). Like Christ, the whale is not recognized for what he is and so must suffer death to "become like us," a sacrifice only the poet seems to notice and acknowledge. Like Christ, the whale comes to us out of its "primeval element," to be "delivered to the mercy of time."

The poem ends with a prayer:

> ... you turned, like a god in exile,
> out of your wide primeval element,
>   delivered to the mercy of time.
>   Master of the whale-roads,
> let the white wings of the gulls
>   spread out their cover.
>   You have become like us,
> disgraced and mortal.

The gulls are transformed finally into angels spreading their wings like a pall to cover the dead deity. An interesting motif involving the gulls is woven throughout the poem: they appear first as merely part of the scenery in section two, a "lazy drift" of birds, unthreatening, detached, then reappear in section four to peck at the body of the whale, violent and dispassionate as some of the onlookers, and finally in section five where they come to represent angels, mournful and protective, escorting the spirit of the dead whale back into its "primeval element."

In a final stroke of brilliance, Kunitz resurrects the word "disgraced" for us, which in this context takes on it most primary meaning. In most instances, "disgrace" has a specific, secular meaning: "Loss of reputation as the result of dishonorable action" (*Compact Oxford English Dictionary*) or "embarrassment and the loss of other people's respect" (*Cambridge Online Dictionary*). But here, Kunitz restores the word to its original meaning: "dis-" again becomes a prefix expressing negation of what will follow—as in "dis-inclined, dis-enchanted"—and "grace" takes on its theological significance of being held highly in God's esteem. The whale, in this poem, is dis-graced. That is: stripped of grace, violated, profaned.

The narrative sections of this poem might be re-imagined as a short story entitled "The Wellfleet Whale" without too much difficulty. The perspective might change—either that of one of the characters on the beach, or several of them—but the events themselves could supply material for a summer idyll in which the beaching of a whale affects the lives of people in a seaside resort, and perhaps the whale and occurrences surrounding its appearance and fate take on symbolic proportions. It would be a far different reading experience, however, in comparison to Kunitz's poem. "The Wellfleet Whale" as a poem is a hybrid form that combines aspects of narrative fiction and lyrical poetry. It is a story poem, or a poem that tells a story. But it is more than that. The "more" that it is results from the compression of that story into highly-charged, evocative lines of poetry and a visionary imagination that has more than plot or character development in mind. This way is open to anyone who would like to gain back some of the ground ceded to fiction in being able to write a more engaging poem.

10

Reading Hopkins' Nun

At a party in Colorado, when I was much younger than I am now, I reached for a small volume of poetry—a fine edition of the work of Gerard Manley Hopkins which resided on a bookshelf nearby. I was sitting in a comfortable armchair in the corner of the room, and while the party raged around me—I recall Jimi Hendrix and his guitar shredding the air and the clamorous voices of my friends raised in conversation and laughter—I opened Hopkins' *Selected Poetry* and began reading the following poem:

HEAVEN—HAVEN

A nun takes the veil

I have desired to go
  Where springs not fail,
To fields where flies no sharp and sided hail
  And a few lilies blow.

And I have asked to be
  Where no storms come,
Where the green swell is in the havens dumb,
  And out of the swing of the sea.

I say "began reading" because for the next hour or so I sat in that chair and read those two quatrains over and over again, each time thrilled with the texture of their language and what seemed to me the balanced purity of their form. In the interests of full disclosure, I must add that I was in a state—shall we say—of enhanced consciousness, and as I read I sipped from a glass of fine cabernet which someone who knew something about wine had brought to the party to share.

So I was comfortable, completely open to what I was reading, the kind of focus and receptivity any author would be happy to have from a stranger who just happened to pick up his or her book. And the irony of the subject matter compared to what was going on in the room was not lost on me, either. Still, only my early and natural mania for language—and poetry in particular—can explain why I sat there reading a single poem over and over while my friends shouted jibes at one another and sang aloud to the music, and the music pulsed out of two large speaker boxes resting on the floor, one quite close to where I sat obliviously reading.

I'm not going to claim that this is one of the greatest poems in English literature, nor even that it is one of Hopkins' best or most import-ant poems. In many ways, it is a modest poem, given its single-minded focus and length. But I *will* claim that it is a very fine poem, a marvel of linguistic engineering, a lapidary beauty of a poem that only a first-rate poet could have written, and that it exhibits the not inconsiderable virtues of symmetry and balance, harmony of elements, concentration and expansion, depth of vision, attention to sound, and form mirroring content if that traditional idea can bear up anymore under the weight of postmodern protestations to the contrary. In poetry, size *doesn't* matter. A short poem can concentrate so much meaning and feeling into a confined space that it can sometimes feel cosmic in its dimensions—though the way it looks on the page might seem to belie that idea. Think of Emily Dickinson, and the concept of an acorn containing a cosmos will be clear. Or Blake's "world in a grain of sand." As I sat there reading, those two seemingly meager quatrains—eight short lines—I was carried away into a universe of thought and feeling that, for the duration of the spell I was under, seemed to have no bounds.

To begin with, I did not, and still do not have, any real interest in the poem's religious content. This might seem a curious thing to say, seeing as Hopkins was a Jesuit priest and his poem is openly about a wom-an renouncing the world by taking holy orders and entering a nunnery. But the poem transcends that limitation of meaning if we agree that it might be interpreted in a larger sense to address the desire anyone might have to retire, even temporarily, from the *sturm und drang* of the world.

Who doesn't wish from time to time for a safe place away from obligations, doubts, threats, anxieties, pressures, the constant chaos of daily living? Though I do feel that the full meaning and impact of Hopkins' poem probably depends on a religious interpretation finally (I'm certain Hopkins would agree), I choose to view it in this wider, secular sense, and empathize with the woman in the poem who is looking for a haven from the "storms of life," a metaphor that might not rise above the level of cliché in other hands. One of the things a poet can do is to blow new life into the lungs of a dead metaphor.

Hopkins begins by reminding us of how closely the two words "Heaven" and "Haven" resemble each other. The two might be used in a poem to make a consonantal, or slant rhyme. Only one vowel separates them from becoming the same word. Linking them with a hyphen, as Hopkins does here, might suggest that they are etymologically related. But they are not. The word "heaven" comes to us from the Old English word, "heofon," which meant "home of God," and earlier, simply "sky." "Haven" comes down to us from the Old Norse word, "höfn," which meant "place that holds (ships)." Further, we find that the Old Norse word "haf" and the Old English word, "haef," both meant "sea," and that the word "haven" is probably related somehow to the common verb "have," meaning to seize, hold, or contain. Perhaps too much etymological explanation is tedious, but it is needed to show that what Hopkins means here is not that the two words are related at their roots, but that he is posing a metaphor in the very title of the poem itself—conceptually, the idea of "heaven" as a sanctuary or shelter in the presence of God is very much like the idea of a "haven," or harbor, which is a place of safety for ships. It is this idea, presented in the most compressed way possible, that Hopkins will explore and develop further in the poem to follow.

Some readers might pick up on the fact that "Heaven-Haven" is about a nun preparing to enter holy orders had Hopkins not included the parenthetical information that appears directly under the title of his poem, but many probably would not. It could just as easily be about a monk entering a monastery. Or someone—anyone—mortally wounded or sick praying to be taken to heaven after death. Or none of the above. Less astute readers might have no idea at all what the poem is about without the helpful information Hopkins offers. Because he is forthcoming, Hopkins allows the reader to enter the poem with direct knowledge of the situation of the speaker. This knowledge contextualizes the poem, so all fumbling after character, circumstances, and setting is foreclosed upon before any confusion can arise. We know who is speaking and we know what's happening so there is no need—as with some poems—to figure this out for ourselves before we can begin interpreting what the poem might mean. Many poems work exactly by withholding such information, so that one of the major satisfactions for the reader is to figure out such information. This is the idea of a poem as a puzzle or conundrum of some kind. What the poem *means* is less important—less enjoyable—than figuring out its basic situation, who's speaking and what's going on. Hopkins doesn't want us to waste a second on such gamesmanship. For him, the pleasure of a poem lies elsewhere.

After reading the poem for the first time—or even glancing at its physical appearance on the page—it is obvious that it is a formal poem and that the two quatrains resemble one another in shape. It is obvious, too, that the third line of each stanza is longer than the other three. These observations are important, and more than merely coincidental. They suggest, as balanced stanzas often do, a bipartite structure, in which we might expect that the two stanzas will complement each other in some way, that there will be a connection between them as the form suggests. Perhaps the second stanza will develop a theme introduced in the first stanza or reverse it by arguing, or maybe the second stanza will reintroduce the theme of the first from a different perspective. It is clear, as well, that the first and fourth lines rhyme, while the second and third lines rhyme on a different sound. This kind of sandwich stanza, in which a middle couplet—lines two and three—are enclosed by a larger couplet—lines one and four—might be recognizable to readers familiar with many other poems that employ the same form. Most notably, Tennyson's elegy, "In Memoriam," a poem so etched into the minds of readers of English verse that the stanza itself has come to be called the "in Memoriam" stanza. But even if we do not have this historical background, we can still see the rhyme scheme clearly and wonder what part it will play in the enfolding of the poem.

There *is* an essential connection between the two stanzas, which I will address shortly, but after taking stock of the general shape and structure of a poem, it's a good idea to determine what sort of meter it is written in as this, too, will play a role in how the poem develops and how it will make its meaning not only understood, but felt.

Determining the base meter of a poem is usually easy enough by reading through the poem and listening to what kind of foot occurs most frequently. The predominant meter will assert itself with enough insistence—if the poem *has* a predominant meter—for the reader to detect what it is. A rule of thumb: A poem with more than fifty percent of one kind of metrical foot is written in that base meter (even with a high degree of substituted feet); a poem that exhibits much less than fifty percent of a repeated metrical foot is usually a free verse poem that might be said to exhibit a certain degree of regularly metered lines. There are no rules in poetry, of course, but this generality is good to keep in mind. There are enough iambic lines in "Heaven-Haven" for us to say that it is written in an iambic meter, though there are not enough lines of equal length to say for certain what the length of those lines will be. We can see clearly that "Where springs not fail" is an iambic dimeter line. But this line is written in iambic pentameter: "To fields where flies no sharp and sided hail." Likewise, the first line of the second stanza is an iambic trimeter line, and the following line— "Where the green swell is in the havens dumb"—might be described as an iambic pentameter line, with a double iamb in the first two feet (a pyrrhic foot followed by a spondaic foot, followed by three fairly regular iambic feet). One could even argue that the second line of the second stanza is an iambic dimeter line (like the second line of the first stanza), by demoting the word "storms" to a lesser degree of stress than "no" or "come." Perhaps it's a line with one iambic foot followed by a spondaic foot. Either way, it's a line that has two feet, at least one of them iambic. To sum up: "Haven—Haven" is written in iambic feet with lines of mixed length which contains some interesting and highly expressive substitutions.

If we consider the line "Where the green swell is in the havens dumb" and scan it as I have suggested above (an iambic pentameter line with a double iamb in the first two feet) we might mark it this way:

˘ ˘ ˈ ˈ ˘ ˈ ˘ ˈ ˘ ˈ

Where the | green swell | is in | the hav | ens dumb

This allows that spondee in the second foot to physically reflect the sense of what is being said at that point in the line: a double stress will slow a line down, suggest heaviness or sluggishness (in certain contexts) and, in this case, "swell" the line by arresting, even for a moment, the forward thrust of the sentence to which this clause belongs. The line itself bulges metrically, just as the sea itself heaves up into a wave. The use of spondees—sometimes matched with stresses from surrounding iambs or trochees to extend the effect—has been a staple of English verse for centuries, where heaviness, difficulty, or arrested movement is being discussed. When Horatio is telling Hamlet about his father's ghost walking the parapets of Elsinore at night, he describes the two sentries, Marcellus and Bernardo, as being rooted with terror and awe to the spot on the battlements where the ghost appears:

> ... Whilst they, distill'd
> Almost to jelly with the act of fear,
> Stand dumb, and speak not to him.

The phrase "stand dumb" not only expresses, but metrically enacts, the sense of what is being said. The line literally stops at that point (I detect a slight hesitation, or caesura after those two heavily stressed words), before moving on. Another famous example serves to express harrowing experiences or sights that "thick men's blood with cold" where four stressed monosyllables crowed around a single unstressed syllable ("with"). But the line from Hopkins offers another example of how the physical attributes of a line may reflect the sense of what is being said in that line.

We have already noted that the third line of each stanza is longer than the other three lines, which are relatively equal (though not perfectly). Another form of metrical variation is mixing lines of different lengths in a single stanza or poem. Here Hopkins contrives to "swell" his line to a full pentameter, which distinguishes it from the dimeter and trimeter lines that surround it. Just as the sea expands into waves, the line extends itself, stretches out to accommodate Hopkins' meaning: The vast swelling of the sea, which, when it is finally confined in a harbor (or "haven"), will cease to be tumultuous and destructive. Taken together then—the spondee in the second foot and the expansion of the line into a pentameter—these effects combine to underscore and mirror Hopkins' meaning, his description of the sea as a wide, open, boundless place. We understand this, we feel it, through the formal aspects of the line and its place in the stanza. And the long line in the first stanza is no different. It, too, functions as a way of reflecting open space, a wide view of a place relatively unbounded, in which certain smaller things will be highlighted by contrast.

The field in which a full-blown hailstorm is taking place must be by definition large enough to contain such a storm. The nun desires to go to a field as large, but free of all disturbances, a field of safety and tranquility. The two fields stand in contrast to each other atmospherically, but not geographically. They both contain much space, which the length of the line itself reflects. What's important here is that the next line—the fourth line of the first stanza—contracts suddenly and drastically to highlight "a few lilies" growing, one might suppose, in a small corner of that field. The smaller line, then, represents graphically the modest cluster of lilies bunched together in a vast place. Such a sudden contraction after an expanded line serves Hopkins' purposes beautifully. The lilies and the field remind us of Jesus telling his disciples: "Consider the lilies of the field, how they grow... " Just as Jesus' lilies are humble, few, and frail, but glorious in their humility, so the nun will join the small host of those who are saved and dwell in heaven where the danger of worldly fields with their violent storms will be no more. That beauty, that utter safety and calm, is what the nun desires. She wants to be one of the lilies, delicate but protected, vibrant but meek, and radiant in the never-ending light of God's love and care. And the purity of their petals, their white spotlessness, surely alludes to the white raiment of saints, if only obliquely.

The most startling and effective use of metrical variation, however, occurs in the very last line of the poem. Here's how I would scan it:

And out | of the swing | of the sea.

This reading underscores the emotional and psychological release the nun believes she will feel once she is inducted into holy orders, once she renounces the dangers and temptations of the temporal world. Just as the meter here—for the first time—breaks away from the base meter of the poem (iambic) and swings out into the freer cadence of an anapestic rhythm, so she will be freed from suffering and the constraints of a worldly life. And, we can feel the "swing" of the sea, too, the long rolling pulse of its waves as they move forward and finally break upon the shore. It is a moment of metrical and spiritual release, a simultaneous liberation. Even half-drunk and slumped in my chair, I hadn't missed that joyful moment of change, that letting go of the more restrictive meter that had preceded it. I read it over and over. It made me want to get up and dance.

The pleasures of "music," of a melodic, self-consciously wrought lyricism, are—as with all Hopkins' work—on abundant display here. Anyone might pick up the end rhymes, which is to be expected in poems composed in traditional meter and form. Critics have argued that sound relationships between rhyming words suggest semantic relationships as well. If words rhyme, do they share a similar content of meaning? Whether they do here or not, the rhymes "go" and "blow," "fail" and "hail," as well as "be" and "sea," "come" and "numb" conspicuously provide a coherent structure to the stanzas, a balanced resonance that mirrors the matched shape of the stanzas on the page. The ear confirms the eye, and symmetry—one of the classical qualities of beauty—exists in both concrete and abstract ways. Those with a subtler ear might note Hopkins' use of alliteration—those fluent F's and I's in the first stanza, along with the long I's of *desired*, *flies*, and *sided*, and the seething S's throughout—especially in the second stanza—wholly appropriate to a passage describing the movement of the sea. In addition to such onomatopoeic effects, assonance may underscore or bind certain words together: *desired*, *flies*, and *sided*, for instance, are key words in stanza one and contain much of the meaning expressed there. *Fields*, *flies*, and *few* are bound together by alliteration, and once again link important concepts, deepening our sense of a correspondence between content and sound wherever they might occur. Taken together, the picture of words existing in a resonant equipoise, repeating various vowel and consonant sounds, or both, appears to be more than arbitrary. Syllabic stress may be one way of emphasizing words in a line of poetry, recurrent sound may be another.

Perhaps all of this means nothing more than that every word of a poem ultimately contributes to its final meaning whether sound patterns exist or not. Still, it's hard to ignore that the overall meaning here is tightly knit, enmeshed, solidified by the various skeins and patterns of sound that cross and re-cross its lines constantly echoing what's been emphasized and expressed, a sonic stitching holding words and meaning firmly together in a rich, semantic tapestry. Even without a consideration of intricate webs of sound and how they might support and contribute to meaning, such patterns in and of themselves provide pleasure for the ear and don't require any more justification for their existence than that. We take pleasure in sound for itself—music is a great sensuous experience— and the intellectual effort of interpreting their meaningful relationships is only an added pleasure for those who can appreciate it.

I am interested, as well, in Hopkins' word choices at certain moments in the poem. Diction can illuminate a line, bring it to life, and deepen its meaning, sending out waves of suggestiveness beyond the mere denotation of those words. Specifically, his choice of "sided" in the first stanza, and "dumb" in the second. Even during my initial reading of "Heaven-Haven," these words stood out for me because they seemed so unexpected and curious, words I might never have chosen myself, and certainly different from the largely common terms that occur in the rest of the poem. Hopkins is making sure that we envision hail—not rounded and smooth, like pearls—but edged, with sharp sides like hard jewels that might cut anything they strike on the way down. And "dumb" in stanza two doesn't mean, of course, simple-minded or stupid as it does in colloquial speech, but relatively soundless, not crashing and seething, sounds that turbulent water makes during a storm on the open sea. Violence of motion is one aspect of a storm, but violence of sound is another. Both frighten and appall.

What most interests me about "Heaven-Haven" is the parallelism that exists between the two stanzas, in the form of a theme repeated—but slightly altered—through the modification of a central metaphor. But even before this thematic parallelism occurs, a hint of the presence of parallelism might be detected even in the repetition of grammatical elements at the beginning of each stanza: "I have... " "And I have... "

which immediately signal an equation of thought. Before we pursue the idea of parallelism, however, I want to point out that the phrases "I have desired" and "I have asked" suggest the Christian process of moving towards salvation. First, the supplicant must desire, which leads inevitably toward asking, an echo of the Bible's assertion, "Ask, and it shall be given you, seek, and ye shall find." Hopkins' nun desires shelter and safety, so she asks for it in metaphors both compelling and apt.

The controlling metaphor is the idea of a storm. Life is often compared to a tempest wherein the individual is buffeted and often injured or ruined by slights, reversals, betrayals and so forth, a ship tossed about on the waves of a gale. This is the aspect of human experience the nun wishes to avoid. She seeks tranquility of spirit, peace of body and mind, and she believes that this exists in the "harbor" of God's grace. But in the first stanza, the storm described takes place on land—a hailstorm in a field. A hailstorm is a particularly damaging sort of storm and one we wish to avoid. The unprotected lilies would be easily torn apart by hail stones, left in tatters. In the second stanza, the storm becomes a tempest at sea from which the nun seeks to flee by entering the haven of God's protection. The sea storm offers terrors of its own, and in some ways is even more frightening as there is no place to hide. One is at the mercy of the elements and can only pray for the winds to abate. So, the central metaphor of "Heaven-Haven" is broached in stanza one and repeated in stanza two with a slight but important modification. Parallelism is the final balance, in a structure of several balances, that the poem has to offer. And balance is a form of order and stability all its own.

Hopkins' point is that there is no safe haven anywhere, on land or sea. Without presenting both, in a parallel structure, the picture of earthly danger would not be complete. When Hopkins later came to write "The Wreck of the Deutschland," surely one of his most famous poems, about the drowning of five Franciscan nuns when their ship ran aground in a storm, he recycled the phrase "heaven-haven" and placed it deftly into the final stanza:

Remember us in the roads, the heaven-haven of the Reward...

Obviously, Hopkins was attached to the title of his earlier poem and the metaphor embedded in it and wanted to pick up the idea again of God's heaven as a place of solace and safety after life's incessant turmoil. And the death of the German nuns must surely have reminded him of the nun in his previous work. It is unusual, but not unheard of, for a poet to adopt a phrase or an image from an earlier poem and incorporate it into the text of a later one, and it is a good example of how some ideas and images may become a motif in a writer's work, cross-referencing it and binding it together.

But to return to "Heaven-Haven"—this is a lot to make of a short poem. Still, slumped in that chair so many years ago in the midst of a raging party, I was able to slip off into something like an aesthetic trance to enjoy the imaginative world of Gerard Manly Hopkins and, whether I was conscious of it or not, respond fully and completely on some level—many levels!—to almost every aspect of "Heaven-Haven" I have detailed above. It has taken me all these years to collect my thoughts and acquire the skills to articulate that response and realize what it was about the poem that so thoroughly captivated my mind and held me spellbound in the chaos that surrounded me. When I read the poem now, the ensuing years evaporate, and I am back in that timeless moment of insight and perception. So what if I couldn't have explained my ravishment then? Better late than never.

ASSESSMENT

11

Nature and the Poet:

On the Work of Mary Oliver

For decades, Mary Oliver has been producing books that have garnered awards and created a large and admiring audience for her work. Earlier collections like *American Primitive*[1], *House of Light*[2], *Dream Work*[3], and *Twelve Moons*[4] are filled with poems of technical precision, emotional intensity, and penetrating vision into the mysteries of the natural world. Perhaps one of the last American Transcendentalists whose work can be taken seriously, Oliver promises in poem after poem to lift us beyond ourselves, beyond the confines of humdrum existence to a place of revelation. It is a difficult task, one which requires the highest poetic skills and the deepest passionate understanding of the non-human world. Oliver seems to possess a natural empathy that approaches religious devotion.

"Leaving the house," she says in the first line of the first poem in a recent book, "I went out to see / the frog, for example, / in her shining green skin" and we become aware a certain expectation has been set up, the expectation that her famous vision, her heightened sensibility will be acute and powerful enough to lead us back into Paradise once again, that place of pristine first vision when the doors of perception were wide open, letting the light of heaven stream in. It is a world apprehended with a consciousness not unlike that of a child, witnessed with an adult's respectful—and grateful—sense of awe. In language both simple and precise, Oliver creates images that enrapture our senses, that make us see and feel again what it is like to perceive the world as if for the first time. In the light of that perception, we are made to observe the frog's eggs "like a slippery veil; / and her eyes / with their golden rims." In that world, the pond lies unruffled "with its risen lilies," for it is a world where resurrection and eternal life are not merely promises, but facts, a world where "the white heron / like a dropped cloud" wanders languidly "through the still waters" echoing the comforting words of the 23rd Psalm.

Oliver's vision is Blakean, the Blake who could see angels lounging in trees, glimpse the soul of a flea, and address the seasons with an unselfconscious directness, as he does, for instance, in "To Spring" which opens, "O thou, with dewy locks, who lookest down / through the clear windows of the morning..." That sense of "looking down through the clear windows of the morning" unsullied by the modern world's disbelief and bitter cynicism, its sophisticated rejection of the marvelous, is everywhere apparent in Oliver's work. She takes Whitman, another forebear, at his word:

> Long enough have you dream'd contemptible dreams,
> Now I wash the gum from your eyes,
> You must habit yourself to the dazzle of the light and
> of every moment of your life.

The last two lines of Whitman's injunction, especially, might serve as an epigraph to the whole body of Oliver's work. She is one who has challenged us to experience the world once more in its prelapsarian purity, before Adam fell and with him, according to Puritan doctrine, the whole multitudinous, pristine enterprise of nature, right down to the least bird, fish, and flower. Her work is punctuated by reminders that life is a precious gift, as in "The Summer Day" from *House of Light* which ends: "Tell me what is it you plan to do / with your one wild and precious life?" or in a poem entitled "Black Snake" from *What Do We Know*[5], which asks, "... if you would praise the world, what is it that you would leave out?" For the inevitable result of such seeing, the poems all but literally assert, can be nothing but spontaneous celebration and praise.

And that is part of the problem with Oliver's work. Though many readers and critics have pointed out the pains Oliver takes to avoid sentimentalizing nature, it can hardly be doubted that she comes perilously close in many of her poems. In the poem mentioned above, for instance, "The Summer Day" from *House of Light*, Oliver observes a grasshopper, "the one who has flung herself out of the grass, / the one who is eating sugar out of my hand." A grasshopper eating sugar? Out of a human hand? Surely this is a fond fancy, a poetically contrived moment when emotion and the fervency of belief overcome reality. The grasshopper in the poem has been transformed into something cute, like a pony, which—for human beings, at least—is much easier to love than the many-limbed, chitinous, bug-eyed reality of an insect. And Oliver's further attempts to disguise the grasshopper's more alien features—she says it has "enormous and complicated eyes" and "pale forearms"—fail to convince. Now the grasshopper has become a beautiful, dark-eyed girl. But anyone who has studied a grasshopper closely knows that it is nothing like a pony or a girl. The triangular mask of its face, its twitching mandibles, dragon-like body, serrated appendages and jutting threadlike antennae bear no resemblance to anything cuddly or adorable. And its eyes—opaque, fixated, bulging—are complicated, yes, but not with the intricacies of beauty. Rather, the complexities of function and necessity. A particularly repellant feature of grasshoppers is that they have dirty brown blood and a soft segmented body not much more appealing than a maggot's. It is possible to admire grasshoppers for the way in which their bodies are adapted to their environment and their ability to persist over geologic time. But to love them? Perhaps in flight, when they "snap their wings open and float away." Even this, however, is not quite accurate. Less flight than awkward leap, they flop into the air to land with an inaudible thud wherever the trajectory of their oversized femurs happens to propel them. Yet these powerful hind-legs exhibit, oddly enough, the only real aesthetic feature of their gangly frame, marked as they are by garnet rows of chevrons from hip to knee.

Likewise, in the prose poem "Black Snake" from *What Do We Know*, Oliver seeks to redeem the much-maligned reputation of the snake as being on one hand slimy and shifty, and on the other a symbol of ultimate evil. Observing a snake sunning on a rock, she muses: "He has cousins who have teeth that spring up and down and are full of the sap of death, but what of that, so have we all." Fair enough. But when she depicts the snake devouring its prey and says, "he can catch a mouse and swallow it like a soft stone," we may balk at the obvious way in which she avoids the real horror here. The mouse is not a "soft stone," but has consciousness and feeling, and must be rigid with terror at being ingested whole, completely aware and alive. Until overpowered by constriction and the peristaltic action of the snake's body, the mouse kicks for all it's worth to back away from that ghastly, rippling maw. We can accept and "forgive" the snake, of course, knowing it has no choice and is simply following the dictates of its genes. Like the grasshopper, we can even admire it and certainly respect it for its lethal power. But we must not prettify the brutal facts of the situation, or the mouse's fear. In fact, we may do them more honor by accepting them for what they are than falsifying or domesticating them in order to make them more sympathetic to humans.

A poem is not a zoological treatise. A poem is an imaginative act and need not conform to physical reality. At the same time, poems must not falsify psychological and emotional truth. We cannot be brought to feel what we do not feel, no matter how much we may wish to feel it, and no matter how commendable that wish may be. Nor can we be forced to deny what we assuredly know. If Oliver's poetic ambition is to bring herself—and her readers—to love all nature regardless of its more repulsive and downright horrifying aspects, she must do so honestly. Perhaps it is possible to love the grasshopper and the snake in a doctrinal sense, a Platonic spiritual sense, as legitimate representatives of God's abundant creation, but not—as Oliver would have us believe—in a personal, erotic, physical sense. It will be a long time before some of us are prepared to lie down easily with the scorpion or the black-tailed rattler.

The image of an idealized nature, of the lion reclining with the lamb, comes to us from a long tradition of Biblical belief. Once humanity—and with it all of co-corrupted nature—has been redeemed, the conventional animosities and competitions between animals will cease. We are not told what the animals will eat or how they will live, but we are assured that harmony and mutual love will reign among beasts. The wish for physical contact—safe, affectionate, reciprocal—is often expressed in Oliver's work in ways which we can more readily accept than the wish to consort with bugs or deadly serpents. In "The Roses," for instance, Oliver walks all day on the dunes of Cape Cod "from one thick raft of the wrinkled salt roses to another." Overcome by their allure, she addresses them: "O sweetness pure and simple, may I join you?" And in typical Oliverian fashion, feels the desire to be in contact. "I lie down next to them, on the sand." We may think this odd or not, but there is nothing inherently repugnant in the act because roses are both beautiful and harmless. Moreover, most of us have dreamed of lying down in a field of flowers. It's the following lines that perplex: "But to tell / what happens next, truly I need help. / Will somebody or something please start to sing?" What does happen next? Something inconceivable? A floral orgy? We do not know, because the poem stops here. Oliver implies that she has fallen into a kind of erotic-spiritual swoon and cannot speak, like Theresa of Avila. There's little for the reader to do but discreetly avert his eyes and move on.

This kind of omni-eroticism is not new in American poetry. Whitman was the first to express it in "Song of Myself" and many of his ensuing poems. The desire is announced in his opening lines:

> The atmosphere is not a perfume, it has no taste of
> the distillation, it is odorless,
> It is for my mouth forever, I am in love with it,
> I will go down to the bank by the wood, and become
> undisguised and naked,
> I am mad for it to be in contact with me.

Later, Whitman implores: "Press close, bare-bosomed night!" and, addressing the earth, says "Smile, for your lover comes!" From beginning to end, "Song of Myself" ripples with sexual energy that sometimes bursts out to manifest itself in passages of unusual frankness—unusual for the nineteenth century. This is the new world, and Whitman is the new Adam returning to Eden. The idea has a long and venerable tradition for both Transcendentalists and Puritans.

Oliver's assignation with the roses is not her only fling with nature either. In "The Return" she finds an abandoned seal pup along the beach and lies down on the sand "with my back toward it, and / pretty soon it rolled over, and rolled over / until the length of its body lay along / the length of my body." And in the poem, "Ghosts," from *American Primitive*, she dreams of the vanished buffalo sprawled across the Great Plains. In the final section of the poem, a cow gives birth to a calf:

> ... in a warm corner
> of the clear night
> in the fragrant grass
> in the wild domains
> of the prairie spring... I asked them,
> in my dream I knelt down and asked them
> to make room for me.

It is a surprising and evocative moment, a moment when, through the poet's catalytic imagination, an ancient wish to commune with the animals is fulfilled, poetically at least.

But roses, baby seals, and bison are easy to love. We may be more easily persuaded to love them than other species more distant from us on the evolutionary chain. The closer the link, the better. By investing animals or plants with human attributes, we are drawn closer to them. And once we begin to identify with them, our sympathies are readily engaged. This is accomplished regularly with Oliver's mockingbirds, loons, ravens, egrets, larks, and the like, and other mammals such as the bobcat, skunk, whale, fawn, and wild goose. With some imagination, and Oliver has plenty, we can be brought to empathize with mussels, clams, dogfish, bats, and turtles, though some of the cold-blooded creatures and scavengers are harder to adore. Insects, reptiles, and vermin are perhaps the hardest sell of all. Sometimes, as with the grasshopper, the stretch to identify personally with something and therefore to love it is too great. No matter how much language, how much gorgeous and arresting imagery Oliver lavishes on such creatures, we demur. We step back. We hesitate in the face of such closeness to what is so alien and strange. Though Oliver does her best with the black snake,

> ...he can climb a tree and dangle
> like a red-eyed rope out of its branches; he can
> swim...

we cannot quite be brought to believe that a snake is just one of the rascally boys in our neighborhood.

One of her easier persuasions, you might think, would be the dolphin. After all, they almost speak by themselves, frolic in the waves, ostensibly smile, and generally win our hearts with their watery shenanigans. And we all know how intelligent they are. Yet the poem "One Hundred White-sided Dolphins on a Summer Day" is arguably the weakest in her book, *What Do We Know*, perhaps because dolphins already resemble us in so many ways. Thus, the magic of Oliver's transformation is robbed of its initial peculiarity and surprise. There they are, leaping in the sea, "threading through the... foam," and we are sure a moment of transcendental illumination is on the way. How could it be otherwise? Oliver has set herself a daunting task: every time she passes over her threshold we expect nothing less than revelation. Inevitably, predictably, the dolphins rise to meet her challenge: collectively, they become God, who looks "with the moon of his eye / into my heart." And what does God find there?

```
      pure, sudden, steep, sharp, painful
               gratitude
               that falls—

        I don't know—either
            unbearable tons
      or the pale, bearable hand
            of salvation
            on my neck
            lifting me
     from the boat's plain plank seat
            into the world's

        unspeakable kindness...
```

For one thing, Oliver's estimable vocabulary and powers of description seem to fail her here. For another—perhaps because of that failure—we are told what she feels, more than we are shown, which would allow us to experience her feelings for ourselves. The "bearable hand of salvation" is simply too vague an image to effect much of a transcendence. And because our hearts and our imaginations are not transported, we are unable to swallow the assertion towards which the experience is leading. The world is not unspeakably kind, though it is sometimes beautiful even in its savagery. The language of the poem continues to fail before the agenda it has set for itself. After asserting that she almost vanishes into the body of the dolphin—the typical conceit for spiritual union—she sinks to the bottom of the sea "with everything / that ever was, or ever will be." The language here is hackneyed, flat, even blustery in its attempt to convey vastness, hugeness, a sense of awe. What happens next? The animals continue to frolic:

> Then, in our little boat, the dolphins suddenly gone
> we sailed on through the brisk, cheerful day.

It is as if she had written: "…and then we all lived happily ever after." The ending is weak because what preceded it is weak, and the whole project of the poem—to bring us to a visionary understanding of God and salvation—collapses. Even the title of the poem is unconvincing: Were there actually one hundred dolphins? Or is this merely a symbolic number, like one of those exaggerated statistics from the Middle Ages, meaning *lots*. The whole poem has the feeling of a symbolic gesture, the depiction of an abstract grandiose idea rather than an actual, heartfelt experience.

This failure of language is evinced here and there throughout *What Do We Know*. In the poem "The Roses," for instance, there are several lapses in diction, all the more noticeable for a poet who is normally scrupulous about her word choices. Describing the roses, she says their petals are "red as blood or white as snow," comparisons so dull, so frayed and trite we are puzzled and shocked by them. And in a line already quoted above, she addresses the flowers: "Oh sweetness pure and simple, may I join you?" Purely and simply, this is shopworn language. Perhaps these are really lapses in imagination, which are always bound up at the root with language—a lapse in one practically dictating a lapse in the other. Speaking of her beloved egrets once more, she says, "They stand in the marsh like white flowers." Surely this is the conventional image, the expected image, the first and easiest one the mind settles upon when striving after metaphor. And such failures lead, inevitably, to lapses in thought as well. Language-image-thought, they are intricately connected, affecting one another in radical ways. Describing a flurry in "Early Snow," Oliver remarks: "…the gardens began / to vanish as each white, six-pointed / snowflake lay down without a sound…" and later thinks "how not one looks quite like another / though each is exquisite, fanciful." This leads to an image of the snow as "a confident, white blanket / carrying out its / cheerful work…," the kind of facile personification that makes Oliver sound like one of those forgettable nineteenth century lady-versifiers who drove Ezra Pound to distraction.

Perhaps Oliver's silliest metaphors are reserved for "Mockingbird," a poem about writers' sometimes painful inability to marshal language in response to the world's obvious attractions. Wandering through the spring landscape, lonely as a cloud, she complains that she is unable to write a single word, nor even think anything at all "at the window of my heart." This flirts with sentiment and unquestionably works better in popular song than in poetry. Two stanzas later, Oliver commits to paper what may be her most egregious conceit. Referring to the landscape around her, she observes:

> And nothing there anyway knew, don't we know, what a word is,
>   or could parse down from the general liquidity of feeling
> to the spasm and bull's eye of the moment, or the logic,
>   or the instance,
> trimming the fingernails of happiness, entering the house
>   of rhetoric.

The language and thought leading up to "trimming the fingernails of happiness" is a bit turgid, and the phrase, when it occurs, strikes us as unfortunate, if not somewhat ludicrous. Keats, listening intently to his bird, never allows himself to stray so far into the antic and bizarre.

Such failings are curious. In the past, Oliver has employed a precise and resourceful vocabulary—a powerful mode of expression—for the visionary experience. This is achieved not with polysyllabic Latinate terms from the vocabulary of philosophy, but, as is always with true visionaries, the simplest language, the words and images of everyday experience newly conceived. Pick up any of Oliver's earlier books and browse. You will find surprises on almost every page, language so original it seems to fit—to accommodate itself—to reality. So, in *American Primitive*, Oliver writes of the mole who digs "among the pale girders / of apple root" or the thrush, with its "gorgeous amoral voice," or the heron that spreads its wings and "rows forward into flight." Those words, "girder," "amoral," and "row," are precise, almost revelatory in their exactness. From *Dream Work*, possibly her best book, we read of the "one-lunged life" of clams, or starfish who slide "like too many thumbs" up onto the sand, or—a stunning auditory image—the ocean's "black, anonymous roar." In *Twelve Moons*, we read of "the hot blade" of the fish's body, of "silky" ponds and a turtle "hunting, morosely, for something to eat." Could there be a more perfect word than "morosely" to describe the turtle's sluggish, cold-blooded delving? And in *House of Light*, we are presented with fields in "wrappings of mist" and another more believable snake, a snake right out of the mystery of the universe and the poet's image-fusing imagination, a snake who moves "like a stream of glowing syrup." Here, the image is the illumination, not a description of it.

Part of the problem for a poet of exaltation is the exhaustion of language available for descriptive purposes. The stock nouns might include such terms as "sweetness," "joy," "gratitude," "beauty," "purity," "tenderness," "wonder," "kindness," "glory," "mystery," and so forth. Adjectives like "unspeakable," "luminous," "holy," or "unbearable" abound, as well as the words "lovely" and "utterly." All of these words—and/or variations of them—appear in her current work, and to a far lesser extent in the earlier books. When the poet is at her best, it is not in the guise of an explainer, but a presenter, one who invests images of the natural world with a startling newness, as though we had never really looked at landscapes or animals accurately before. The key is in the image, conceived with visionary perspective, and not in the mere testimony of general descriptive words like those above. And further, the image thus drawn must be believed: not the fanciful "pale forearms" of the grasshopper, but the real bodies of sharks,

> sinuous explorers of the blue chambers
> of coastal waters moving
> easy as oil, without a wasted stroke,
> in and out of the warm coves.

It is the difference between thinking and seeing. Always it is the latter that galvanizes and transforms.

At her best, that is, Oliver does not attempt to beautify nature, to decorate the bare facts of reality with attractive anthropomorphic details. Instead, she looks closely with the obsessive focus of a predator's eye, and the words to incarnate reality seem to come to her naturally, though we know how much work it takes to hone the poet's sensibility to just such a keen edge of vision, and how much work it takes to shape that vision into song. Nor does Oliver insist on drawing a comforting moral out of what she sees. In "Sharks," excerpted above from the volume *Twelve Moons*, the swimmers along a beach are called out of the water after "the steep / dark dorsal fin" of a shark is spotted in the distance. A few hours later:

> ... since nothing has happened
> a few figures dare the water to their waists,
> forgetting, as men have always forgotten,
>
> that life's winners are not the rapacious but the patient;
> what triumphs and takes new territory
>
> has learned to lie for centuries in the shadows
> like the shadows of the rocks.

Despite the elevated tone of "life's winners"—a line ringing with the rhetoric of a sports announcer—we are a long way from Oliver's frisking dolphins and their abstract, comforting message. A long way from the mockingbird with its "fingernails of happiness" and the black snake who "looks shyly at nothing and streams away into the grass." The shark, and the images that reveal it, are specific, unvarnished, and dead-on.

Among the more recent poems that convince are ones that retain some of the old fierceness of thought, if not imagery. Standing on the shore of one of the ponds that dot the landscape of Cape Cod, Oliver observes two herons—one blue, one green—neither of which is at that moment fishing. Therefore, "the little fish in their rainbow shirts are gliding peacefully by." Abruptly, the description of the scene is cut short by a narrative:

> There is an old story, often told, of a warrior frightened
> before battle, not so much for his own peril but for the strife
> to come, and the awful taking of life by his own sword.
> Suddenly a figure appears beside him—it is one of the gods
> in the dress of battle and on his face an expression of willingness
> and ferocity. His speech is brief, and all-encouraging.

The poem returns abruptly to the scene at the pond. The green heron, having been asleep, shakes itself awake and begins hunting. And the blue heron walks rapidly "one might say devotedly along the shore. And the water opens willingly for the terrible feet. And the narrow face, the powerful beak, plunge down." The gods, it is implied, not only encourage, but sponsor the carnage of nature. Hunger and death are not immoral in the non-human world. They are part of a divine order.

One of the strongest poems in *What Do We Know* begins with a familiar scene near the edge of woods (at twilight, of course) "when something begins / to sing, like a waterfall / pouring down / through the leaves." We are in familiar poetic territory here, and many other such scenes—from Frost, for example, or Keats—raise themselves up in memory. Ah, "the sweetness of it—those chords, / those pursed twirls… "We relax, prepared for the usual encomium to nature's beauty and the romance of the night. Suddenly, the poem swerves in a different direction when the poet hears "out of the same twilight / the wildest red outcry." The sound is ghoulish, loud, desperate. It silences the thrush that had been singing. Is it the predator or its prey? Now, "the dark grows darker" as the appalling cry seems to eclipse everything, except the moon which has just begun to rise:

> And whatever that wild cry was
>
> it will always remain a mystery
> you have to go home now and live with,
> sometimes with the ease of music, and sometimes in silence,
> for the rest of your life.

This poem achieves the right balance between wonder and fear with regard to the natural world. The most important line in the poem, "out of the same twilight," is crucial. Out of the same inscrutable source—initially appealing—nature sends forth the beautiful and terrible, life and death, music and anguish, as though the merging of the two were not contradictory but somehow proper, logical, natural. It is just this mixture of rapture and dread that confounds us with regard to nature. Many lesser poets choose to ignore horror or gloss it over with decorative metaphors or the comforting technique of personification. But Oliver wisely rejects those possibilities here. The enigma remains—nature is not logical, but paradoxical. A paradox we must live with, whether we like it or not.

That is why, when in "Black Snake" Oliver asks, "if you would praise the world, what is it you would leave out?" answers leap to mind: the horrifying, the evil, the repulsive. How to praise them? Yet, in any serious account of nature they must be included. When emissaries from the savage, non-human side of nature show up, as with the shark or the "black prince" from "Raven with Crows," we must pay them due respect while regarding them with an unblinking fidelity. The raven, we are told, "is not a big bird ... but an / impossibly big bird":

its
chunky, almost blooming black beak

and its large unquenchable eyes
shine
like a small, unheard explosion; it is
no crow, no perky, stiff-winged head-bobbing
corn-meddler...

All great nature poets understand it is not in sameness where the power of their poetry lies. If the animals are just like us, and we like them, what can they teach us? So, it is not in likeness, but in otherness where revelation resides. Once our humanness is thrown into relief against these alien creatures, we begin to discover who and what we really are. And who and what they are, as well. This is why writers from Thoreau to Gary Snyder have argued for the preservation of wilderness and wild species. When we lose them, they contend, we lose a part of ourselves that we may never recover. It is also worth noting that just here, with a less loveable creature, Oliver's imagery returns to something like its former vigor.

For throughout *What Do We Know* the imagery is not only domesticated, but rather generalized, ordinary, even tepid. Here, for example, the ocean's "black, anonymous roar" from *Dream Work* becomes simply "the big voice of the sea," an altogether friendly and companionable presence by comparison. In *American Primitive*, the sea is described as "luminous roughage," an "insucking genesis" and "that roaring flamboyance," images that strive to describe the ocean in terms of its unique otherness, its quintessential nature, not its generic qualities. It has often been asserted, as I have in the first chapter of this book, that the poet's job is Adam's job: to name the things of this world again as though for the first time. They wait, still, always, no matter what the age for their precise names, for the language of poetry to discover them and call them forth. In *Twelve Moons*, the sea becomes "A cold slate / full of swirls" from which waves are "tossed shoreward on dark tines, / lapping with boiling tongues / up the smooth sand," and later in the same poem, "the smashing of the water's gray fists / among the pilings" is heard, and "the blue cauldron / of the sea's immense appetite" is discerned—shadowy, bottomless. In *House of Light,*" the sea / … was slashing along as usual / shouting and hissing/ toward the future." These images have movement, force, a kinetic energy that seeks to capture the spirit of nature in words. When Oliver returns to the sea in *What Do We Know*, it is only for a glance:

> When I went back to the sea
> it wasn't waiting.
> Neither had it gone away.
> All its musics were safe and sound; the circling gulls
> were still commonplace the fluted shells
> rolled on the shore
> more beautiful than money—
> oh yes, more beautiful than money!

Then she notices a number of seals, bobbing in the waves:

> oh bed of silk,
> lie back now on your prairies of blackness your fields of sunlight
> that I may look at you.
>
> I am happy to be home.

This is fine as far as it goes, but the passion for description, the fiery intensity of seeing and imagining, of grasping the world with words, has gone out of it. Once again, the language fails, falling into cliché: the sea is "safe and sound." All the poet can do now is point out a few "common- place" things—the circling gulls, the fluted shells, the seals. Even the adjectives here are the usual ones. The specific, self-identifying sounds of the sea are now generalized into "all its musics." The phrase "prairies of blackness" is promising, but not followed up. The poet here has not gone out into the world where everything is unaccustomed and new, but has come home to where things are old, familiar, and comfortable. We feel it in every line of the poem.

If there is a diminishment of poetic imagination and expression in her most recent work, how can we account for it? Age may play a part. There are many examples—especially among nature poets—of those whose literary powers have flagged with time. Wordsworth is foremost, but one might just as easily mention Lawrence or even Whitman, whom Lawrence called "the white aborigine." These and others have found that as the body ages, one begins to defer to the mind. That is, once the life of the senses begins to recede, so the life of the mind concomitantly takes precedence. As Wordsworth tells us in "Ode: Intimations of Immortality from Recollections of Early Childhood":

> Though nothing can bring back the hour
> Of splendour in the grass, of glory in the flower;
> We will grieve not, rather find
> Strength in what remains behind...

In the years that bring the philosophic mind.

The aging poet moves towards abstraction, toward ideas, away from the physicality of the body and the senses. But the senses are the only direct access the poet has to nature. Move away from them and you move away from the primal world of oceans and snakes and stars. The mind is weak, almost useless, for grasping the immediate facts of creation, for creation is manifestly a place of substance, a place of no-mind, or perhaps not-mind. Insofar as it is alive, it is generally a place of flesh, instincts, reflexes, and genetic mandate. In our egocentricity, human beings like to believe that most other animals have some sort of feeling and thought, an inner life like ours, but the number of animals who actually do amount to a pretty narrow fringe just below us on the evolutionary scale. The vast world of living things has nothing even approximating human consciousness or personality. And then there's the non-living world, the world of inanimate matter, and beyond that emptiness—a nearly atom-less vacuum—which is what 99.99% of the universe is made of, according to cosmologists. The mind there is truly lost.

If the language of the mind is statement, the language of the senses is image. The sense-image when it is powerfully conceived, is both thought and thing. It is thought incarnated as thing. In her best moments, Mary Oliver still understands this. In the poem, "Wind," she writes:

> I am tired of explanations. Unless they are spoken
> by the best mouths. Black bear coming up from
> sleep, growling her happiness. Nighthawks snap-
> ping their way through the dusk. Or the voice of
> the wind itself flailing out of any and every quarter
> of the sky ...

Yet, this poem, like so many others in *What Do We Know* seems barren of compelling images. It is mostly statement—mostly explanation. Unless one considers the final image, "the wind breaks open its silver countries of rain." But this seems more of a mental image than a sense-image, more contrived than felt, as the shark's oily, unimpeded movements through the blue chambers of the sea are obviously felt in *Twelve Moons*. There, the language is as concrete as the object being described. There, the imagination is engaged directly through the senses and the resultant image is palpable, undiluted by abstraction. And when thought does enter the poem, it feels as concrete and physical as the world out of which it has emerged. Recalling the excerpt from "Sharks" when a few people finally decide it's safe enough to wade back into the water, the language is crisp, clear, the thought it conveys as tangible as an object: "...what triumphs and takes new territory / has learned to lie for centuries in the shadows / like the shadows of rocks." We are reminded of Eliot's idea of disso-ciation of sensibility, his assertion that the Metaphysical poets enjoyed a special sensibility that has largely been lost. For Donne, Marvell, or Henry Vaughn, "a thought was an experience..." an experience charac-terized by "a fusion of thought and feeling." They "felt their thought as immediately as the odour of a rose."

If there has been a dissociation of sensibility in the work of Mary Oliver, perhaps it is signaled by a movement in her career towards the prose poem. There are eight prose poems in *What Do We Know*, out of forty overall. Not a high ratio, granted. But none of the earlier books contain a single prose poem. They only begin to appear in 1994 with the publication of *White Pine* and continue through *West Wind* and *Winter Hours* to *What Do We Know*. In fact, *Winter Hours* is overwhelmingly a volume of prose and prose poems. Yet, Oliver is still able to assert: "I can think for a little while; then, it's the world again." In these volumes, poems in traditional lines and stanzas continue to predominate. But if prose is fundamentally the genre of speculation and thought—as in the essay, for instance—or the long narrative that develops a theme—as in the novel—then perhaps the move towards prose, once it has been taken, begins to bleed into the poet's more formal work as well. Perhaps the habit of abstraction begins to shadow the words and images of the tightly controlled lines of verse that once stood out so solidly from the page, and in the mind, as things rather than vehicles for themes or ideas.

Some of the finer moments in *What Do We Know* are not of inspired diction or imagery, but moments of direct statement offered up to the reader for his or her own reflection, like koans. Some have already been mentioned, as the statement in "Black Snake," "if you would praise the world, what is it you would leave out?" and the opening of "Wind," "I am tired of explanations." The book is peppered with others. In "Crows," she remarks: "Somewhere, among all my thoughts, there is a narrow path. / It's attractive, but who could follow it?" and in "The Lark," she asserts: "We are reconciled, I think, / to too much." In "Moonlight," she warns: "Take care you don't know anything in this world / too quickly or easily" which echoes the statements from "Snowy Night" quoted above. One of her best comments appears as the first line of "Blue Iris": "Now that I'm free to be myself, who am I?" At such moments, when she asks such questions and makes such statements, we are disarmed and ready to be convinced. These, and not images and tactile experiences, constitute the true visionary moments in *What Do We Know*. But moments of inspired statement, unfounded—or ungrounded—in the physical are the stock in trade of the essayist, more than of the nature poet. The nature poet's gift is to describe, to show, to re-create the world through images that fairly make us shudder as though we responded to something actual and not an illusion, of art. That's what made Dickinson's pulse race and the hair stand up on the back of her arm—not abstract argument, no matter how intelligent. We respond physically to the physical. Statement only makes us pensive.

Oliver herself seems to guess at the problem afflicting her new work. Finding a huge jellyfish washed up on the shore, she says of her own struggle to describe it: "For all the liveliness of my mind, / I have to work to imagine / its life of gleaming and wandering, / its bulbous, slow, salt comfort…" A curious admission for a poet who seemed, for a while at least, to have found a perfect language to bring forth whatever object or creature she might come upon in the world.

Beneath the note of wonder and joy at the diversity of the natural world with which we are familiar in all her work, we detect an elegiac note, the beginning, perhaps, of a long valedictory. Time and again, the language blurs into hackneyed speech, cliché, easy sentiment, verbosity, a tendency towards the approximate rather than the exact. Is it mere chance that "Mink" is reserved for the final poem in the volume? Out walking again in the snow, Oliver is treated to a rare sight:

> A mink,
> jointless as heat, was
> tip-toeing along
> the edge of the creek,
> which was still in its coat of snow,
> yet singing—I could hear it!—
> the old song
> of brightness.

She can hear it, the "old song of brightness," but can she still reproduce it in powerful, accurate language? The proto-language of Adam articulating the world? It seems not. The banks of the creek wear only an ordinary "coat of snow," and the intricate, glassy, tinkling flow of an icebound brook is reduced to an "old song" whose one quality is an abstraction. She is reminded of Ruskin, but no—he never painted a scene like this.

She notices the trees leaning "this way and that" (a phrase only half a step away from "to and fro"). We can almost feel her straining to grasp some elemental noun, some fresh, animating verb that will bring it all to life. There is the "seed-beaded buckthorn," and the water that slips through the landscape "like a long, / unknotted thread." This is suggestive, but leads back to the mink who has "a hunger in him / bigger than his shadow" which was "gathered / like a sheet of darkness under his / neat feet." She watches as the mink sniffs the air, his way of acutely perceiving the world, but after attempting to imagine what the mink smells in rather bland images, she gives up: "who knows / what his keen nose was / finding out." Now it is possible for her to relax and say what she has to say outright: "for me, it was the gift of winter / to see him." Just seeing him is the gift, not capturing his essence, his spirit in that "old song of brightness." Moreover, it is the gift "of winter," that time of barrenness and endings.

Finally, she turns away altogether, but not without a retrospective glance or two, as if she knows such chances will come less and less now, and the attempt to capture them become increasingly difficult:

> I stood awhile and then walked on
>
> over the white snow: the terrible, gleaming
> loneliness. It took me, I suppose,
> something like six more weeks to reach
> finally a patch of green, I paused so often
> to be glad, and grateful, and even then carefully across
> the vast, deep woods kept looking back.

ADDENDUM:

It is possible that poets whose careers last forty years or more will begin to repeat themselves and become programmatic in their approach. Certain subjects, themes, strategies, and perspectives show up with expected regularity—which is perhaps a comfort, not a liability, to their many readers. In Mary Oliver's latest, as of this writing, collection of poems, *Why I Wake Early*[6], the tokens of her style adorn almost every poem with such predictability it is possible to posit a standard form, hardly more variable than the twelve-bar blues. It goes something like this: I woke up this morning and walked out into the shining world, where I found something amazing, which I observed, and in which I ultimately found sacred truth: the universe is beautiful and good beyond words. This God's-in-his-heaven-and-all's-right-with-the-world approach is evident from the very first poem in the volume:

> Hello, sun in my face.
> Hello, you who make the morning
> and spread it over the fields
> and into the faces of the tulips
> and the nodding morning glories,
> and into the windows of, even, the
> miserable and the crotchety—
>
> best preacher that ever was,
> dear star, that just happens
> to be where you are in the universe
> to keep us from ever-darkness,
> to ease us with warm touching,
> to hold us in the great hands of light—
> good morning, good morning, good morning.
>
> Watch, now, how I start the day
> in happiness, in kindness.

This chirpiness, this irrepressible good humor, is enough to dispense with suffering and death in a single brief line, for what can they matter in the face of such overwhelming and benign existence? "Every Day," the poet assures us in another poem later in the book, "I see or hear / something / that more or less / kills me / with delight… " One can only assume the poet never listens to the radio or reads a newspaper or even speaks to another informed human being. And the facts of natural science are glossed over with indifference, as well. In Oliver's version of reality, a hundred species a day aren't slipping into extinction and the world isn't balanced on the edge of ecological disaster. Instead, she asserts, with characteristic bravura: "Oh Lord, how shining and festive is your gift to us, if we / only look, and see."

Even when the poet tries to accommodate the more terrifying aspects of existence in her poems, she fails notably—a failure that makes itself apparent in both image and diction:

> Don't call this world adorable, or useful, that's not it.
> It's frisky, and a theater for more than fair winds.
> The eyelash of lightning is neither good nor evil.
> The struck tree burns like a pillar of gold.

Not only humanity with its wars and torture chambers, its relentless injustice and wide-spread oppression, but all of nature "red in tooth and claw" is subsumed in that one insipid adjective: frisky. Understatement is hardly adequate to describe the euphemistic quality of "frisky" in this context. And though a bolt of lightning is neither good nor evil, it is a bit more than an eyelash to anyone but an inveterate idealist or an all-powerful god. By this time in her career and given her commitment to praising only the beauty of the world while ignoring the rest, Oliver is bound to beautify images of nature whenever they may appear threatening or ugly. So, a tree after being struck by lightning—splintered and still smoldering—becomes a pillar of gold, something lovely and positively symbolic. But even Yahweh's famous pillar was composed of wild, uncontainable fire, searing the sky, nothing so handsome and aesthetically pleasing as gold.

Why I Wake Early then continues, and even amplifies, the general substance and approach of earlier volumes, an approach that by this time has become almost reflexive. The poet is there to praise (consider the epigraph to this book, from George Herbert: "Lord! who hath praise enough?"), and any attempt to vary from this purpose will meet with immediate resistance from the poet herself: "I would like to write a poem about the world that has in it / nothing fancy," Oliver confesses in the very first line of a poem, "But it seems impossible." The impulse to praise is admirable, even necessary, one of the oldest functions of poetry. But praise must come at the end of struggle, a true and comprehensive assessment of reality, praise that the reader feels has been wrested and won out of the general chaos and violence of existence. It cannot proceed blithely out of a self-satisfied and willful solitude. There is no struggle here, only conviction, something quite different.

In one of the best poems in *Why I Wake Early*, Oliver suddenly confronts her own complacency in lines of unusual frankness and, for once, takes herself task:

THE ARROWHEAD

The Arrowhead,
which I found beside the river,
was glittering and pointed.
I picked it up, and said,
"Now, it's mine."
I thought of showing it to friends.
I thought of putting it—such an imposing trinket—
in a little box, on my desk.
Halfway home, past the cut fields,
the old ghost
stood under the hickories.
"I would rather drink the wind," he said,
"I would rather eat mud and die
than steal as you steal,
than lie as you lie."

12

Winning Neglect:

On the Work of Samuel Menashe

Now and then, a poet and his work are resuscitated—to borrow a word made famous by Ezra Pound, who used it in a more general way to describe the neglected art of highly-crafted poetry. It seems that in every age, there are poets whose work has been largely ignored in their own time only to be rediscovered later and restored to its rightful place in the canon. This would be true of Melville and Dickinson in the last century, though it is also true that one of these writers seems to have courted neglect as much as having it bestowed upon her. The poet's personality and peculiar aesthetic practice have as much to do as anything with how one's work is received and accepted or not. Some poets become famous almost for the mere fact of having been neglected, then rediscovered over and over by admiring readers who are determined not to let their work die. Such is the (happy) fate of poets as divergent as Mina Loy, Weldon Kees, and Basil Bunting. Others suffer neglect during their lifetimes and never quite recover. They vanish into the pages of forgotten anthologies or languish on the back shelves of libraries, never to appear again as the very pages on which their poems are printed disintegrate over time. This is a kind of oblivion from which no poet may reemerge.

A recent case in point involves the work of Samuel Menashe, much of which has been re-issued in the American Poets Project from the Library of America. In fact, the collection is the winner of the first "Neglected Masters Award" established by the Poetry Foundation, which carries a cash prize of $50,000, a nice round sum by any measure. Moreover, each volume is introduced respectfully by a distinguished poet or critic—in this case Christopher Ricks, Warren Professor of the Humanities and co-director of the Editorial Institute at Boston University. It appears, then, that Menashe's long dark night of neglect is over. *New and Selected*

Poems[1] ought to go a long way toward reestablishing him and his work—if not in the minds of the greater culture, at least in the minds and hearts of those who care about and read poetry, admittedly a specialized but important subculture and one that, in the long run, may be the only one that really matters. How did Menashe's neglect come about in the first place? If he is as accomplished and important as this new award suggests he is, how is it possible that such work has gone unnoticed and uncelebrated for so long?

To begin at the beginning: Menashe was born in New York City in 1925, placing him squarely in the generation that produced such acknowledged American poets as John Ashbery, Adrienne Rich, James Wright, James Merrill, Denise Levertov, A.R. Ammons, Allen Ginsberg, Barbara Guest, Galway Kinnell, Robert Bly, Gerald Stern, Robert Creeley, Carolyn Kizer, and Donald Justice. Not bad company, and no one can argue that as a generation these poets share a common style or common concerns or write about the same subjects or resemble each other in any significant way, aesthetically or otherwise. So, Menashe's neglect may have nothing to do with uniqueness, per se, the singularity of his style or voice. Others were singular too, distinct and individual. What, then? After serving in World War II where he saw combat in France, Belgium, and Germany, Menashe stayed in Europe to study in London and later at the Sorbonne before publishing his first book, *The Many Named Beloved*, in 1961. Unable to find a publisher in the United States, Menashe turned to Victor Gollancz Ltd., which specialized in the publication of high-quality literature and popular fiction, including science fiction. It was first to publish many famous authors' books, including George Orwell, Daphne du Maurier, and Kingsley Amis. With a foreword by the likes of Kathleen Raine and positive reviews by Robert Graves, Austin Clarke and others, it seems that Menashe was on his way. Strangely, after this first taste of success—nothing. Nothing of any consequence for decades, as far as public accolades go, even as he continued to write. He produced several collections, including *To Open* in 1970, *No Jerusalem But This* in 1971, *Fringe of Fire* in 1973, and even a *Collected Poems* in 1986, published by the National Poetry Foundation before returning to print with *The Niche Narrows* in 2000. The volume of collected poems proves that someone was tracking his progress, whether the wider world of poetry was aware of it or not.

How to account for Menashe's long eclipse, then, that forty-some-odd-year period during which his poems were virtually abandoned by critics and readers alike? Even a preliminary glance at the work in *New and Selected Poems* will begin to suggest an answer, if we consider what was happening in American poetry at the time. Remember the list of his contemporaries whose work was gaining prominence even as Menashe's was diminishing in readership and critical notice. Here is a not untypical poem, chosen at random, which exhibits many of the hallmarks of his style:

ENLIGHTMENT

He walked in awe
In awe of light
At nightfall, not at dawn
Whatever he saw
Receding from sight
In the sky's afterglow
Was what he wanted
To see, to know

Not a bad poem, in general, but the brusque, high-stepping iambics; the use of dimeter—not seen much in any period of poetry in English; the fairly regular rhyming; the retention of capital letters at the beginning of each verse; the syntactical integrity of the lines (only a single enjamb-ment); the oracular tone in comparison to the intimate, confessional tone of most other lyrics at the time; the moral or philosophical weightiness of the thought; the extreme brevity; the ceremoniousness of style; the slightly cryptic, or gnomic suggestiveness apparent in the last two lines: These combine to separate the piece from much of what was being written after the Second World War. The one concession made to contemporary poetics is the relative lack of punctuation, which another member of his generation, W. S. Merwin, was to make not only suitable, but practically conventional from the 1960s onward.

A poem such as "Enlightenment" must have seemed peculiar and awkward to a generation just discovering the deep-image, South American magical realism, "found" poetry, "concrete" poetry, "naked" poetry, and so on, while all the time engaging in further formal and technical experiments. How must Menashe's poetry have struck the Beats, the Black Mountain Poets, the Confessionalists, or those of the New York School? And how could such truncated meters, deeply imbued with a biblical Romanticism, have drawn the attention of the elegant old formalist masters like Richard Wilbur and Anthony Hecht, whose work was more expansive and modernized in subject and tone? It is not, as I have said, a matter of breaking from the pack and forging one's own style. Everyone was forging his or her own style, and there was a plethora of packs, not just one, from which to break free. Even within those packs there was great variation, and no one would have agreed that they belonged to a pack or school anyway. It is not enough to say that Menashe ran counter to his time. This does not explain his subsequent neglect. On the contrary, this is what happens when one runs counter to one's time, not by way of innovation or experiment, but in retrospect—a refusal or inability to accept the onset of the new or to participate in the making and founding of what is contemporary and modern.

This, then, may account in part for Menashe's neglect. But there is another element involved, an element made clear in a cogent and detailed essay by Barry Ahearn, "Poetry and Synthesis: The Art of Samuel Menashe."[2] Considering one of Menashe's untitled early poems—

A flock of little boats
Tethered to the shore
Drifts in still water...
Prows dip, nibbling

Ahearn performs a brilliant act of close reading, perhaps the closest reading possible. He deconstructs this poem with the precision of someone who carefully lays out, one by one, the miniature springs and gears of a tiny watch:

This poem's components are managed impeccably. The poem divides into two, lines 1 and 2 posit a stasis, lines 3 and 4 a dynamic. This effect arises from the disposition of nouns and verbs. Nouns in the first two lines ("flock," "boats," "shore") outnumber those in the last two ("water," "prows"). In contrast, verbs ("drifts," "dip") are pushed to the last two lines, along with the participle ("nibbling"). Furthermore, the stresses fall on the monosyllabic nouns ending lines 1 and 2, but the more fluid lines 3 and 4 end with trochees. This establishes a distinction between firm stress on stable materials (boats, shore) and the wavering stress on liquid (water) and process (nibbling). In terms of imagery, the poem successfully masquerades as a pastoral scene—but on water. With "flock" we are invited to see the little boats as so many aquatic sheep. Vocabulary aids the effect; animation is granted to the boats by virtue of the poem's observation that they drift in "still" water. To the eye, the water seems motionless. The boats therefore appear to be moving of their own volition. The act of observation itself is a covert subject of the poem. It gradually moves to a closer inspection of the scene, with attention shifting from the flock to the prows. This closer inspection of a particular part of the scene coincides with the narrowing in the number of syllables per line: 6, 5, 5, 4.

Menashe, then, writes with a jeweler's loupe, attending to every syllable. This is a lapidary art, Pounds craftsmanship with a vengeance. If that is true, however, to whom exactly is such poetry aimed? The interested, general reading audience, the scholar, the connoisseur, or the professional critic? There is much to be admired in the deft, miniscule perfections of such an art. But other poets—all good poets, in fact—pay attention to poems at the syllabic level as well. Menashe is not unique in this respect. For most poets, however, syllabic considerations and diction are only part of the story, part of the greater context and overall structure of the poem, not its chief focus or primary achievement. It would be difficult to argue that such poetry could ever find itself at the center of mainstream literature, any more than cloisonné, filigree, or the Fabergé egg could ever establish themselves at the center of mainstream art.

This radical compression, this minute subtlety of technique—wonderful as it is—must contribute to the general neglect of Menashe's work. As Ahearn remarks, speaking of the allusiveness in Menashe's work: "Menashe can afford to remove a good deal from his poems, because he leaves the bare number of signals required for us to make connections to other texts … " and goes on to say, "Reading his poetry, therefore, becomes an exercise in sensing how much lurks at the edge of the words." Exercise is the key word here. It's an exercise, I believe, in which most readers will be unwilling to participate. How much effort can readers be expected to make before they give up and go home, out of breath? Donald Davie even worried that Menashe's tendency to condense when revising would make it harder for him to acquire a readership. Harder, but not impossible. Those who love Menashe's work, and are willing to make the effort—including not only Ahearn, but Christopher Ricks, already noted, Stephen Spender, Derek Mahon and, more recently, Rachal Hadas and Dana Gioia—write glowingly of Menashe's ability to atomize language and thought in order to produce poems that are not only fiercely condensed, but belong to the world's long tradition of wisdom literature.

When Ahearn asks if Menashe's poetry represents a high level of accomplishment, why then has he failed to acquire more than the scantiest critical notice, his answers are different than mine and, I think, more cynical. He refers to Menashe's lack of any academic post, the fact that he doesn't belong to a recognizable school of poetry, and that "Menashe seems to have paid the price for being rigorously individual." Perhaps this oversimplifies the case. It smacks of the bitterness in the ongoing literary wars. Who could have been more individual than E. E. Cummings in his time, or Emily Dickinson in hers, yet these poets have garnered legions of fans, and they continue to do so in our time. Who is quirkier, more adamantly himself, than Bill Knott? And whose work is more linguistically driven and word-bound than Heather McHugh? Furthermore, there are successful poets who have never held a proper academic post (they may have taught here and there) or been editors of an important literary magazine—Jack Gilbert and Linda Gregg come to mind—so, other than the quality of their work, they have never been in the position to "exert influence or solicit favors." Not everyone is a literary opportunist, though many are. Too many perhaps for the culture's good.

Still, those who revere Menashe and his work insist upon his status as a maverick and the unsurpassed artistry of his poems. Their praise is specific and unabashedly full. In his introduction to the present volume,

Christopher Ricks sounds much like other exegetes of Menashe's work, extolling Menashe's craftsmanship and the atomic level of attention it takes to really appreciate what he is doing, not only syllable by syllable, but—as Ricks demonstrates—letter by letter. This is poetry brought to the vanishing point of language. How much, at first glance, might a person be able to make out of the following poem:

> A pot poured out
> Fulfills its spout

Another curious fact with respect to Samuel Menashe's work: the poems can feel trivial at first, then profound after the commentator hauls his academic microscope out and reveals to us the swarming, invisible life evident at the sub-word level. Reading such a poem as the one above, a person might think that it is only a step away from "An apple a day / keeps the doctor away," or, slightly more portentous, the old Puritan saw: "In Adam's fall / We sinned all." But, Ricks contends, Menashe is no mere aphorist or maker of epigrams (the same way Ahearn concedes that, while Menashe owes a debt to imagism, he "moves beyond" it). Ricks describes this as "A minimalist maxim," and goes on to say:

> The poem fulfills itself, just so. How perfectly the verb
> "fulfills" fulfills the promise of a generous thought. A
> promise, a mission, an obligation, a nature: these are
> the kinds of things that it is possible and desirable to
> fulfill... where exactly does it emanate from, this sense
> that the poem, too, is no less full for being so happy
> to give itself entirely away?... When attending to
> Menashe's poems Donald Davie found himself de-
> scending the scale of units, from verse-line to word to
> foot to syllable... Why not then to the very letter? For
> Menashe has something of Lucretius's cosmic comic
> pleasure in the thought that the atoms that constitute

all that is physical are also the letters that constitute all
that is verbal: elementa. Menashe's art pours together
the elementary and the elemental. See how the word
pot pours itself out into "poured out." See how, fulfilled
but not done with, the word is poured forth again: pot
living again within "spout."

Ingenious? No doubt. It takes a focused, alert mind to ferret out such minutiae. But Ricks is not through. There are even more subtle linguistic points to be made:

But these are not the only fulfillments: how fluidly "out"
is taken up, without damage or distortion, effortlessly
within "spout." Not just *le mot juste*, but *la letter juste*.
For Menashe (mindful that he is grateful to Britain for
first publishing a book of his, as it had done for Robert
Frost) has pointed out that his is precisely an American
poem. British English, in adopting the spelling "fulfils,"
would forfeit the full acknowledgment of the word "fills"
that American English proffers so calmly in "fulfills."

It is often difficult to distinguish between Menashe's brilliance and that of his critics. Certainly, his deftness and uncanny wit compel our respect. But can any poet consistently demand such ravenous attention to detail and still expect his work to have the kind of wide-ranging appeal it takes to win and hold a large and loyal audience over time? I am not suggesting that a poet ought to pander to the lowest common denominator of taste, treating readers as if they were incapable of appreciating subtle literary techniques or delicate effects. Far from it. Only that, if his critics are to be believed, the difficulty involved in Menashe's work is of another order altogether. It is difficulty doubled by concentration, imagination packed into a matchbox. Difficulty has always been a problem in modern poetry. From the beginning there have been accusations of impenetrableness and obscurity. But there is a vast difference between the expansive, generous allusiveness of "The Waste Land" and the confined, pressurized, almost fastidious complexity of Menashe's work. These poems are complex in a very special way: the poem as microchip, as Rubik's Cube.

Given the situation, then, I suspect that Menashe, like the poets mentioned above—Loy, Kees, and Bunting—will continue to fall into neglect, only to be rediscovered by coteries of devoted critics and fans every few decades or so, then to fall back into neglect when they fail to reach a wider audience, to be rediscovered again by a new generation of poets a few decades later, and so on. Their work deserves notice, but it is so specialized, so attuned to particular obsessions and the more complicated pleasures of technique that it may never take its place firmly at the center of the canon. Such poets exist in a twilit historical space, a limbo between oblivion and full renown. It is an immortality of sorts, but a frustrating niche to inhabit. Their work is simply too good to forget, yet too difficult in the end to prosper.

13

Does Postmodern Poetry "Work?":

A Review of Spencer Short's *Tremolo*

Snappy, self-conscious, whimsical, brash—Spencer Short's poems exemplify all the lessons learned by a younger generation of poets at the hands of the first wave of postmodernist writers—especially John Ashbery and the so-called New York School. Such poems, we have come to expect, are dodgy, elliptical, random, and committed solely to their own inwardness and whimsical sense of language. They thrive on illogical shifts, grammatical cul-de-sacs. The Self, highly suspect of course, is banished, a mere servant of the reprehensible Ego. Emotion is embarrassing. Memory a synonym for nostalgia. Most notably, postmodernist poems like this play hide-and-seek with substance, contriving to avoid—at all costs—that moment when language inevitably tends toward syntactical coherence and meaning.

In a blurb on the back cover of *Tremolo*[1], Billy Collins—who chose this book for the National Poetry Series—proclaims: "He [Short] lifts his reader far above the dreary fields of subject matter." Meaning, one must suppose, the poems' virtue lies in the fact that they are not about anything in particular, or perhaps anything at all. That would require a certain belief in the mind's ability to apprehend definable truth, an intentionality postmodernism emphatically rejects. Instead, Collins continues, Short's poems convey the reader "into an ionosphere of verbal surprise and insightful play." Playfulness is abundantly displayed, to be sure, often leading to surprising metaphors and combinations of words. But the term "insightful" implies subject matter. What else can one be insightful about but a subject?

Here are excerpts from a typical poem—typical of one kind of Short poem—that begins with a line taken from Berryman's Dream Songs

SWEDES DON'T EXIST, SCANDINAVIANS IN
GENERAL DO NOT EXIST

> & it's the truth innit? Seasons agog w/
> their slow dissociation, despair tramping its genera
> on the rusty fire-escape & all night we
> drift through the city as through
> the corridors of expendable wealth—

And so on and on. One poem of this kind is as good as another for illustration because, as Mark Levine puts it (in another blurb adorning the back cover of Short's book), "the mechanical effusions of postmodern style" are easily generated out of a lack of subject matter. If, as Robert Frost quipped, writing free verse is "like playing tennis with the net down," then writing the postmodern poem further dispenses with the ball. The postmodern poet shows up in white shorts and sneakers, holding a racquet—but that's about as far as it goes. No challenge, no game, no outcome. Only an allusion to these, a lot of posing coquettishly for the camera. Later in the same poem Short writes:

>   — the news
> reconfigured us like a haircut,
> touched us like a *sense sublime*. Pshaw-pshaw
> sluice the black cabs past the rain-soaked
> carports & for 4 yrs. I lived only for the radio

It's the very arbitrariness of this kind of postmodern poem that begins to wear one down. Why not "the news / reconfigured us like a facelift" (or "tea leaves," or "a fisheye lens")? Again, the lack of subject matter allows for interchangeable metaphors because true metaphor is connected, at its root, to the core meaning of a poem. Break that connection—or dispense with it—and anything goes. This is not the same thing as freedom. It is artistic anarchy. The results of such an approach are inevitably meaningless and superficial. But who cares! This poetry is so much fun:

> "O Delores who sleeps just so,
> arms crossed, a crux, sheets tossed:
> I fear everything & am afraid of nothing.
> The yard is electric. Mail the coupon today."

This is the end of the poem excerpted above. It is the final disjunction, or set of disjunctions, that represent one of the most salient features of postmodernist technique—the omnipresence of non-sequitur. It is not the same thing as Robert Bly's notion of "leaping" in poetry. "Leaping" implies association, connection, even if it occurs over a considerable gap in the logical sequence of thought. Connection, that is, to the outspoken or implied subject of the poem. The wildest poem by Lorca or Vallejo still revolves around a subject. It is not arbitrary. There is no sense of Lorca's lines—or Vallejo's, or Bly's for that matter—being blurted out indiscriminately.

Another prevalent feature of postmodernist verse is paradox. Consider the interesting line above: "I fear everything & am afraid of nothing." As the following entry on paradox in *A Dictionary of Literary, Dramatic, and Cinematic Terms* by Barnet, Berman, and Burto clearly demonstrates, paradox has long been a staple of the best poetry:

> Paradox. Usually a statement or situation that seems—
> but need not be—self-contradictory. When in one of
> his "Holy Sonnets" John Donne wishes his proud spirit
> broken so that he may achieve salvation, he appeals
> to God paradoxically; "That I may rise and stand,
> o'erthrow me."[2]

The difference between Donne's use of paradox and Short's is immediately apparent. Short's comment doesn't just seem self-contradictory. It is self-contradictory. No deeper truth or meaning emerges from it upon closer inspection. It's only a trick, a simple rhetorical inversion. But when we contemplate Donne's statement, we see that—clearly—it only seems contradictory, but in fact reveals a deeper truth about the process of Christian salvation.

Literary paradox is not inconsistent, but ultimately logical, a traditional functional element in poems. The postmodernist program, by contrast, revels in nonsense. That is to say, non-sense, darting quickly away from any pretense of knowledge or "truth." Truth is suspect, a chimera, like the so-called "Self" that pretends to possess it. So for the postmodernist poet, paradox remains empty, mere self-contradiction. Like disjunction or dissociation, paradox in the postmodernist's hands is finally just another technique, a way to short-circuit the inevitable tendency of language in its drift towards meaning.

What if these poems do revolve around subjects, as Mark Levine claims in his blurb? According to Levine, Short's poems reveal "symptoms of anxiety and yearning" (*despair tramping its genera / on the rusty fire-escape*). And why not? I'm convinced that such symptoms might be found here and there among the poems if searched for diligently enough. And scraps and glimpses of other subjects, as well, as many as the reader might care to project. The postmodernist poet avoids a single viable interpretation in favor of multiple interpretations. Postmodernist poems are prisms through which many possible meanings pass and are refracted, bending the reader's mind back upon itself. Here is a true poetry of indeterminacy. The poem seems to ask: you want me to mean this? OK. You want me to mean that? OK, too. One does not observe the objective world, in a postmodernist poem, but one's own mind in the act of interpreting the poem. The real world, whatever it is, may never be seen.

And that must be the ultimate rationale for postmodernist poetry. To be intractable and indeterminate, noncommittal, coyly mysterious. To mean all things to all people at all times, and yet mean nothing in particular. This is a poetry for the cynical and self-indulgent, a literature preening itself before the mirror of theory. And yet Spencer Short is not completely without talent. At any moment, in poems or parts of poems, Short may transcend himself and write something inventive and meaningful, if only tentatively so. This is the case with the following poem, somewhat enigmatically titled:

IT WILL BUT SHAKE AND TOTTER

Many poems have been written about the turgid sea.
For instance: The one about the man and his lover on the cliffs above
    the turgid sea.
It is the English Channel
& he is Matthew Arnold in 1851.
Across from him: "ignorant armies," "clashing by night."

The armies are not French.
They might be stars if what we've always thought of as stars
turned out to be the fading chalk of a fading language,
turned out to be nothing but the small sparks of rocks
being struck by chains in the corners of the sky.

Like a Russian novel the sea roils & cedes, roils & cedes.
Fish do their fish-like work among its atavistic depths.
Notice how the moonlight glisters like lacquer
between the crests & troughs, the smell of the brine,
the heavy, salt-stung air.

All night the moon rings and rings.
All night the wind searches the cliffs for a flag,
a kite, a woman's hat.

Love, I say, let us be true. Let us be.
The world is but a darkling plain. A hill of beans.
We are the few & the far between.

Here Short achieves something rarely experienced in his other work—precisely because the poem has a subject (our absolute unimportance in the universe) and most everything is connected to that subject, no matter how discursive it may get along the way. Breezy, prosaic, the first stanza sets the situation up with little loss of energy or time. In the second stanza—the most associative—Short ventures out imaginatively farther than it was possible for Matthew Arnold 150 years ago: chaos and obscurity, for someone at the end of the twentieth century, exist in more than worldly events (personal tragedy or political upheaval) but in the greater enigma of the non-human world, the vast cosmos we have come to discover beyond our understanding. Not armies, but gigantic exploding stars provide symbols of appalling violence, a kind of language the mind cannot begin to interpret. And stars, no matter how immense and powerful, are still only "sparks" tossed off by "rocks / being struck by chains in the corners of the sky."

But Short, wisely, brings the poem back to earth in the third stanza, finding cosmic emblems in the sea, with its "atavistic depths," and the moonlight which "glisters like lacquer" on the waves. Like Frost before him, he can recognize unsettling evidence of desert places right here at home. The relaxed tone of the opening stanza has completely disappeared, along with any impulse Short might have had to entertain us with poetic inanities. Except for a slight miscalculation, one of those verbal jokes we have come to expect from postmodern authors (the moon has rings, so maybe it rings and rings like a telephone?), the subject has gotten serious. If this were a real postmodernist poem, we might expect the ending—which parallels the ending of "Dover Beach"—to be flip, ironic, quirky, a perfect moment to pull the rug out from under the weight of emotion that has accumulated. Instead, Short plays it straight, offering a haunting image of nature void of humanity: "All night the wind searches the cliffs for a flag, / a kite, a woman's hat." Then he paraphrases Arnold's famous line, "Ah, love, let us be true / to one another!" by stripping it of its nineteenth century romantic tone: "Love, I say, let us be true." and adds, as if in desperation: "Let us be." Another paraphrase of Arnold follows: "The world is but a darkling plain" to which Short adds what might, in another poem, be a superficial postmodern quip: "A hill of beans." But here, because the poem has accumulated so much darkness, the phrase rings like gallows humor, a smirk of pathos. The final line resounds ominously: humanity is "few" and whatever spots of life exist in other parts of the universe are "far between."

"It Will But Shake And Totter" is a clever take off of "Dover Beach." There are many other places in *Tremolo* where Short achieves something interesting. Images like "Lloyd shoots pool like he's standing / in a puddle being prodded with live wires" or "the moon drifts, a pink egg in a big / jar" or "the yard percolating with crickets" lodge in the mind, enter-taining at least in their freshness. It's not in the particulars or local effects that this poetry fails, when it fails, but in the permission Short too often gives himself to ramble and spout indiscriminately, trying the patience of even the most devoted reader:

> The blackbird eclipse reworked as beauty
> mark. In the eye of the beholder. Must
> be fully described/Must exhaust its own
> significance: Thusly March licks a last
> salt from its body & like a boy blown
> on a bridge over the busy thruway
> a new world opens redolent with? Fear?
> If spring comes now will it ever again?
> The boy is undone. Reworked as————.

There is a lot of pizzazz in *Tremolo*, moments of passing insight and ver-bal fun. But that is not enough. "Surprise and play" are not enough. Wit alone cannot make up for lack of substance, lack of depth. Judgment and discipline are required as well—those somber chaperones. Cleverness and wit can be virtues in poetry, of course (see Shakespeare, see Pope), but not if that is all there is.

14

Good Poetry Never Ages:

A Review of

The Captain of the Butterflies

by Cees Nooteboom

Some poems are unreadable. Others one reads out of a sense of duty and therefore with some effort. But some are irresistible. They compel you to stop whatever else you are doing and pay attention. This is the case with *The Captain of the Butterflies*, the first collection of poetry by Dutch novelist Cees Nooteboom, translated into English by Leonard Nathan and Herlinde Spahr. Though published more than a decade ago, the book is worth revisiting. Rereading it is a lesson on how good poetry never ages.

A surrealist, Nooteboom sees the everyday physical world with one eye and the hidden, mysterious, abstract world with the other. This double-vision serves him well in poem after poem, reminding us of how divided consciousness is, or may become. The firm, sparkling, manifest world of order and quotidian ritual floats perilously on an ocean of impenetrable depths, an abyss the human mind cannot fathom. Nooteboom peers through the surface-sparkle of phenomena to apprehend the movements of this shadowy world, a world both threatening and beautiful, where intuition and hunch are better guides—and more reliable guardians—than reason. The ancient role of poetry has always been just this: to glimpse the sacred through the profane and bring news of that other existence back to us in oracle and song.

One of the first poems in the book demonstrates this admirably:

THE POEM OF DEATH

Along the cold thought of the moon
the light drifts
the wings of the birds are brilliantly painted

this is the poem of death
which begs and tumbles
in the long drawn arches of the evening,
nobody hears it.

nobody hears it, such winged sounds
fly right by the saints
silent, and stuck in the sand,
they are immobile in the drought.

on the hollow path
the painted birds.
in the carved white night
the enchanted voice.
among the swaying trumpets of the angels
those in masks whisper

a house is no house
a thing is no thing
life does not exist.

The poem restores an imbalance between the two primary realities: life and death. As far as death is concerned, life hardly exists; it is so tentative and short. How can life—with its frail houses and hallucinatory things—make any claim towards ontological value or importance? Viewed from the perspective of death, life is illusory, fleeting, utterly negligible. A thing of little substance and staying power flickering across the dying mind. Death, on the other hand, is eternal. Life withers to a "cold thought" drifting across the face of the moon. The poem of death, the "enchanted voice," cannot be heard by human beings, not even by those entrusted with our spiritual welfare. Religion is a human "thing." The saints are "silent, and stuck in the sand" of limited human perception, "they are immobile in the drought" of human ignorance and error. And even when we get to see the angels, those who really know, they are wearing masks—so we can't see them completely either. The poem both reveals and discreetly obscures final knowledge, which after all can never be apprehended.

The poems in *The Captain of the Butterflies* are haunted by the reality of death and night and our impotence in the face of them. Another poem, "In Memoriam Leo L.," opens with a startling image of Nooteboom's friend, to whom this elegy is addressed, curled up in a hospital bed awaiting his end:

> Only a week ago
> like a fetus in bed.
> Real eyes. Real nails...

The smile of this dying invalid is "a lock," something which cannot be accessed or deciphered. When the dying turn fully towards death, the living may no longer communicate with them. Whatever expressions their faces wear are enigmatic to those who stand around their beds, mourning. Again, the ineffectuality of religion for Nooteboom is stressed in no uncertain terms:

> Tomorrow the dance
> of the odd priest
> Latin shaman
> without magic

Once the forms and rituals that console those left behind have been accomplished, the dying may truly leave this world of houses and things, saints and ghostly insubstantial moons:

only then the fire
of inaudible voices,
the eternal tracks

toward home.

Repeatedly we are reminded of the failure of religion in dealing effectively with absolute reality—or perhaps, a plurality of realities. In another poem, the gods simply sleep "in their gold-lacquered beds...wild and useless in their loneliness." These are the old gods of the Greeks and the Romans, gods of Egypt and Mesopotamia. But they represent any gods, really, from any civilization at any epoch. The poem ends, "...a thousand years the gods sleep and then, another thousand / dreaming the merciful salt of death."

For Nooteboom's "Captain of the Butterflies", "reality is the greatest contagion." The self is "...established in its solitude / like a shipwreck cast in bronze." "There is nothing pretty about these poems," Nooteboom asserts, and we understand he refers to their otherworldly, non-human character. No sentiment. No easy consolation. Only the self-alienation of human consciousness without its customary mask, without the protective layer of myths, rituals, and fond dreams with which we surround ourselves in order to survive. It's as though the blanket of ozone around our planet was burned away, once and for all, and we stand naked in a deadly stream of solar rays: the final illumination.

All religions prohibit looking directly at the gods. Rilke knows he couldn't survive even in the presence of an angel, that he would "shrivel... next to its greater existence." Even everyday reality, if we could truly apprehend it, would probably drive us mad. Nooteboom describes the shattered self in unsettling terms: "someone, somebody scattered, / the uncollected persona / in converse with himself, dreaming and thinking / present, invisible." In many ways, then, these are troubling poems. At least those in the first section, "Self and Others," that depict the dissolution of identity, the core of the individuated personality: "Midday of glittering hours / that will not fit together, / and himself cut up by himself / sitting in various chairs / with almost everywhere a soul or body."

Nooteboom observes that "no hand…controls all this," emphasizing the chaotic nature of such an existence, akin to the harrowing pathology of schizophrenia.

The poems in the second section, "Travels and Visions," extend Nooteboom's method of intense penetration to cities, sites, and landscapes around the world. Nooteboom sees not what the tourist sees, but the inner reality of a place, the ethos of a landscape, its hidden character compacted of history, culture, nature, and geography. So, in Arcadia, Greece, he senses "the shepherds of noon" and hears "crickets argue for death / urns of annihilation." In Bogotá, "the rooster is beaten a third time / because in the dark he saw the light." At Mt. Fuji, Nooteboom observes that "all of Japan hangs on it like a gondola full of dreams / which it lifts and cherishes and carries along / through the sky / beyond the tract of time." The least successful poems in this section are anthropomorphic persona poems in which the speaker is a rock, a plant, the sun, the sea. Perhaps this is because personification is too familiar a poetic technique to draw the reader in easily.

Section III comprises several poems that meditate on the nature of poetry and the poet's art. In "The Page on the Lily," the poet

> …sits there posturing on the edge of his grave
> and listens to the gulping of time
> in the poem across from him,
> the never-to-be-grasped.

In "Golden Fiction," Nooteboom refers to the poet as a "traitor," ostensibly because he doesn't live life, but merely sits apart in his study to record it:

> The traitor sits in his room and writes it down.
> Out of which lives does he write? Which time?
> Will the real life ever come to him
> and take him with it?

No it will never take him with it.
The traitor sits in his room and writes
what the voices tell him to write.

In "Homer on Ithaca," the essential poet is described—separate, dreaming alone, eyes blind to anything but the inward drama of Imagination. The poet is steward of memory, time's amanuensis, slave to the Muse which bids him "Sing!"

The book's final section includes poems about the mind's ability, or non-ability, to grasp ultimate truth. Throughout, Nooteboom's poems are seeded with references to locks, seals, distances, space, blindness, and invisibility, all terms that indicate our inadequacy for discovering what is hidden or secret, what cannot be easily revealed—or revealed at all. The attempt to illuminate even a tiny fraction of reality requires Herculean imaginative and intellectual effort over years, often centuries, and by the most perspicacious minds available. This is best presented in Nooteboom's poem, "Grail," which is worth quoting in its entirety:

Remember the time
that we were searching for something,
something quite precise,
a concept, paraphrase, definition,
a summa of what we did not know,
something we wished
to assume or measure or tally
between all things obscure?
You know, don't you know
how we always wandered off, dividing
the concept and the quest,
Augustine the brothels, Albert the Numbers,
Jorge the mirrors, Immanuel home, Pablo the forms,
Wolfgang the colors,
Teresa, Blaise, Friedrich, Leonardo, Augustus,
always tallying and measuring between words and notes,

> thinking
> among nuns, soldiers and poets,
> breaking, looking, splitting,
> till the bones, the shadow,
> a glimmer, a narrowing down
> in senses or images,
> until in a glass or a number
> but always so briefly
> a hiccup of a thought, of a way,
> so endlessly vague became visible.

All that vast effort to arrive finally at the mere "hiccup of a thought," something so small and frail that—once again—human effort is portrayed as negligible, the entire history of ideas as insubstantial as a flicker of light. All things remain, essentially, obscure. The human mind is continually defeated in its effort to grasp even the edges of ultimate truth.

Throughout this review I have used phrases like "absolute reality," "the sacred and the profane," "ultimate truth," and so forth. I have referred to "the hidden, mysterious, abstract world" as if such a thing were to be taken for granted. But many will find such ideas merely romantic, a naïve throwback to obsolete theories about poets and the poetic art. In the *New Princeton Encyclopedia of Poetry and Poetics*, the editors describe the poet, in part, in the following way:

> Some cultures make a formal distinction between the
> sacred and the profane; others do not. In those that do,
> the poet has a public and sacral status as the conveyor of
> wisdom and knowledge of a very high order. In those that
> do not, however—which includes all modern Western
> industrial societies—the poet can present only knowledge
> that is personal and private, appealing to his or her readers,
> in essence, to judge for themselves whether or not the
> knowledge and experience described is not also their own.[2]

Not many people would argue with such an assessment of poetry and poets in contemporary society. That there has been a diminishment of value, a contraction of cultural cachet and influence with regard to the poet, is hardly deniable. Confessionalism, with all its limitations, is the result of a thoroughly discredited Romanticism. Yet, a poet like Nooteboom gives us pause: Is it possible that, regardless of how the contemporary world views them, poets of real vision and insight, poets who can speak with ancient, oracular authority, exist and do their work uninhibited by an almost universal disregard? This idea may seem romantic, a kind of Harry Potter idea of poets operating secretly within the stifling milieu of suburban, bourgeois society.

Yet here, at the opening of the twenty-first century, it is not so clear that the sacred has been so easily defeated, so completely relegated and cast side during the nineteenth and twentieth centuries. Seemingly endless, festering religious conflicts—with more and bigger ones on the horizon—make us question whether the sacred might not be staging a comeback, whether the ascendancy of the profane in a scientific and rational age may not ultimately prove a chimera, something which seemed undeniable for a time until time reversed itself. No one would welcome back an age of superstition. But the poet's otherworldliness is not religious so much as intuitive, imaginative, psychological. What has been "sacred" to the poet of the modern era is not the received doctrine of organized religions, but the realm of the subconscious, and even deeper— the unconscious—where important human truths and realities may lie. More than personal, but less than absolute, such truth involves the very meaning of human consciousness and being. It all depends on how you define the sacred, and what we can possibly know—or guess at—with the limited instrument of the human mind.

Poets like Nooteboom operate within the territory of the mythic and archetypal. It is almost impossible to read Nooteboom and feel he is presenting "only knowledge that is personal and private." The images cast up for examination feel more universal than that, more unsettling but familiar, more like our own shadowy imaginings and doubts, our own fears and dreams. It has been said, "A myth is a public dream, while a dream is a private myth." Nooteboom, it would seem, is someone with a powerful enough imagination to dream for us all. To confine the substance and meaning of his poems to personal and private knowledge would feel not only like a misjudgment of his real achievement, but a betrayal of his gift—the gift of these penetrating, revelatory poems.

15

Exuding Gold:

Cracking Open Bill Knott's

Plaza de Loco[1]

Wallace Stevens has written somewhere that all true poetry is experimental poetry. He meant, I suppose, that true poetry—authentic poetry—is inherently original. It does not *aspire* to originality, it is original at its core, its source, which is the poet's own unique sensibility. All other poetry, no matter how well written, is more or less derivative. It falls short of what only the true poet can achieve. This is a rigorous criterion for poetry, severe in its expectations and demands. But when it attains this high ideal, we know it.

Knott is a true contortionist of verse—like Berryman or cummings—twisting words, grammar, and syntax everywhichway to wring the last possible drop of meaning out of a phrase. And meaning is central to Knott's poetic ambitions. No matter how convoluted and oblique, it is apparent that Knott's poems aren't meant to hide or deflect meaning but to illuminate it. It is, finally, our perspective that is being wrenched to allow us to regard reality in a new and surprising light. This is mind-bending verse: one feels oneself (almost physically) being forced by the imaginative logic in these poems. The experience is a bit disorienting, and not a little exhilarating:

STORY OF OR

to Pauline Réage

To pose nakedness is
To refute it. A pose

Is a clothes. Like
Stanzaic arrangements of

The word which should
Ideally be in pain against
Its w and its d. No slack
Is why such heaves of or

To denude itself could
Make us exude gold, yet when
Was that ever opposite enough

What scream or epigram
This sperm has come
To measure our mouths for.

Like all of Knott's work, "Story of Or" is radically condensed, its materials compressed to generate manifold possibilities. But Knott follows this, on the same page, with a companion poem masquerading as prose:

> Note:
> For "or" to free itself from "word," it must strain
> ("heave") against the "w" and the "d" that enclose
> it. If, via this strenuous (perhaps squeamish)
> process, the meaning of "or" is transmuted from
> the English into the French as a sort of homage
> to the pseudonymous author of 'Story of O' (*Histoire
> d'O*), then, alchemically speaking, (or so an Aurealist
> might suggest) it will have risen from the pose of
> its measures to or-emerge as an else-gasm.

Detractors might dismiss the above as mere whimsy. But, some serious issues about language and reality are at stake here. To begin with, Knott makes an assertion about exhibitionism as opposed to real openness and disclosure. Projecting an image of self is not the same thing as revealing self. Those women, unfurled out of the middle of men's magazines, are not "naked" in any true sense. Air-brushed, coifed, powdered, lipsticked, glistening through filters and self-consciously posed, they present—not themselves—but a fantasy image of themselves. In Knott's terms, they refute nakedness and might as well be wearing clothes for all we can see of their actual human reality: not revelation, but illusion is the result of such manipulation of our senses.

Knott quickly finds an analog in poetry, which turns the poem in another direction: formal arrangements of language—stanzas, lines, metaphors, typographical shapes—can also be a pose, a self-conscious arrangement of words that has little connection to our everyday experience of language. Most poetry is language gussied-up to project an alluring image—the verbal constructs we call "poetry." But Knott is looking for the naked essence of language which can only be found by splitting words open (trading alchemy for physics), as if they were atoms waiting to release devastating hidden energies. When this happens, words "exude gold," which is to say: real poetry. The "or" (ore) embedded in w(or)ds emerges translated into the French "or," which means "gold." What results is language as basic—as visceral—as a scream, as contracted as an epigram, a kind of "sperm" that measures (considers or fits) our mouths in order to utter new truths. Truth is one kind of explosion, and the rawness of experience unmediated by the strategies of language and the mind.

To crack words open, then, is Knott's project: his poetic ambition. Yet, with typical irony, Knott's word-splitting manifesto is itself presented in a very formal arrangement of language: the stanzas, lines, and images he seems to be denouncing as potential elements of poetic illusion. But to crack things open—whether it be atoms or words—requires force, pressure, and pressure in poetry is supplied by form. "No slack" is what allows words to "exude gold." Knott is no agitator for a freer, wilder outpouring of poetry, no dervish flinging poems out in a mindless frenzy, but a deliberate craftsman bearing down on his materials in order to liberate the secret shapes of beauty and truth they contain. Scratch any great experimentalist and you will find a traditionalist—someone who has mastered traditional forms and uses them to create a new poetic idiom. Concealed in one of cummings' linguistic and typographical odd-ities—like the imprint of an ancient fern—we find a perfect sonnet; behind Berryman's seemingly improvised stanzas we detect the six-line strophe of Yeats.

Here's a backwards sonnet—unrhymed, but metered—in which Knott reverses the normal order of the form by starting with the couplet usually reserved for the end:

BECKON GONE

Now I see they put the world together
at an angle that goes wrong to the earth.

Tables and chairs have a density in this,
flawed beyond all hopes of wood. The wind
rivering through the bare branches gathers
their withering rather than my growth.

Shadow sutured to the eventual skin of
our ascendance, your swami crannies
fail me. Amadeus, Amadeus,
the sky calls. Beckon gone, go, go on home—

Nothing blunts my perfume as I become,
as I attempt to exude from within
the most faintly effigy I can. North
of birthfants, south of deathdults, where am I?

And here's another sonnet—rhymed this time—in which Knott reveals something unforeseen about the form: The traditional quatrains may be transformed into triplets rather neatly and still retain the nature of a con-ventional sonnet. There is even—semantically and grammatically (the first nine lines form a single sentence)—the slight sense of a volta, and a dramatic pause before delivering the conclusion of the final couplet:

HERE ARE THE HEIRS OF HARVEST

The lunatic walls that hide in front of love
Are right to hide, though the eye tries to find them
More undercover than the skull above

Which the face finds your face, to coffer share
A suffice of yes, an enough of no:
Is that still credible in the morning where

(Pillowjam/bedbutter spread, shed behind drapes)
Our distance occurs, our demarcation
Destinations are aimed at a landscape.

Immured by dawns, the horizon trusts
Only the space we vacate, plotting to rear
An inherent figure, no longer us—

That which waits concealed will yield our founding place.
We must paint the house with what its grounds waste.

Though written in Knott's crabbed, notational style, it's easy enough to pick out the echoes: "A suffice of yes, an enough of no" is straight out of cummings, while "That which waits concealed will yield our founding place" is unmistakably Shakespearean. Such moments emphasize how Knott's outlandish experiments are firmly rooted in tradition. But for the most part, this is pure Knott: gymnastic, near-impenetrable, wound tighter than copper wire on a coil. If real poetry "communicates before it is understood," as Eliot averred, then we must be careful to keep all our receptors in good working order if we are to detect the subliminal messages these poems emit.

Finally, a poem must be understood—not merely intuited. Its full force must be felt, and this requires a conversion of the subliminal into conscious apprehension. How hard can the reader be expected to work? In poem after poem Knott challenges us to be pliable, attentive, patient, willing to follow the contortions of his logic, to "stretch" our imaginations in the old sense even as we decipher the highly condensed meaning of his phrases. How does he do this? By "loading each rift with ore" (we're back to gold). There's hardly a line, a single word or syllable that hasn't been carefully considered, shaped, and polished to fit exactly into its determined place. These poems scintillate with verbal energy. A selection of representative lines makes this clear:

> "From gaze-and-gone, that mine-or-yours is where
> I remember us..."

> "The birch-upsurge of a sapling
> separates my buttocks..."

> "May vidsnaps and ground zeroes grow on their graves."

> "Am I similar to slime enough, be-
> Mimic with muck?"

Such taut, self-conscious phrase-making reminds one of Dylan Thomas's equally terse inventions—and they can be every bit as enigmatic. Some may argue that they are too arcane. But one can hardly argue that they are predictable or boring, or the mere superficial linguistic nonsense of language verse. Meaning inheres in these lines the way emotion inheres in staves of music: a seamless coalescing.

Other lines are clearer, more direct and arresting in their playfulness:

> "The way a ballerina boards a gunboat..."

> "A dead dog in the bottom of my pram..."

> "According to the Dictionary of / Glossolalia..."

> "Only a fishhook can play Hamlet adequately—"

Still other lines haunt with the beauty of their rhythm, sound, and imagery:

"I am that serene derided echo / known as form..."

"Now, while memory disciplines the occasion..."

"... even the sea lay / in stills of inertia..."

"Failure has surrounded me with flesh..."

One need only compare this to the proliferation of flat, loose-jointed, amorphous verse in order to appreciate Knott's classical ear for organizing shapely and effective language and making it "exude gold." For many poets, writing in prosy, free-verse forms is (still) enough to qualify as modern or experimental. Real avant-garde verse, however, doesn't simply abandon the classical. It transfigures it into something unexpected and strange, liberating a new beauty from the old.

Consider the following by Thomas Hardy, a visionary poem about what we now know as DNA, but which Hardy intuited as a persistent tendency in human beings to replicate essential, distinguishing features:

HEREDITY

I am the family face;
Flesh perishes, I live on,
Projecting trait and trace
Through time to times anon,
And leaping from place to place
Over oblivion.

The years-heired feature that can
In curve and voice and eye
Despise the human span

Of durance—that is I;
The eternal thing in man,
That heeds no call to die.

How would such a theme be handled by a poet today, with all the advanced knowledge of heredity we've gained through bio-technical research? What new language, metaphors, and images might be employed to update this theme, transfiguring it into something unexpected and strange, revealing new beauty? The following poem by Bill Knott answers these questions:

SENTENCE

Since the sentence of my head,
punctuated by ears for commas
and eyebrows dashes, eyes
and so forth, nose, or as

the period the mouth merely
paraphrases those features
everyone must compose in order
to parse it, why does my neck

hold it so studiously
close—so marked and ready—for
my body to peruse: to read

what? an Nth-generation xerox
evolving toward Neanderthal;
a fossil-legible face; a scrawl.

I don't mean to imply that Knott read Hardy's poem (or anyone else's poem on this theme) and set out consciously to "update" it. I only mean to show how a contemporary, up-to-date poet transmutes classical forms and themes as a matter of course by some natural (and thereafter cultivated) instinct of renewal—gained through a lifetime of attentiveness and hard work. Knott isn't *trying* to be modern and avant-garde; he *is* modern and avant-garde. Think of Pound congratulating Eliot on having "modernised" himself without the aid of contemporary models. For poets at the beginning of this century, it must have seemed that Eliot appeared out of nowhere, but we know better. After studying and absorbing the work of the past, Knott has taken the best features of postmodernist verse and made of them the basis for a seminal poetry.

The problem with much of Knott's verse is that its elements are so pressurized and distilled—so shorn of all but the quintessential—they can feel encrypted. How far can logic bend before it breaks? And how much tension can language stand when it is torqued down to the level of syllable and letter, yet still be expected to yield meaning? One is often defeated, reading these poems, by the sheer effort of concentration required. Some lines sound more like stutters ("My pencil-popped oh tweezers species sex") or brain teasers ("time truer to one's due self than you") than discrete, meaningful lines of poetry. At such times one is tempted to renounce Knott's poems as gibberish, "the ruins of great intentions" as Pound said of D. H. Lawrence's poems at the beginning of this century. But as Pound was wrong—on the whole—so would we be wrong to judge Knott's work as rubbish. It may not always be easy to discern what Knott is up to, but whatever he is doing there is too much brilliance in it to summarily turn away.

16

The Shameless,
Absurdist Poetry of Russell Edson's
The Rooster's Wife

In a review of the collection of short stories, *Bacacay*, by Polish novelist, Witold Gombrowicz, Thomas D'Adamo quotes Gombrowicz himself, from the preface to his absurdist fiction, *Pornografia*:

> Man, tortured by his mask, fabricates secretly, for his
> own usage as sort of "subculture": a world made out
> of the refuse of a higher world of culture, a domain
> of trash, immature myth, inadmissible passions…
> a secondary domain of compensation. That is
> where a certain shameful poetry is born, a certain
> uncompromising beauty.[1]

D'Adamo goes on to comment further on Gombrowicz's writing:

> No carefully plotted clockworks these, each story obeys
> an internal logic as unique as its creator's fingerprints.
> Rebellion against the infantilization wrought by the
> tyranny of cultural forms and norms is a persistent theme
> throughout Gombrowicz's work. In most cases, rebellion
> expresses itself in fetishes or bizarre ritual behaviors.

Here he might as well be describing the poetry of Russell Edson, which makes full use of fetish, bizarre ritual behaviors, and a strange internal logic that often leads to poems of weird, uncompromising beauty.

Circular logic is one of Edson's specialties, and he employs it in a variety of ingenious ways. The results are disorienting, like an M. C. Escher drawing where bridges or stairways double back on themselves until we understand there is no beginning or end. This is accomplished in poetry by following an idea to its ultimate conclusion, or lack of conclusion, as in "The Hollow Pig,"[2] where a butcher eviscerates a pig into which he wants to crawl to make a pig costume (don't ask why) and is concerned about what he will do with the pig's intestines. He could "hollow out" another pig, of course, and put them there, but then what to do with the intestines of the second pig? Hollow out a third, and so forth, until he has hollowed out all the pigs in the world—but what to do with the intestines of the last pig? It is simply not possible, in Edson's world, to ask why the butcher can't destroy the intestines of the first pig, or why he must worry about what to do with the pig's intestines at all. Once the question has been posed, it must be pursued with maniacal purpose, as though to avoid the question altogether would somehow be immoral.

Edson plays tricks with perspective as well. In "Vignette," a man "inside one distance" looks down into another and sees his mother. So, he climbs down into her perspective to join her. When he gets there, "she is as small as she was in the distance." This predicament calls forth one of Edson's signature arguments, in which people scream insults at each other in ridiculous frustration: "But why are you so small?" the son cries. "It's you," his mother cries in return, "You're still in your own glutton foreground, optical spendthrift!" When asked why she doesn't swell (i.e., grow larger) when he approaches, the poem takes a typical associative turn—typical for Edson—as the mother proclaims, "I don't swell anymore, I'm too old." The son is advised to find somebody else if he wishes to be born again.

Edson's method is clear: pose some preposterous situation at the beginning of a poem, then follow its absurd implications as far as they will go. He comments on his own strategy in "Let Us Consider" by presenting a laundry list of irrational situations any one of which might be developed into a full-blown Edson poem of its own:

> Let us consider the farmer who makes his straw hat
> his sweetheart; or the old woman who makes a floor lamp
> her son; or the young woman who has set herself the
> task of scraping her shadow off the wall...

and after another full paragraph of zany propositions, ends:

> Let us consider the man who fried roses for his dinner,
> whose kitchen smelled like a burning rose garden; or the
> man who disguised himself as a moth and ate his overcoat,
> and for dessert served himself a chilled fedora...

The poem is a catalog of illogical events, as though Edson could invent wildly imaginative situations at will. And if he can, it doesn't diminish the power of his strange, absurdist fables in the least. They have the intensity of fairy tales, but fairy tales imbued with the philosophical and psychological savvy of a full-grown contemporary adult who knows his Schopenhauer and Freud. Anyone who thinks it is easy to access the myth-making subconscious realm as successfully as this, time and again, ought to try it. Most people, attempting absurdist fantasy, come off sounding silly.

I have hesitated calling Edson a surrealist, because it seems to me surrealism derives from another method—and arrives at a different result. Surrealism has a grim, humorless quality, that feels more willed and automatic. It is poetry written out of aesthetic theory and as such suffers from the usual dullness theories impart to actual poetic practice. Edson's eerie little stories, on the other hand, feel as though they had been written directly by the id, which would only defecate on an artistic theory if it could conceive of one. The id simply acts, grabs, devours, creates, destroys, but never thinks. And it has more immediate desires and purposes than dreams, as odd as those purposes may be.

The bizarre atmosphere of an Edson poem is often heightened by deliberately dumbed-down, primitive pidgin language that approximates baby talk in the crudeness of its elements. In "What It Is of the Wood," Edson writes:

> There was an old woman who would open her shawl and
> glide in a wood, squatting now and again on the branch of
> a tree to do urine.
>
> Her husband asked her what it was of the wood.

It is as though Edson wishes the grotesque nature of a given situation to
be mirrored in the very expressions he uses to describe it. So, form danc-
es once again with content, though the dance here is macabre—certainly
not graceful or elegant. The anti-poetic nature of Gombrowicz's art is
employed by Edson to counter and compensate for the highly decorative,
lyrical utterances we expect from most poetry.

In "History," Edson uses sentence fragments and elision marks to
accentuate the slightly menacing quality his poems often create, and to
suggest the unsayable:

> Structure and sense that dreams from the corners
> of a room ... .
>
> Table edges that remind us of tensions drawn from
> exacting boundaries, falling finally up from the patterns
> of a rug ... .
>
> Those drapes hanging by that window, draped like
> classical stone, shifting with subtle compliance to an
> atmosphere softly breathing from a distant meadow ... .
>
> Above us a monstrous artifact of clouds that've lain
> together for centuries like sleeping swine ... .
>
> The drift ... .

The predicates here are all off somewhere happily discussing the philosophical profundities implied to which we, as readers, are not privy. Yet, the very subjects themselves are pregnant with unstated meaning pointing toward some grand conclusion about history and time.

Mostly, Edson is working within the domain of "immature myth" and "inadmissible passions." He dramatizes the grotesque, allowing us to peek into the "secondary domain" behind the mask of imposed civility. There we witness a swarm of unlikely characters going about their improbable business. It is a domain in which Freud, Jung, Gombrowicz, Lewis Carol's Alice stories, and a host of other dreamers tortured by the constraints of society would feel right at home. There, we can see enacted the secret desires we commonly suppress, the thoughts and images that come to us only through the warps and cracks of the everyday self at odd, unguarded moments. And we can do it without the slightest fear of censure or punishment. This is shameless poetry with a beauty all its own.

17

Shannon and the

Twentieth Century Narrative

Campbell McGrath's book-length work, *Shannon: A Poem of the Lewis and Clark Expedition*[1], is exemplary in many ways, not the least of which is McGrath's ability to evoke a life lived in a radically different set of circumstances in a vastly different place and time. McGrath's recreation of a nineteenth century voice and writing style is nearly pitch-perfect. One of the measures of his success is how McGrath creates the illusion that what the reader is holding in his hands is not a poem written in the early part of the twenty-first century, but the actual text of a journal written by a young man in desperate circumstances two hundred years ago. One must keep reminding oneself that this is so, marveling again at the power of the deception.

To create the convincing sense of an historical figure, more than impersonation is needed. Anyone might inhabit a character using only the broadest strokes, the literary equivalent of caricature, which registers that person's most salient features. But, as any good novelist knows, people—fictional or historical—come to life through an assiduous and cumulative presentation of details, those small, precise strokes that reveal a character in all his or her complicated and manifold dimensions. So McGrath has created for us a young adventurer, George Shannon, who is vain, tender, philosophical, fearful, brave, lonely, resourceful, confused, needy, and self-sufficient at the same time, someone who is capable of loving and missing his girl back home while at the same time remembering the grave mission to which he is attached, and admonishing himself:

> Startled awake stiff & dreaming
> Upon the breasts of Constance Ebson.
> Fine as they are, it disturbs me
> To be tracked into this wilderness by such desires.

It's just this kind of detail that offers a glimpse into Shannon's prickly self: both sensual and puritanical, youthful and adult, fun-loving and practical, he's everything you might think a teenaged recruit who is trying to impress his adult superiors might be. He constantly refers to Lewis or Clark in reverent tones, looking up to them as models, as any young buck might who has been placed in the care of seasoned, knowledgeable veterans. He is desperate to garner their attention with his prowess or, lacking that, his courage and willingness to accept difficult tasks.

On the one hand, then, he is a capable young man proud of his reputation so far:

> Eighteen and years in the backwoods
> I am a better hunter than most back home.

And proud, too, of being the one who recovers two stray horses while his companion, Drouillard, finally has to give up and return to the main company, having separated from Shannon as a tactic to cover more territory (this is how Shannon comes to be lost in the first place):

> Again I do regret not obtaining provisions
> Of Drouillard when we split our search party
> Happy as I was to be shed of him
> He being a master tracker & I so eager
> For sole glory.

Yet later, after days and days of being lost and suffering from hunger, he is forced to exclaim:

> Fain to admit but I did
> Despair and weep
> Some while this evening.

This multi-dimensionality creates what novelists call a fully-rounded character. Shannon appears to us in all his half-fledged youthfulness and bravado.

Besides Shannon's emotional complexity, his intellectual life is rich for someone born and bred on the Kentucky frontier. He has apparently had some early schooling and can read and write, accomplishments not shared by many of his companions on the Corps of Discovery. Shannon says of himself:

> I wish I were supplied as Capt. Lewis
> With notebook paper & as gifted
> Alike with Capt. Clark
> Though he is the less well-lettered of the two.
> Capt. Lewis is a fine writer
> Whose education exceeds my own
> But he knows I might proceed to keep a journal
> In his place if need be.

Later, he adds:

> It is my intention upon completion of this journey
> To continue my proper education
> At the Transylvania University in Kentucky

and reveals that he intends to study law there, because "This is a coun-
try of freedom / From tyranny now / & of laws..." These may seem
high ambitions for someone raised at the end of the eighteenth century
in Pennsylvania and Kentucky. But Shannon, as McGrath has correctly
portrayed him, was a man of some talent and ability and the descendent
of a good family. One of his relatives was the governor of the state, and
three of Shannon's brothers served in both state and federal governments.
Both Meriwether Lewis and William Clark considered Shannon a social
equal, albeit younger and more inexperienced during their famous trek
across America to find a river passage to the Pacific Ocean.

Shannon's thoughts, in fact, revolve around several main themes as he
wanders the prairie alone somewhere on the banks of the Missouri River
in South Dakota in the summer of 1804. Besides dreams of continuing
his education upon returning home following the Corps' expedition west,
Shannon recalls scenes of family life back east—memories of his mother,
his father (whose voice and rustic homilies echo in Shannon's ears), his
brothers, and of course his would-be girlfriend, Constance Ebson. This is
natural for a man lost and homesick, separated from all others on one of the
largest grasslands on earth. Those grasslands themselves constitute anoth-
er focus of his attention as he treks a landscape few other European settlers
had ever seen. It's hard not to imagine him as a new American Adam in a
New World Paradise, surveying the land from horizon to horizon rich with
resources and untold possibilities. As he himself acknowledges:

> Thoughts and reflections flow through me here
> Alone in these lands I might consider myself
> The first American to have walked
> Surely, & observations of the land generally
> & such animals as I have discovered.

But as Shannon's ordeal continues, his thoughts turn toward his deep-
ening plight and the hunger that threatens to destroy him if he cannot
find a way to obtain food in that trackless wilderness. He has used up all
his bullets and most of his gunpowder, so he has few if any ways to find

sustenance except by scavenging berries and trying to figure out a way to kill something—anything—prairie dog, deer, turkey, rabbit, by whatever means possible. He sees buffalo, myriads of them, but knows it will be impossible to bring one of them down. Or elk, which he notices fording the river. It is a measure of McGrath's narrative skill that Shannon's obsession with food deepens, almost imperceptibly, as the narrative progresses and begins to eclipse all other concerns until hunger—and the necessity of finding the Corps—become the only things on his mind. As he becomes more desperate, his mind wanders and he acts a little crazy, which at first he himself realizes as when he observes a badger and imagines that he, too, is a badger. "Is it the hunger / thus drawing me out of myself" he muses, "or some deeper cause?" This is the first sign of his unhinging, though it will get worse and his reveries become as complicated as his rational thoughts upon theology or the law. A second sign occurs when he begins to lose track of time and the days blur one into another. He eats a grasshopper. He argues with himself.

Then, in section thirteen, Shannon seems to disappear altogether at certain points as McGrath (the twenty-first century poet) elbows Shannon (the nineteenth century journalist) aside and the verse becomes more self-conscious, more poetic—or perhaps McGrath means to indicate Shannon's final dizzy descent into the madness hunger has brought on:

> let there be light upon the prairie dust
>
> light & the germ of it
> within the dewdrop infused, parched light
> of the moon reflected constellations
> pearl on yucca, immortal diamond
> crown of thorn & stars ...
>
> take this sword of light, this ruin ...
>
> dewdrop, the source, fog of breath
> & the river of light widening towards sunrise
> this astonishment of grass, this extravagance ...

It's difficult not to hear the voice of the poet McGrath here rather than Shannon's. Difficult to imagine Shannon writing, or saying "immortal diamond" or "this astonishment of grass." And scattering the word "buffalo" around several pages is an effective typographical strategy to indicate the ubiquity of the herd, but a decidedly Modernist, even postmodernist technique. If section thirteen is meant to manifest Shannon's deepening delirium, it is only partially successful because the poet's willful management of the material is far more evident than in earlier sections. McGrath even chooses to drop the nineteenth century convention of capitalizing the first letter of the first word of each verse, thereby reflecting a more Modernist sensibility in the very look of the lines, their casual contemporary formality.

Whatever the case, Shannon seems to come back to his senses (and McGrath to withdraw again into his character) in the following section as he returns to the urgent necessity of finding food. Even Shannon's wayward imaginings—he watches some ants and conceives of himself as an Ant-God—seem far more "reasonable" than in the prior section, as even he himself recognizes: "What purpose to carry on / About Ant-Gods, am I losing all sense?" Yet his discourse on ants and their behavior becomes a logical argument close to blasphemy, from a Christian standpoint, as he has in prior sections when pondering religious doctrine. As revealed by McGrath, Shannon seems to be a nineteenth century materialist, or Deist, a natural inheritor of the prior century's clock-maker God, a late child of the Enlightenment like most of the Founding Fathers, including Jefferson, whom Shannon reveres. It's little wonder, then, that he sees the ant as "a creature of laws / Orderly & warranted / In all actions by such directives" meaning the practical need for food and shelter, and to extrapolate from their condition and behavior a natural analog for human beings as well. This is what Shannon has been driving at all along. "See," he finally says, "how I am transformed / From a believer / Into a Democrat & a Man of Science?" In this, he has become the first model for the new American in the new continent, self-reliant (a la Emerson), pragmatic, free of Old World superstitions and ready to establish a new country based on reason and the law. God exists, for Shannon, but He resembles nothing like the ghostly, all-manipulative, irrational God of Parson Macready back home whom Shannon has suspected of pious ignorance from the beginning.

But these considerations pale as hunger returns to gnaw at Shannon and trump all other thoughts. Shannon is quickly reduced to a physical thing, like the skull of an antelope he sees in the grass, and this as much as anything else contributes to his political and theological outlook.

In the end, Shannon decides to give up and retire to the banks of the Missouri River in case a fur trapper or other boatman might wander by and save him. He thinks the chance highly unlikely, but resigns himself to his fate, giving up all hope of ever finding Lewis and Clark or any of the other members of the Corps of Discovery again:

> I have a conception of my soul
> Being taken up in the prairie's austerity and solitude
> To be devoured
> By the stars
> & mind it no longer.

He does not know, as he thinks this, that he has out-walked the Corps that had been struggling up the river at a slower pace and that they will find him, or he will find them, when they catch up at last, just in time to keep him from starving.

There are only a few moments when the poem falters, as when Shannon's otherwise sober narrative voice descends into frontier vernacular and he is in danger of becoming a conventional American prototype. "Git on, horse," he demands of his nag, "Git on." Or the memory of his father intoning advice that prefigures Norman Vincent Peale's *Power of Positive Thinking*: "Soldier on, George my boy," he hears the voice of his father chirp, "soldier on." Such language in the first instance hovers close to stereotype (the American cowboy, still almost half a century away) and in the second instance, a folksiness is introduced into what is essentially a more dignified literary style. I believe such alterations of character are meant to counter-balance the headier, more philosophical passages that precede and follow them. And they almost do. More successful in this regard are passages of situational humor, as when Shannon disturbs a family of skunks—which he calls pole-cats—in a thicket while searching for berries, and the mother skunk chases him back to his own camp "with no injury" but to his pride. And later, he falls into the river stalking a swan and comments: "... the current is fleet. / It would be a poor idea & a peril to drown." And once, I winced at the use of one of our most cherished national clichés that might better have been left out or rephrased, as when George temporarily hunkered down on the prairie in a rain storm, muses about the future he envisions for himself:

> ... America
> Is a land of opportunities
> Best seized by those with schooling

a philosophy that might have appeared on a billboard in the same landscape years later, with the image of a father and a son depicted by Norman Rockwell. No matter that it was, and is, true. Poetry at its best depends upon originality of expression, not platitudes.

But these are quibbles when compared to what McGrath has achieved here. Shannon's observations of the pristine American heartland and his premonitions about the future are couched in historical poetry of the first order. Reading *Shannon* is a great pleasure and adds to McGrath's other achievement in the genre, "William Bartram Beset by Crocodiles or Alligators" in *Florida Poems*, which borrows the eighteenth century naturalist's voice accurately.

There is a caveat, however. Historical poetic narratives hardly receive the notice they deserve, any more than verse fiction, or even book-length meditative poems. Who remembers—or more importantly, reads—Stephen Vincent Benet's sweeping verse epic, *John Brown's Body*, a literary achievement successfully mixing many forms to tell the story of the Civil War; or Andrew Hudgin's more recent treatment, *After the Lost War*, depicting the life of veteran, poet, and musician Sidney Lanier; or Benet's other ambitious work, a poetic treatment of the early history of the United States and the opening of the country, *Western Star*, for which he received a Pulitzer Prize in 1944; or Robert Penn Warren's *Chief Joseph of the Nez Perce Who Call Themselves The Nimipu "The*

Real People," which appears on the eighth page of his works listed on Amazon.com, and even then without a cover image; or Winfield Townley Scott's *The Dark Sister* which James Dickey hails as a contemporary masterpiece, telling the story of Leif Ericson's sister, Freydis, and their journey to the New World in the tenth century (for that matter, who remembers Winfield Townley Scott?); or Archibald MacLeish's saga of Spanish conquest in the New World, *Conquistador*; or even John Berryman's *Homage to Mistress Bradstreet* compared to the almost universal acclaim he received for his later collection, *The Dream Songs*. These are but a few examples of historical verse from the twentieth century. Why these important and ambitious poems should be almost entirely forgotten is anyone's guess, but I would think it has something to do with the novel's almost complete usurpation of the narrative form over the past one hundred years or so.

I suspect McGrath's *Shannon* will eventually languish in libraries along with the rest of the historical narratives written by American poets and met largely with indifference by the reading public. This will have nothing to do with its quality. Americans seem to love learning about themselves and their history in novels, films, and television miniseries. But poetry in the twentieth century has largely been confined to the lyric, and sound bites have reduced attention spans to near zero. Long poems, on any subject, are difficult to market. Still, *Shannon* is worth anyone's time and will repay the reader with an engrossing view of America's past and raise questions about this country's origins at a particularly important juncture in its history. Private George Shannon, the youngest member of the Lewis and Clark expedition, is a lucid and intelligent guide to that past. His ideas about the new territory and the as-yet unformed future are incisive, and sometimes profound. Hunger, drowning, the threat of hostile Indians, to these he begins to sense another danger, one with which Americans even in the present age will be familiar:

> For all my caution of drowning
> In the Missouri River
> It may be the vastness of this land
> That consumes me.

233

18

The Zany Reaches of Imagination:

A Young Poet Comes Into His Own

There are several new poets who are producing the kind of work that may eventually renew the art. This is the function of young poets, after all. What is needed, always, from generation to generation is a fresh perspective, novel ideas, a rejuvenation of language, expeditions into unexplored territories of imagination. Matthew Rohrer belongs to this group of newcomers whose work is everywhere marked by originality and freshness. There is a pristine quality to his work that wakes one up and clears the senses, promising in poem after poem to re-imagine the world.

    Rohrer bypasses the pitfalls associated with younger writers—the wish to appear intelligent and avant-garde—and goes right to the source of things: poetry's uncanny ability to see through false surfaces and transform our understanding. The opening lines of "Epithalamium" in *Satellite*[1] demonstrate this clearly:

> In the middle garden is the secret wedding,
> that hides always under the other one
> and under the shiny things of the other one.

The rest of the poem is no less penetrating for its grasp of unsettling truths:

> Under a tree
> one hand reaches through the grainy dusk toward another.
> Two right hands. The ring is a weed that will surely die.

> There is no one else for miles,
> and even those people far away are deaf and blind.
> There is no one to bless this.
> There are the dark trees, and just beyond the trees.

The assertion of the ring as a kind of weed, common and perishable, is matched by other startling comparisons throughout the book: "When the satellites trickled through the stars / like a pinball machine..." (Sunday Night); "... listening to a song / replay in his memory. / He fools with it a little, like candy cooling" (Philosophy in the Boudoir); "... trees were softening / and the roofs warming up like pans" (The Hunger of the Lemur).

Rohrer does not give in to the present trend for disjunction, nonsense, ellipsis, or interruption. Instead, his poems move with the kind of dreamy, compelling logic of those who are explorative and truly engaged. He will let the poem take him wherever it will, as long as it is taking him somewhere.

The sense that he is in charge, and not the language, not the poem, is evident. Yet there is a feeling of liberation, of openness and possibility in every one of these poems. A feeling that anything may happen, as anything does, with a few apparently simple strokes: "They learned to turn off the gravity in an auditorium / and we all rose into the air" (Childhood Stories); "The pins that held her bare feet on glittered in moonlight" (The Robotroid Girlfriend); "Mockingbirds mastered police sirens / and now the city is on edge." (Mockingbirds). His approach is spontaneous, but deft, lending the poems an atmosphere of expectancy and surprise.

The acid test for any book of poems—or any writing, for that matter—is whether you feel constrained to keep on reading without experiencing a lapse in attention. This requires that each poem, each line, each word sustain itself against the overall excellence of the book. Even a slight miscalculation, any pretense, any attempt to palm off what is second rate will result in disappointment.

Satellite rarely disappoints. At times, however, Rohrer gives in to a temptation—endemic in surrealism, at least the American brand—to simply play around with language, abandoning imagination, when it falters, in hopes of creating ideas out of verbal jokes. This happens in "Comet," where the following lines appear: "My heart sinks into the couch / Yours into the sink." Such facile gestures fall short, causing us to groan at their obviousness. A few lines later, speaking about love, he does it again: "We want to pin it to a constant / Let's pin it to a comet," though he pulls this out at the last minute with the final line, "It'll return."

And Rohrer's ability to end a poem effectively is one of the true pleasures of his work. Whether culminating with a provocative idea, as in the example above, or leaving us pondering a resonant image, the poems in *Satellite* achieve closure firmly, and with conviction. Consider the ending of "Epithalamium," or the ultimate line of "Beautiful Things," which begins:

> When we say something is beautiful
> We mean we can laterally bisect it…

and, after listing examples of the beauty of symmetry, ends:

> Even the five-pointed starfish fits into our group.
> The best time to bisect a starfish is at night
> after a shipwreck when they grip the shore.
> They say they are the hands of sailors who didn't make it.

From time to time, there is a feeling that Rohrer loses his way. That he is simply generating a new image in an attempt to make something happen, and not because it is radically connected to the subject of the poem. But generally, on second thought, or third reading, a subject emerges around which the poem orbits with an unerring sense of what is important, and matters.

The subject of these poems may not always be easy to find or express, and certainly not approached in any conventional or deliberate way. But, as a result of his true engagement with the world—no matter how surrealistic his technique—Rohrer explores ideas long associated with the best poetry: a sense of the ravages of history and political corruption; the strangeness of the individual pitted against the group; childhood in its delightfully charming ignorance; love and its intricate losses; the

oddness of time; and the incomprehensibility of death (to which he adds
a few twenty-first century concerns, like paranoia and the eeriness of
electronic culture). That said, no one could characterize Rohrer as a con-
ventional poet. It's what we make of subjects in poetry that is unique, not
the subjects themselves.

As the passage above from "Beautiful Things" demonstrates, Rohrer
is not afraid of emotion if the situation warrants it. When a poem moves
in that direction, he will not shy away or suppress what he feels. Honest,
controlled emotion permeates his work, arising sometimes out of the most
preposterous circumstances, as in "Starfish Waving to Me from the Sand":

> When I pay close attention to my senses I become immobile.
> I'm stuck living each moment
> instead of taking great strides across them.
> And these are lonely moments.
> Without her this desiccated starfish is my only friend,
> Starfish waving to me from the sand.
> Last night an overcoat beckoned to me from the closet.
> But that was the whole of our frustrating discussion.
> I went back to stare at her portrait by the bed,
> to fall asleep and dream of her portrait rippling
> on the Ghost Ship's sails.
> The rigging creaking was somebody's sighs,
> but what kind, and whose?

Even Tomaz Salamun's epigraph attests to Rohrer's allegiance to the
truth of empathy and feeling:

> The worst imaginable kind of fascism would be
> If the soul belonged only to the living
> and not to the dust and stones!

What Rohrer sees, or wants to see, is consciousness—hence, feeling—everywhere, even in the dust and stones. In an age that denies even the existence of the self, much less any authentic, unsocially constructed feelings, the very mention of a soul is unusual.

Like any poet, Rohrer has tics and obsessions: The sky is always orange and filled with satellites, for instance. But this is only a reflection of the most current, up-to-date version of reality. Our skies burn with poisons, and technology is everywhere. And Rohrer has poet models and influences easily discerned in the general fabric of his work—Russell Edson, Bill Knott, Charles Simic, John Ashbery, perhaps. Though no model is more obvious than James Tate, whose presence hovers behind this book like a stage manager at a play. In "From the World At Night," the kind of zany, surrealistic narrative for which Tate is famous, Rohrer goes to a party, drinks "a glass of poison" offered by the hostess, and begins to throw up on the subway home, when he is brought to exclaim: "My mind was actually / seven or eight minds, all but one of them / composed of helicopters." At such moments, one feels Tate's hand on Rohrer's hand.

It is when we feel Rohrer breaking away from his mentors to create work of his own, unpredictable and unique, that we realize he has the potential to carry on alone. Such moments occur often in *Satellite*. In the course of reeling on the subway during the poem quoted above, Rohrer also says, "Without any meaning, time / accreted to things in funny shapes—" and we know we have left the sphere of past influences. We feel it again when Rohrer refers to neon as "fried light."

Tropes like this make it clear that Rohrer can forge a new voice for himself, developing a style and body of work that might stretch American surrealism—even a little—taking us a step deeper into the zanier reaches of imagination. *Satellite* is an impressive book, and Matthew Rohrer a poet to watch.

19

The Unexpected Imagery

and Astonishing Metaphor

in Emma Jones's

The Striped World

A new poet requires that we take note, then make our adjustments. These involve both a new angle of seeing, and a new texture of speech to which we must become accustomed before we can adequately respond to what we're reading. Subject matter is hardly ever the issue—who has truly introduced new subject matter? How, even, could that be possible? Human nature has not changed since the ancients first began to compose poetry. And rarely, except during true periods of foment in the arts, do we encounter genuine formal innovation. The line is the line as the stanza is the stanza. And all variations of scattering words around the page have seemingly been tried and are recognizable enough for us by now to be comfortable with them. An unconventional touch here and there—odd punctuation, spelling, syntax—but not radical change at the foundations of the art. A new "voice" announces itself not so much through tone, attitude, or opinion as through imagery, diction, and personal obsession. A new mood is created, and we acclimate ourselves to it the way we adjust to anything we have not experienced before.

The texture of Emma Jones's poetry in *The Striped World*,[1] the sound and rhythm and peculiar feel of its language, is recognizable as personal and distinct. There is a terse, tense, bitten-off quality to her verses that draws our attention first. We have the sense that there will be scant room for excess, no posturing or circumlocutions of any kind. The lines seem to clip off units of thought with little or no flourish, then move on:

> When the sun, that gradual sepoy
> rose, then clouds occurred;
> the sea came, and hung like a man;
> the tankers boiled,
> and a wind rifled the trees.

The imagery arrests our attention because we are forced to look at the world from a new perspective, one which is not our own—and certainly not stereotypical—but to which we can accommodate ourselves with some imagination and effort. How is the sun like a "sepoy?" A dictionary will tell us that it refers to a situation that existed in India under British rule. Native Indians sometimes became soldiers and served under British command. The word "sepoy" refers to them, especially, if they served in the British East India Company. So, it is possible that the sun is envisioned here as a kind of lackey, or servant, that willingly submits to its task of lighting up the world each day. This has socio-political implications, though the poem does not develop them. The following images are just as unusual: the sea that came and "hung like a man," tankers boiling on the horizon, and wind that rifles (not "riffles") the trees. It could be argued that all good images are unusual, so what's so unusual about these? Perhaps the slight threat, or latent violence suggested in the verbs: "hung," "boiled," and "rifled." Perhaps the fact that the images strenuously avoid the sentimentality that often accompanies images of nature. Maybe even the rapid-fire succession in which the images appear, each adding another vigorous stroke to the landscape the poet is portraying.

Then there's this curious phrase: "clouds occurred." Why the abstract verb, where everything else is concrete? And why the use of "occurred" in the active tense, rather than the passive, as in normal usage? The alliteration is pleasing. But it also has the sense of depersonalizing nature, of characterizing it in mechanical terms, rather than cozily anthropomorphizing it. Clouds simply "occur," they are not personified Actors on the great stage of Nature, playing their parts in the Grand Scheme of Things. I am taking the time to point out these details because I think they clarify the most prominent features of Jones's style: abrupt phraseology; aggressive patterns of imagery; radical compression of thought; unsentimental depictions of nature and human experience; and spare, everyday language mixed occasionally with unusual and surprising diction. Realizing all of this is part of the process of acclimatizing oneself to her work. Still, even with familiarization, it is possible for Jones's poems to surprise. One never gets quite accustomed to the oddness of her style, the next unexpected word choice, the next far-fetched but astonishing metaphor.

These hallmarks of her writing might be found anywhere, in any poem, in any stanza. In a poem about a painter setting his easel up *en plein air* near the seacoast, a poem that might be about the relationship between reality and art, she begins:

> Everyone's souls, which didn't exist, were playing up,
> and they flocked as the shadows we left on the ground
> when the tired sun—that midday man—was an artist.
> And they surfaced in our sweat, which made, for us,
> a soft lunar garment worn abroad...

Here, she contradicts herself in the first line and by doing so, seems to be able to have it both ways: souls may not exist, but still they play and flock. The abruptness of the phrase at the end of the line is peculiar too: Playing up... to what, or whom? Obviously, she means something like "acting up" or "playing around," but by phrasing it the way she has, she is able to suggest more—that the souls had an audience and were behaving in a self-conscious way. The imagery, again, is entirely unpredictable. The sun is a "midday man," an artist of shadows, whose chiaroscuro work is most visible in the afternoon. And, like swimmers, those same souls "surface" in sweat characterized as a "soft lunar garment." These images couldn't be more peculiar. And the diction once more arrests us: That word "lunar" stands out as an inspired choice, especially since the sun has just been the subject of the previous image, and it is the sun which brings sweat to the surface. Suppose, for consistency, Jones had written, "a soft solar garment." Not bad, but the word "lunar" offers up another contradiction, one that adds complexity to an already complex image.

In "Window," Jones presents us with one of poetry's oldest enigmas: the inner life of contemplation versus the outer life of action, and the problem of having to choose between the two.

> His sadness was double,
> it had two edges.

> One looked out—
> onto skylines,
> and streets with ice-cream
> men, and cars,
> and clouds
> like cut cotton.

> The other stayed in
> to watch
> his memories unbuckle
> and his hairs
> all repeat
> in the washstand.

> Both were impatient.
> Sometimes they'd meet
> and make a window.

> "Look at the world!" said the glass.
> "Look at the glass!" said the world.

By conflating the idea of undressing inside the room with a person's memories, Jones devises another startling image made possible through an unexpected word choice: "his memories unbuckle..." And once more we find an abrupt, snapped-off phrase suggesting two things at once: "his hairs / all repeat..." Repeat what, you might ask? But she means that his hairs continue to fall out, that the word "repeat" refers to the aging process, not to something said. Though, if they could talk, they would admonish: "You are getting old, old!" We are reminded that time is wasting for the contemplative, while the world outside passes by unconcerned.

Other poems in this volume address various definable subjects in idiosyncratic ways. There's a kind of existential rant ("Conversation") poised precariously on a short periodic sentence; a vast urban landscape completely void of people ("Hush"); a rambling, bizarre re-write of Genesis ("Creator,")—Jones is fond of one-word titles—; a hip, jazzy monologue spoken by the Virgin Mary to her dead son, Jesus, ("Pieta") which might have been written by Lord Buckley; a perfectly conventional sonnet about spring, called "Sonnet," in decasyllabics; and a rambling paean to writing, childhood, and geography ("Waiting") studded with unforeseen, colorful terms.

In the eleventh stanza, for instance, she refers to a "cracked gardenia / strewing its level scents." What could the adjective "level" mean in this context? And yet "level" seems apt, inevitable, if only because it sounds right, its short "e" setting up an echo with the next word, "scents." In fact, a crisp and clear-cut lyricism might be added to the distinguishing features of Jones's work. She writes as much by ear as by subject, with the result that content often gives way to sound, an ongoing set of repeating notes, as in a musical score.

The heart of the book, its center of gravity even though it comes near the end of the volume, is an ambitious poem, "Zoos for the Dead," which substitutes animals for people—mainly an extraordinary blue parrot— who seems to take the role of Sybil or socio-historical-spiritual guide for the poem's unnamed narrator. The poem's subject is announced in an epigraph, which reminds the reader of the sad history of Australia's aboriginal population—especially aboriginal children—at the hands of racist governments from the late nineteenth century to the 1960s. The parrot, Narcissus, is the child of another parrot who is a surrogate for one of the aboriginal children captured and abused by the state. Confusing? The poem is certainly complex—both in its quirky symbolism and narrative manner—but there are stunning images throughout that make the poem worthwhile reading whether it hangs together easily or not.

For example, the narrator's first description of Narcissus is astonishing in its weird particularity: "...his Goya - / etching face was first scooped from the gloom of his shirt-front / and angled me two white eyes winched on a lamé collar." When the parrot and narrator scuba dive into the sea off Australia to inspect the wreck of a ship called Miranda, the imagery is compelling: "We found the wreck, squinting, / and we'd move above it like birds in slow circles, stung by some centre, / and find the loam of its beams, the twisted skins of its coins..." The images may be clear, but the allusion is not. The only reference I could find to a vessel in Australia named Miranda describes a wreck in Apollo Bay in southwestern Victoria in 1881: the ship was loading potatoes when a huge sea swell dashed it against the rocks on shore. For some reason, the wreckage has never been found. The connection between the story of the Miranda and the deracinated and abused aboriginal children is anyone's guess, but we have to make room for foreign histories and cultural cues which may not be immediately apparent to readers in other countries.

Though she's obviously influenced by current postmodernist theory, she hasn't fallen prey completely to the non-narrative craze. Despite the eccentricity of her approach, her subjects are never far from view. She may improvise around them, as she does with the sonic patterns or bizarre metaphors I've discussed, but she never entirely abandons content. Her poems are built up with layers of meaning, sound, rhythm, and metaphor, none of which completely dominate and all of which play themselves out as the poem progresses. The reader may feel intrigued, or temporarily puzzled, but never thoroughly lost.

Though Jones's writing is highly stylized and self-conscious, her work feels natural, natural to her, not overtly labored. Her incisive intelligence and canniness work together to assure that—while calculated—her poems seem fresh and uncontrived. This is one of the keys to her success. A twenty-eight-year-old poet from Australia, this is Jones's first book. The question to ask of any young poet just launching a career might be, Will there be growth? But some poets arrive more fledged than others. How much growth can we expect by way of innovation on an already accomplished style? Perhaps the question, in some cases, is more than the reader can ask.

20

How to Rhyme:

Balancing Sense with Sound

in Todd Boss's

Yellowrocket

Every year or so, a first book of poems is published by an unknown poet that makes readers take notice. Tastes will vary, but recently many were drawn to Todd Boss's debut collection, *Yellowrocket*.[1] There are good reasons for this attention, including an exquisite ear for the sounds language makes, and how to orchestrate them; a homely and whimsical imagination that is at the same time more than merely fanciful; a strong narrative voice that has important things to say about rural life, endurance, and the delicate negotiations living with a family requires; and has a feel for effective and appropriate forms and the rhythms words inevitably make when linked together as they march staunchly across a page. Iterations of sound, the most salient feature of Boss's poetry, is what initially draws the reader's attention and it is best to start there in assessing his poems and discussing how and when they succeed, and why.

When comparing the characteristics of traditional verse to free verse, the poet William Matthews used to say that he had nothing against rhyme. He just didn't see why it had to be lined up rigidly—vertically—on the right-hand edge of the poem. Why couldn't like-sounding syllables and words echo off each other all over the text, anywhere they occurred in the lines? Todd Boss exemplifies that aesthetic perfectly. Call it wayward or vagrant rhyme—not internal, interior, or medial—as Boss's rhymes might occur just as easily at the beginning and ends of lines as in the middle, anywhere, really, as if by whim. Of course, this kind of rhyming has been with us for some time now, though Boss is so deft at using it that he draws attention to its virtues and seems to create it all over again as though it were a device he had just invented.

Rhyme must be a surprise—or at least unpredictable—to be successful as a technique in poetry. This is true even though the regular pattern set up in a traditional rhymed and metered poem is wholly predictable—not in the words involved, but in their positioning at the ends of lines. In Boss's poems the words, as well as their position in the lines, are unpredictable. Surprise is doubly built into the technique. In fact, Boss goes out of his way to make sure that rhymes do not usually occur at the ends of lines, but anywhere, everywhere, suddenly and delightfully, perhaps when we least expect it. A typical Boss poem presents us with a rich texture of irregular rhyme, not a rigid, anticipated pattern.

Still, Boss often teeters on the edge of excess. It is a measure of his artistry that he rarely falls into mindless iterations of sound, overdoing what—in sensible balance and proportion—gives considerable pleasure to the ear. In passages like the following, which refers to those on a neighboring farm whose fortunes are tentative at best:

> Their heyday
> > a payday
> away

Boss risks sonic bathos, packing so many flat A sounds so closely together. One more word ending in "ay," one more syllable of the same ilk, and the poem would sink into the kind of incessant rhyming only a child could appreciate. But Boss knows when to stop—short of monotony—and quickly goes on to establish another set of vowels and consonants that echo off each other and allow us to accept the five identical rhyming syllables that have preceded it:

> Pride,
> > Ruin's bride-to-be,

            paced our property
                in the long
  laced gowns
  of afternoons

The originality of the metaphor helps to mediate the repetitions of sound here, as well. Some of our attention is focused on interpreting it, and thereby diverted from the rhyme so that an effective balance is maintained.

When that balance is ignored and restraint cast aside, the results can be distracting, if not laughable. We can see what happens in that case in the second section of Boss's poem, "Turbulence: Three Exercises" where his compulsive rhyming seems to get the better of him and runs amok:

2. A FIGHT

  might nightly
  light like
  lightning
  any frightening

  sight in white
  reverse, might
  write it on our lids
  like a curse...

Here the technique falls into a parody of itself, producing a carillon of rhyme that drowns out all proportion and sense. Occasional rhyme requires that enough space occurs between homophonic syllables so that other sounds might intervene and provide some relief, holding monotony at bay. Closely packed, jangling rhyme is not only annoying, but obscures any other virtues the verse might possess—including meaning. With this kind of rhyming, discretion is everything.

In one poem, "Wood Burning," Boss substitutes grammatical repetition for rhyme, stacking the indefinite article "a" at the ends of his short lines like the butt ends of sawn logs:

WOOD BURNING

To my father, a
woods is not a
woods without a
wood pile in it, a
brush mess near it
where the lesser limbs
landed...

This creates an arresting visual effect on the page—a special instance of eye-rhyme—though it provides nothing in the way of reiterated sound. Once again, though, had Boss continued in this vein much longer the poem would suffer from making its point too often, and too much. Such special effects, like the sounds of cannons, wind, or bells in a musical composition, had better be used sparingly, or not at all. They become gimmicky when used too often.

It's worth noting, however, that when Boss abandons sporadic rhyme and writes what amounts to straightforward contemporary free-verse, the results are far less interesting and effective. This may be because for Boss rhyme is less a rote structural element than a principal of composition. Rhyme helps him to write, helps him to generate the poem, by leading him from thought to thought along a pathway of sound—rather than the other way around—an associative/connective approach whereby the cognitive process and the rhyming process become one. Something like this must be true for all poets whose work is densely rich with sound: Dylan Thomas, Gerard Manly Hopkins, Swinburne. To read the highly alliterative poetry of Mina Loy and not to understand that she is doing something more than merely flirting with consonants is to miss the point. Alliteration in her work functions like meter in a traditional poem. It provides a regular pattern, a framework of language off which her meanings might resonate and her imagination play. For such poets, sound carries as much matter and emotion as structure, syntax, and meter.

But if rhyming or visual tricks were all that Boss had to offer, these poems would be less worthy of our attention and a good deal more superficial than they are. Boss is acutely aware of the fragility of life, and the possibility of many types of disaster. There's plenty of violence in these poems, but it's largely natural: wind, rain, fire, quake, squalls, turbulence of all sorts play major roles in his work and provide much of the drama to be found there. This is what you might expect from someone who grew up on a farm, knows weather, watches it carefully, and feels personally affected by it. Nature is not only beautiful to the farmer, it is chiefly productive and sometimes dangerous, an enormous machine that can blow up and go awry, ruining not only crops, but lives and livelihoods as well. In a poem about an overnight storm, "In the Morning We Found," which Boss describes in his notes as "the single worst natural disaster in Wisconsin state history," his parents walk "alone and paired" in the wind-damaged fields and observe "downed trees still / green and breathing" and which remind them of the carnage after a massive battle. The snapped, mangled trunks lie there "fallen / as in a war." He knows that nature both provides and destroys, sometimes in spectacular ways.

Violence, too, sometimes threatens his marriage—emotional violence—and in a number of unsparing poems he figures at least one marital squabble as a storm. In "Tangled Hangers and All," his wife, in a fury, throws his clothes down a stairwell. After referring to "the falling waters of our marriage," he describes the scene:

> I
>
> stand idly by as the river swells deep and high
> with necktie twists,
>
> balled fists of socks, a bandy-legged affair
> of thermal underwear
> suit jackets shoulder to shoulder in trysts.

Another poem describes the desolation of six nights spent away from home at a hotel by himself, presumably after another vehement argument. And in still another poem, when couples gathered at a party begin to tell the relatively happy stories of how they met, Boss admits that for him and his wife, "love was always complex." Such unflinching honesty stops the dinner conversation cold. Adult love is real for Boss, but infinitely complicated by experience. In a particularly tight-knit mixed metaphor, Boss again figures love as difficult, but true:

THE DEEPER THE DICTIONARY

The more complex the lexicon.

Take you and me.
The sheets like pages, pulled on

and torn off in a rage!
The long-dead languages! Ah—

but the core of our love
is six thousand sheets down!

And here we are, shamming
counterpanes, when

the mattress, the box spring,
coil with origins.

Love may be hard, but it exists. When Boss turns exclusively to "the core" of love, he gives himself over to a more sentimentalized, romanticized version of it. In a poem entitled "To a Wild Rose," he adopts the oldest trope in the book to symbolize his love and the beauty of his beloved (the rose, adhering to convention, grows in a recess in the woods and is never seen except by the lucky observer). And in another erotic poem, Boss witnesses an albino deer stepping out of a misty patch of woods and, of course, it becomes a surrogate for his wife in its startling beauty and the feminine delicacy of its step. Swooning at the sight, the poet becomes excited and rather rhetorical: "All white and white / and white she was… " This line might just as plausibly have been written by Wyatt or Spenser. Other moments of poetic inversion occur elsewhere in the poem, as though once you adopt a classical trope, traditional language must follow: "What grace, / what art, what eloquence she bore!" We can practically see Boss, sitting behind the wheel of his car, throwing the back of his hand to his forehead and sighing. This is what happens when a poet sets out deliberately to write a love poem, rather than having a love poem emerge out of some unlikely experience or event. Self-consciousness wrecks the whole enterprise, and whatever originality the poet may possess flies out the door.

But when he writes of his love for his son and daughter, such stale rhetorical gestures largely disappear. Invention and originality replace outworn conventions, though it's true that filial love hazards its own set of literary mannerisms. His son puts on his pants backwards, so Boss ties his tie cockeyed and "out we / trip into / the great / disheveled" world, like a pair of vagabonds or clowns without a care. When he drives his daughter to school "through the jeweled / morning light" they sigh "What a lovely morning" and call out together "Wake up, old Mr. Sun." Love here is untainted by irony or the past. It is as clear and simple as the morning through which Boss and his daughter pass, and the play of rhyme and imagery seems entirely appropriate to the situation. Appropriately, too, the light-heartedness of the moment must deepen into something more in the end:

> I need to think she saw it all
> as it sped by—
> the rink in spun
> chain link, the outlet mall
> in mist—and loved
> the pinks and golds
> as I do. She is so young.
> If I can't train her eyes
> to love, how else then

praise the lapidary,
who cuts our days
like diamonds
from the carbon cold above?

At his best Boss balances sound with sense, reflects meaning through music, and adapts content to form. When the elements of his poems do not outweigh, but complement, each other, Boss's work can be both satisfying and unsettling, playful and poignant, as it is in the following poem which, I think, shows him at his best. In "Patiently, the Partial Brides," the sentimental is undercut by pathos, wit makes us wince as much as smile, and the odd, inanimate tailor's dummies still manage to exhibit much that is recognizably human:

PATIENTLY, THE PARTIAL BRIDES

in the bridal shop window

wait.

The shop's
closed up for the night

and yet

they wait
with the diligence

of the dead

and the mis-
understood. —See how she's

lost her head,

how she her arms, how she
is nothing but a shelf

display,
as if there'd been a tussle
for a thrown bouquet.
This one

is nothing but a bride-
shaped

cage.

They stand around on needles
and pins,

strangled

by the silences they sing.
The morning will cue no

voluntary.

There is no telling
for whom the little front

door bell will ring.

ADDENDUM

An Ambitious Raid on the Sublime:

Horror and Kurt Brown's *ABDUCTION*

by David J. Rothman

After Kurt's death in 2013, I discovered in my papers what is, as far as I know, the only copy of "Abduction," a long poem that was never published during his lifetime. He had sent it to me about thirty years earlier (there is no date on it, just an address from Boulder, where he earned an MFA in the mid-1980s). I deeply admired the poem then, but whenever I suggested publishing it in one journal or another I was involved with, Kurt would always demur. I can understand why. The poem is unusual for him. At 228 lines (38 six-line stanzas) it is far longer than any other poem of his that I know; it is also explicitly narrative and luridly violent, a fictional recreation of Ted Bundy's murder of Caryn Campbell in Snowmass, Colorado in 1975 (Kurt was living in Aspen at the time). I don't think he ever wrote anything else like it.

"Abduction" first appeared in the journal *THINK* (which at the time I edited with Susan Spear), about three years after Kurt's death, in volume 7.1 (Fall 2016). I believe Kurt would have respected the decision to publish it even if it made him uneasy. It is a sustained, sublime, and terrifying narrative in the tradition of the best poems and stories of its kind, bearing comparison with Poe, Jeffers, and the entire Gothic tradition. Hewing quite closely to the facts as they emerged in the investigation of Bundy's crime, Kurt weaves them into a story that pushes at the edge of what we can imagine.

The first recognizable modern horror novels were what we now call Gothic, beginning with Horace Walpole's *Castle of Otranto* (1765) and then continuing most famously in the work of Anne Radcliffe a few decades later. Those works and scores of others like them were filled with historically-specific trappings of ruin and decay that led to the generic "Gothic" designation, and that continue to appear up to the present day in a number of fantasy and horror sub-genres (the ruined castle, the catacomb, the abandoned monastery, the malicious and sadistic villain, the innocent heroine…).The more literary turn in the genre came in the nineteenth century with works such as Frankenstein and Dracula, along with Poe's and Hawthorne's stories. While many of these works were also set in distant times and places, what gives them greater strength than the earlier work is how they use their lurid content to provoke meditations on a wide range of serious topics, from advances in science to the psychology of revenge, from politics to the behavior of mobs and the deep experience of guilt or anxiety. They are not only designed to give readers a sense of delight in the symbolic experience of fear, terror, and horror, but also, at their best, to give insight into those feelings, both their sources and how they work in us. "The Telltale Heart" and "Young Goodman Brown" have more to say than what they merely do to us.

Most of the great writers of horror have worked in prose. Very few poets have accomplished or even attempted it, with Poe preeminent in English, yet even he did not write long poems in the genre ("The Raven" is only 108 lines). Assuming we do not reclassify Dante's *Inferno* as horror, or other epic visits to the underworld (which are certainly part of the background and inspiration for modern horror, but in a different line), there isn't much. In this and in other ways, Kurt's poem suggests the only other great modern poet to have worked in a similar way at times, Robinson Jeffers, whose many mid-length and book-length narratives always involve depictions of believable murder, mayhem, and some kind of horrific holocaust.

Kurt's poem belongs in this fine company. While the poem is relentlessly, explicitly, brutally terrifying, it goes far beyond the lurid, evoking inhuman transcendence as powerfully as anything Jeffers ever wrote. The tension builds throughout the poem to its inevitable and obscene close, in which Campbell, abducted by chance out of an elevator in her hotel, is split open by Bundy's knife in a field and he puts his head into the cavity:

> his awful head thrust deeply
> into the split walls of your chest
> crooning something unthinkable
> as an animal   ecstatic with hunger
> buries its head in carrion
>
> He is speaking directly into
> your wounds   into your brain
> making the shapes of words crawl
> inward   until they become your own
> secret voice   opening your lips
> to ask   Mercy   Mercy

In the end, Campbell's body is left in the field, emerging rotting in the spring and eaten by animals, "fallen to the hunger of beasts," each of which, as it devours part of her, carries "in / the brute crèche or its skull / the vision of a woman charmed by / candlelight... "

Why contemplate something so gruesome? Kurt offers us no moral, no obvious redemption. Nothing softens the blow. Nothing redeems the psychosis, sadism, and brutality. And yet, the poem has astonishing power, a power that lies not merely in its theme, but in the way Kurt makes us respond to it. As powerfully as any poet ever has, Brown tests Wilde's pronouncement that no artist is ever morbid. As in a great tragedy, "Abduction," in all its horror, creates a sense of life—of its beauty, of its preciousness—even when it is being violated and destroyed by a murderous madman. He does not do this by telling us this is how we should or even might feel, but by showing life being purposefully and systematically desecrated, at the same time as he pays loving attention to it. Even the way the fictionalized Bundy is represented with his head in the butchered torso of his victim,

> crooning something unthinkable
> as an animal   ecstatic with hunger
> buries its head in carrion

creates an image almost too terrible to contemplate, and yet poetically astonishing, the tender song combining with a vicious animal appetite. The value of the poem doesn't come from the fact that it is based on something true, but from looking so steadfastly at something inarticulately true, perhaps the merciless, inhuman suffering of the universe, made even worse because people inflict it on each other, and here not even as a means, but simply because they wish to, and can. It may seem odd to call such a depiction of suffering "beautiful," but, as with Jeffers, that is a testimony to the power of the poetry, which places us in such an intense contradiction. "Abduction" may not be to everyone's taste (I wouldn't read it before bed), but it stands as an ambitious raid on the sublime, a masterpiece not only of horror, but perhaps ironically also of vitality, even of something sacred. As to how Kurt achieves that, the critical essays in this book testify to the range of techniques he uses to such powerful effect in the poem.

ABDUCTION

All sitting together by the one
candle   their known faces floating
in its aura   a fragrance of wine
rising   flare of silver   the one
candle with its spellbound flame
lulling them to the center

The table in front of you arranged
and rearranged with grave precision
as if it were a gameboard   does not
leave the floor   but stands plainly
under the feast   with names
trumped up from another language

You are the one to rise and go
from that harmless light   from their
laughter   into the mercy of something
trivial   a warm sweater   a forgotten
package of cigarettes   the last
joke still wearing your features

A number hauls you patiently
through floors where people recline
by fires   which spring up   at
a touch   not caring if their clothes
are taken   or the lights   into
the locked arms of their exhaustion

You sing yourself the hymn
of boredom   bend close into the
hovering room's metal reflection
to check the double of a woman borne
adorningly above the heads of lovers
like a sacred figure in a chair

He is waiting for the wall to open
for anyone to step out   now   as
you do   lost in their pockets   still
amused by the recent wine of hallways
the sealed rooms they have paid for
denying them   closing them out

He fumbles for you like a key
the coded teeth remembering entry
half a step into that box of light
draws you out of a cry   the last door
holding your life open on a bound
black sky riddled with stars

He's picking you up in style tonight
the one you're forbidden to see
the one from the wrong neighborhood
For a minute in the strapped-down
car   as it glides among the beds
and tables   the ice and gingerbread

of this resort   you scream   a single
walker crossing the road at this hour
not three feet from your voice   Behind
you the windows of the village dwindle
to a birthday cake   though this
is the long evening of your death

They are only now pronouncing your
name like a formula   calling you back
into another world where you take
your place again at the table   speak
privately to the one on your left
some words imagining the future

Under the same star-drawn men
that climbed your roof each night
as a child   brandishing their weapons
you ride   hands cuffed behind you
like two pale witches in the stocks
as if you were the criminal

Soon the only lights abroad
are yours   surprising each object
in its place and fixing it against
the snow   simple   abstract forms
stripped to a thought of themselves
half-buried in the landscape

When he cuts them altogether
the shocked country huddles
and withdraws   giving back a wall
a cottage   a field   stone by stone
in a spectral light made earthly
by the absence of any light

In the center of that waste
he stops   with such abrupt and
foreknown ease that neither of you
moves   or speaks   but sit
distracted   like a pair
of mannequins in a test crash

Silence itself becomes
an element   something physical
in which you pose   a frieze
perpetuating what is about to
happen   a moment between
moments when the heart stops

Until your voice comes back
to you   from outside   where it has
flown above the snow   the animals
driven deeply into the earth
turning to it in their sleep
beginning to dream of their prey

When the door swings open
he steps away from you in the cold
from the probing light that winces
on and off like a surgeon's lamp
photographing the last image of your
face in the blackened glass

For an instant   he appears
before you   exact and motionless
against the faint glimmer of
the hill   the figure of your own
shadow   outcast   adrift   wanting
only to re-enter the body

Then he is lifting you out
of that intimate place into a vast
and absolute dark   holding you
tightly in his arms against
the icy distances   like a child
at the end of a long journey

He carries you into the fields
each step puncturing the thin
carapace of snow   the way a swimmer
carries his awed victim up onto
the beach   still half-possessed
of the water's indifference

In the farthest field   over
glazed ridges flayed empty as
bone   where the stars writhe closer
eating the blackness   he leans
almost kneels at a huge stone
to place your body there

With your hands still pinned
behind you in prayer   he must
cut you from your clothing   paring
it away until you lie   finally
an effigy beneath him   the first
sculpture of the woman he wants

It is then you claim your body
an utter self-possession that
denies him   until he almost
vanishes above you   though you
wanted to retreat into a figment
the oldest ghost of yourself

You think your flesh is stone
hard enough to expel the blade
that plumbs you   obscenely   a frank
splinter of cold nailing you into
rock   shattering all self-conjured
images   any world but this

He tears you upwards letting
each half open under the blind eyes
of the figures bent above you   as
another bent to free you from your
garments   coming apart like
something hinged in his fingers

The pain ruptures in you   and
subsides   a clenching agony
that reaches outward from the hard
depth of your wound   shaking you
completely from the root of yourself
until you think you're free

In the half-transported light
you watch the stars disappear   the
sky grays empties   like a field
from which a massive flight of
birds has been startled
by a sudden   piercing cry

But he draws you back at once
his awful head thrust deeply
into the split walls of your chest
crooning something unthinkable
as an animal   ecstatic with hunger
buries its head in carrion

He is speaking directly into
your wounds   into your brain
making the shapes of words crawl
inward   until they become your own
secret voice   opening your lips
to ask   Mercy   Mercy

Entering further   he can feel
your breath close down around him
feel your pulse become his own
as someone   out of breath   slows
down beside himself   to wait
for his laboring heart

Until he can see   with your
last look   the brute shape poised
above you   watch his own head
withdraw   the unknown face float up
into the darkness for a terrible
moment   painted with your blood

He will leave before the sun
lifts   stumbling into his own tracks
already half absolved   as the sky
changes and the constellations
drift   groveling in the snow to
scrape the stigma from his face

The first light takes the field
advances   hesitates   crawls forward
like someone testing ice on a pond
each thing catching it and tearing
a shadow in its wake   finding you
sprawled on the open rock

This day   and every day   for
months   the sun returns earlier
each morning   later each night
witnessing   over and over   the
simple gesture   your body makes
alone in a blazing field

And those that are raised   come
forth   purged of somnolence and ice
into the baffled light   having
only the one   pure   unshakeable
thought of emptiness driving them
blindly from another world

They will come to you   at first
in the middle of the country's wild
obsessive green   without thought
of what aroused them   jamming
their muzzles into the starved
bowl of your ribs

On foot or flying   or sliding
with a long   convulsive step   they
will take you into the death of
their living   the wolf   the night
owl   the blackbird   crossing
with its blood-spotted wings

Each will carry with it   in
the brute crèche of its skull
the vision of a woman charmed by
candlelight   among the hard glitter
of knives   calm   unassailable
fallen to the hunger of beasts

ENDNOTES

Chapter 1—Poetry and the Language of Adam

1. In his short biography of the life of Dante, Giovanni Boccaccio offers his own theory about the origin of poetry. Describing the beginnings of religion in earliest times, Boccaccio refers to the first priests whose job it was to ritualize the worship of "the imagined divine essence," or God, and that this began with the shaping of statues, but it soon required something more: "And in order that to so great a power a silent and mute honor might not be paid, it seemed to them that they should humble themselves before it with words of lofty sound, and render it propitious to their needs. And as they thought that this power exceeded everything else in nobility, they wished to find words far from the ordinary plebian or public style of speaking, and worthy of the divinity, in which they could offer their sacred praise. Moreover, in order that these words might seem to have more efficacy, they wanted them composed according to laws of rhythm, by which pleasures might be felt and resentment and annoyance removed. And it was clearly appropriate that this should be done, not in a vulgar or accustomed form of speech, but in one that was artistic, exquisite and unusual. This form the Greeks called *poetes*. So it arose that what was made in this form was called *poesis*, and those who made or used such a manner of speaking were called *poets*. This then was the origin of the name of poetry, and consequently of poets." For Boccacio, then, poetry began — not mythologically with Adam naming the animals — but much later in a practical way with the beginnings of the liturgy. Boccaccio notes, however: "Others argue differently, but this notion pleases me most."

2. Dickey, James. "The Movement of Fish." *The Whole Motion: Collected Poems, 1945–1992.* Middletown: Wesleyan University Press, 1992.

3. Dickey, James. "Diabetes." *Poetry,*
   vol. 114, no. 3, 1969, pp. 151-152.

4. Kinnell, Galway. "Under the Maud Moon." *The Book of
   Nightmares.* New York: Houghton Mifflin Company, 1971.

5. Kinnell, Galway. "The Fly." *Body Rags.* New
   York: Houghton Mifflin Company, 1967.

6. Hulme, T.E. "Romanticism and Classicism."
   T.E. Hulme: Selected Writings, edited by Patrick
   McGuinness. New York: Routledge USA, 2003.

7. Bly, Robert. *Leaping Poetry: An Idea with Poems
   and Translations.* Pittsburgh:
   University of Pittsburgh Press, 2008.

8. Kinnell, Galway. "The Path Among the Stones."
   The Book of Nightmares. New York:
   Houghton Mifflin Company, 1971.

9. Pinsky, Robert. "Shirt." *The Want Bone.* New
   York: HarperCollins Publishers, 1991.

10. Melville, Herman. *Moby Dick.* New York:
    Simon & Schuster, 1991, pp. 285.

Chapter 2—Divorced Couplets and the Evolution of a Form

1. Wormser, Baron. *The Road Washes Out in Spring:
   A Poet's Memoir of Living Off the Grid.* Lebanon,
   NH: University Press of New England, 2006.

2. Matthews, William. "Masterful." *Search Party.* New
   York: Houghton Mifflin Company, 2004.

3. Preminger, Alex and T.V.F. Brogan, eds. *The New Princeton Encyclopedia of Poetry and Poetics.* Princeton: Princeton University Press, 1993.

4. Zapruder, Matthew. "The Path to the Orchard." *American Linden: Poems.* New Adams: Tupelo Press, 2002.

5. White, Jared. "The Cure Is Love." *Meridian.* Issue 19, 2007.

6. Fussell, Paul. *Poetic Meter & Poetic Form.* New York: McGraw-Hill Education, 1979.

7. Hoagland, Tony. *Real Sofistikashun: Essays on Poetry and Craft.* Minneapolis: Graywolf Press, 2006.

8. Scholes, Robert E. *Elements of Poetry.* New York: Oxford University Press, 1969.

9. Musei Vaticani. http://www.museivaticani.va/ content/museivaticani/en/collezioni/musei/ cappella-sistina/volta.html. Accessed 10/18/2018.

Chapter 3—Poetry and Restraint

1. Glück, Louise. "Disruption, Hesitation, Silence." *The American Poetry Review,* vol. 22, no. 5 1993, pp. 30-32.

2. Ginsburg, Allen. "Howl." *Collected Poems, 1947-1980.* New York: HarperPerennial, 2001.

3. McGrath, Campbell. "Angels and the Bars of Manhattan." New York: Ecco, 1994.

4. Haines, John. "Marigold." *The Stone Harp.* Middletown: Wesleyan University Press, 1971.

5. Hayden, Robert. "Those Winter Sundays." *Collected Poems of Robert Hayden.* New York: Liveright, 2013.

6. Orr, David. "Rough Gems." *The New York Times Sunday Book Review,* April 2, 2006, https://www.nytimes.com/2006/04/02/books/review/02orr.html.

7. Stafford, William. "Traveling Through the Dark." *The Way It Is: New and Selected Poem. St. Paul: Graywolf Press, 1998..*

8. Dobyns, Stephen. *Best Words, Best Order: Essays on Poetry, 2nd Edition.* New York: Palgrave Macmillan, 2003.

Chapter 4—On the Immortality of Images

1. Woods, John. "The Deaths at Paragon, Indiana." *The Kenyon Review,* vol. 16, no. 3, 1954, pp. 442–445.

2. Crane, Hart. "Cape Hatteras." *The Bridge.* New York: Liveright, 2001.

3. Reed, J.D. "The Weather Is Brought to You." *Expressways.* New York: Simon & Schuster, 1969.

4. Bronk, William. "Veni Creator Spiritus." *Life Supports: New and Collected Poems.* Northfield: Talisman House, Publishers, 1997.

5. ———. "The Torment." *Life Supports: New and Collected Poems.* Northfield: Talisman House, Publishers, 1997.

6. Phillips, Patrick. "Heaven." *Boy.* Athens: University of Georgia Press, 2008.

7. Williams, William Carlos. "Nantucket." *The Collected Poems of William Carlos Williams, Vol. 1: 1909-1939.* New York: New Directions, 1991.

Chapter 5—Beyond Description

1. Sterle, Francine. "Snake." *Every Bird Is One Bird*. North Adams: Tupelo Press, 2001.

2. Bishop, Elizabeth. "At the Fishhouses." *The Complete Poems, 1927-1979*. New York: Farrar, Straus and Giroux, 1983.

3. Bishop, Elizabeth. "The Fish." *Poems*. New York: Farrar, Straus and Giroux, 2011.

4. Bloom, Harold. *The Art of Reading Poetry*. New York: Harper Perennial, 2005.

5. Bishop, Elizabeth. "The Moose." *The Complete Poems, 1927-1979*. New York: Farrar, Straus and Giroux, 1983.

6. Williams, C.K. "Waking Jed." *Tar*. New York: Vintage, 1983.

Chapter 6—Time and the Lyric

1. Thomas, Dylan. "Ballad of the Long-Legged Bait." *Dylan Thomas: Selected Poems, 1934-1952*. New York: New Directions, 1971.

2. Haines, John. "Marigold." *The Stone Harp*. Middletown: Wesleyan University Press, 1971.

3. Addonizio, Kim. "Rain." *Tell Me*. Rochester: BOA Editions, Ltd, 2000.

4. Simic, Charles. "Elegy." *Selected Poems: 1963-2003*. New York: Faber & Faber, 2004.

5. Lax, Robert. *A Thing That Is*. New York: Overlook Press, 1997.

Chapter 7—Six Bullets Ripped into My Chest

1. Simic, Charles. "The Partial Explanation." *Selected Early Poems*. New York: George Braziller Publishers, 1999.

2. Edson, Russell. "The Automobile." *The Childhood of an Equestrian*. New York: Harper & Row, 1973.

3. Lux, Thomas. "Traveling Exhibit of Torture Instruments." *The Drowned River*. New York: Houghton Mifflin, 1990.

4. Roethke, Theodore. "In a Dark Time." *The Collected Poems of Theodore Roethke*. New York: Doubleday, 1961.

5. Weigl, Bruce. *After the Others*. Chicago: Triquarterly, 1999.

6. Frost, Robert. "Stopping by Woods on a Snowy Evening." *The Poetry of Robert Frost: The Collected Poems*. New York: Holt Paperbacks, 2002.

7. Harrison, Jeffrey. "My Worst Job Interview." *Incomplete Knowledge*. New York: Four Way Books, 2006.

8. Hoagland, Tony. *Sweet Ruin*. Madison: The University of Wisconsin Press, 1992.

9. ——. *Donkey Gospel: Poems*. Minneapolis: Graywolf Press, 1998.

10. ——. *What Narcissism Means to Me: Selected Poems*. Northumberland, UK: Bloodaxe Books, 2005.

11. Twichell, Chase. "A Lamb by Its Ma." *Horses Where the Answers Should Have Been: New and Selected Poems*. Port Townsend: Copper Canyon Press, 2010.

12. Matthews, Sebastian. *Coming to Flood.*
    Venice, CA: Hollyridge Press, 2005.

Chapter 8—Writing Habits and How to Kick Them

1. Simic, Charles. "Fork." *Charles Simic: Selected Early Poems.* New York: George Braziller, Inc., 1999.

2. ——. *The Metaphysician in the Dark.* Ann Arbor: University of Michigan Press, 2003.

Chapter 9—Long Story Short

1. Holden, Jonathan. *The Fate of American Poetry.* Athens: The University of Georgia Press, 1991.

2. Turner, Frederick. *Genesis: An Epic Poem of the Terraforming of Mars.* Spokane Valley: Ilium Press, 2011 (orig. 1988 by Saybrook Publishing Company).

3. Walcott, Derek. *Omeros.* New York: Faber & Faber, 1990.

4. ——. "The Schooner *Flight.*" *The Star-Apple Kingdom.* New York: Farrar, Straus and Giroux, 2014.

5. Barr, John. *Grace.* Los Angeles: Story Line Press, 1999.

6. Kunitz, Stanley. "The Wellfleet Whale." *The Wellfleet Whale and Companion Poems.* Rhinebeck, NY: Sheep Meadow Press, 1983.

Chapter 11—Nature and the Poet

1. Oliver, Mary. *American Primitive.* New York: Back Bay Books, 1983.

2. ———. *House of Light.* Boston: Beacon Press, 1992.

3. ———. *Dream Work.* New York: The Atlantic Monthly Press, 1994.

4. ———. *Twelve Moons.* New York: Back Bay Books, 1979.

5. ———. *What Do We Know.* Cambridge: Da Capo Press, 2003.

6. ———. *Why I Wake Early.* Boston: Beacon Press, 2005.

Chapter 12—Winning Neglect

1. Menashe, Samuel. *Samuel Menashe: New and Selected Poems.* New York: Library of America, 2005.

2. Ahearn, Barry. "Poetry and Synthesis: The Art of Samuel Menashe." *Twentieth Century Literature,* Vol. 42, No. 2 (Summer, 1996), pp. 294-308.

Chapter 13— Does Postmodern Poetry "Work?"

1. Short, Spencer. *Tremolo.* New York: Perennial, 2001.

2. Barnet, Sylvan; Morton Berman; and William Burto. *A Dictionary of Literary, Dramatic, and Cinematic Terms,* 2nd ed. New York: Little, Brown & Co., 1971.

Chapter 14—Good Poetry Never Ages

1. Nooteboom, Cees. *The Captain of the Butterflies.*
   Translated by Leonard Nathan and Herlinde Spahr.
   Los Angeles: Sun & Moon Press, 1997.

2. Preminger, Alex and Terry V.F. Brogan, eds. *The New
   Princeton Encyclopedia of Poetry and Poetics, 3rd
   Edition.* Princeton: Princeton University Press, 1993.

Chapter 15—Exuding Gold

1. Knott, Bill. *Plaza de Loco: New Poems.* Self-published, 1998.

Chapter 16—The Shameless, Absurdist Poetry
of Russell Edson's *The Rooster's Wife*

1. D'Adamo, Thomas. "Thomas D'Adamo on *Bacacay.*"
   BOOKFORUM, issue Feb/Mar 2005, pg 6.

2. Edson, Russell. *The Rooster's Wife.* Rochester:
   BOA Editions, 2005.

Chapter 17—*Shannon* and the Twentieth Century Narrative

1. McGrath, Campbell. *Shannon: A Poem of the Lewis and
   Clark Expedition.* New York: Ecco Press, 2009.

Chapter 18—The Zany Reaches of Imagination

1. Rohrer, Matthew. *Satellite.* Seattle: Verse Press, 2001.

Chapter 19—The Unexpected Imagery and Astonishing Metaphor in Emma Jones's *The Striped World*

1. Jones, Emma. *The Striped World.* New York: Faber and Faber, 2009.

Chapter 20—How to Rhyme

1. Boss, Todd. *Yellowrocket: Poems.* New York: W. W. Norton and Co., 2010.

CREDITS